Celebrating
PALOUSE
COUNTRY

T0417956

Celebrating PALOUSE COUNTRY

A History of the Landscape in Text and Images

30th Anniversary Edition

Richard D. Scheuerman and John Clement

Foreword by Alexander C. McGregor

BASALT BOOKS

Pullman, Washington

BASALT BOOKS

Basalt Books
PO Box 645910
Pullman, Washington 99164-5910
Phone: 800-354-7360
Email: basalt.books@wsu.edu
Website: basaltbooks.wsu.edu

Library of Congress Cataloging-in-Publication Data
Names: Scheuerman, Richard D., author. | Clement, John, photographer. |
  McGregor, Alexander C. (Alexander Campbell), writer of foreword.
Title: Celebrating Palouse country : a history of the landscape in text and
  images / Richard D. Scheuerman and John Clement ; foreword by Alexander
  C. McGregor.
Other titles: Palouse country
Description: 30th anniversary edition. | Pullman, Washington : Basalt
  Books, [2024] | Includes bibliographical references and index.
Identifiers: LCCN 2024003483 | ISBN 9781638640288 (hardback) | ISBN
  9781638640264 (paperback)
Subjects: LCSH: Palouse River Valley (Idaho and Wash.)--History. | Paloos
  Indians--History. | BISAC: HISTORY / United States / State & Local /
  Pacific Northwest (OR, WA) | SOCIAL SCIENCE / Sociology / Rural
Classification: LCC F752.P25 S34 2024 | DDC 979.7/39--dc23/eng/20240125
LC record available at https://lccn.loc.gov/2024003483

Basalt Books is an imprint of Washington State University Press.

The Washington State University Pullman campus is located on the homelands of the Niimíipuu (Nez Perce) Tribe and the Palus people. We acknowledge their presence here since time immemorial and recognize their continuing connection to the land, to the water, and to their ancestors. WSU Press is committed to publishing works that foster a deeper understanding of the Pacific Northwest and the contributions of its Native peoples.

Cover image: John Clement, *Sunrise Glory*, near Spangle, Washington
Frontispiece: John Clement, *Steptoe Wheat*, looking north from Steptoe Butte
Cover design by Jeffry E. Hipp
Interior design by Tracy Randall

Dedication

For John Clement and Alex McGregor,
longtime companions in many Palouse Country adventures—
from yesteryear's Hooper footraces to recent treks along our favorite river

Palouse River Fall   south of Elberton, Washington

Contents

facing page

Kamiak Butte Morning

north of
Pullman, Washington

List of Color Plates

List of Maps

Foreword

Alexander C. McGregor

"In the far Northwest of the United States lies an unusual land," historical geographer Donald Meinig wrote more than a half century ago. "So sharply is it set apart from its surroundings that it can be recognized immediately, at a mere glance." Rolling hills of grain, the rippling fields of green on a spring day, the stark rugged canyons incised through layer after layer of basalt, exposed by massive Ice Age floods that scoured them, and the gnarled black locust trees surrounding homesteads and barns of an earlier time.

Richard Scheuerman, John Clement, and I have felt the powerful pull of this land throughout our working careers. "The Three Amigos," we call ourselves, and we've pitched in together to celebrate this land across the decades. Dick's ancestors, of Russian-German stock, made the long trek here generations after pledges made by Catherine the Great to encourage settlement on the Volga steppes were forgotten. He grew up near what had been "the Palouse Colony," where many other families of the same heritage got their starts. As an educator and historian, Dick's contributions to our historical knowledge of the region have been dramatic—in particular his studies of the Snake River-Palouse tribe, the emigrants attracted to this land from around the globe, and the agricultural panoramas captured with artists over many generations have broadened our knowledge of the lives of people on the land.

John Clement has been capturing images of the Palouse (and beyond) for many years, traversing hills and valleys through lightning storms, blizzards, and dust, whatever it takes to illustrate its dramatic panoramas. Among his finest, in my view, are images of pioneer churches isolated in rural fields and bracing for a storm (Freeze Church near Potlatch, Idaho and Egypt Lutheran north of Davenport, Washington) or of old farm equipment and barns no longer called to duty on adjacent acres but reminding us of families before who once cared for them.

Every fall I have to make a tough judgment call. Which Clement photos are the most powerful for the Northwest Drylands calendar we will share with farmers across the Inland Northwest when the new year arrives? We have a good track record, not really because of my skill as judge but because John has so many gems from which to choose. Dick, John, and I have collaborated on speeches, articles, books, and events for many years. My roots run deep here too, dating back to territorial days when four desperately poor Scottish-Canadian brothers—my grandfather and three uncles—got their start herding sheep in the rugged Channeled Scablands. Like my friend Dick, I did my tour of duty studying the history of this land and its people in graduate school and have been sharing and learning ever since.

Both of us have had the opportunity to interview people who came to hew out a living on the land. As he puts it, "While the pioneering experiences of our first-generation relatives living throughout the region were as varied as the languages they spoke, a common theme framed the stories they told us children: 'The Palouse was a Promised Land for which we chosen ones living here should be profoundly grateful.'"

facing page

Hilly Harvest

west of
Colfax, Washington

There were many times of hardship along the way which must have stretched the gratitude thin at times—crops hit by freezing winds or drought, livestock isolated in snowbanks in "cow-killing" winters. My family was sued for trespass for grazing sheep on unfenced railroad ground, forced to lease and then buy land under court order—sometimes obstacles turned out to be opportunities. I once asked my cousin, Bill McGregor, long-time manager of our ranch, how early settlers persevered, putting down roots in an unfamiliar land. Three traits, he said, were key: unquenchable optimism, a wry self-deprecating sense of humor that helped them through the tough times, and a tenacity verging on stubbornness. Traits, he went on to say, that were useful then, are useful now, and will be useful in the future.

Working together over the years we have told of pioneer farmers—their tools captured in John's images, their stories shared by Dick and me—and about the changing world in which farm families persevere, and sometimes prosper. Dick focuses on philosophy, artistic images of agriculture, cultural tensions and a passion for the land and its people. My focus has been upon reaching out on behalf of those families, dedicated stewards of 96% of our agricultural lands, to tell legislators and urban neighbors of their achievements and the vital role they play. It's a tough trade in which the biggest rewards are not financial. Ask any farmer what matters most—and we've all known many over the years on this land—and you are likely to hear three responses: the pride in benefitting from agricultural science and their own hard work in seeing that the land will be in better shape than it was when they began their tour of stewardship. The satisfaction of producing healthy, hearty meals for people around the nation and the globe. A great place to raise the next generation.

You'll find here powerful stories of the ethnic origins of settlers on the land based upon prior books Scheuerman has written, including the Snake River-Palouse Indians (*River Song*), the Russian-German pioneers (*Hardship to Homeland*, with Clifford Trafzer), a history of Inland Northwest agriculture (*Harvest Heritage*, with me), and three popular editions of *Palouse Country: A Land and Its People* (with John Clement).

This, the thirtieth-year anniversary edition, titled *Celebrating Palouse Country*, features historical photographs and artwork. It represents an important contribution towards a fuller understanding of the region's First Peoples. Devastated by diseases and warfare before the arrival of large groups of immigrants, the native Palouse Indians had "maintained an intimate relationship with the land." A great-grandson of one of the immigrant families, Scheuerman shares his love of the land, a thorough knowledge of conditions in the distant lands from which many Palouse immigrants came, and an appreciation for the diverse peoples who came to settle on the rolling prairie.

Living conditions were primitive in the early years and farm tools makeshift at best—such as the crude harrows cut of hawthorn bushes and tied to long poles designed by German families of Spokane County. Dick skillfully weaves the stories of these families and immigrant groups together with the overall fabric of the pioneering process, describing their search for available farm-ground, methods of land acquisition, development of towns, and changes in farming practices as settlers advanced from hand broadcasting seed and subsistence crops toward commercial production in their new homeland.

The process of Euro-American settlement was largely completed around World War I, although considerable property along the Snake River remained under Native American title through the provisions of the Indian Homestead Act. My great uncle, a state senator, helped one of the last residents of the village at the mouth of the Palouse, Sam Fisher, keep his land. The family worked hard to keep caves with artifacts a secret until Washington State College archaeologists had funding to study them. By then the Palouse had become "settled up" and was becoming known for "producing more wheat per acre any other place its size in the world."

While the enclaves of foreign-born immigrants became amalgamated in time with the broader population, a rich heritage of distinctive cultural ties is still reflected in the communities, churches, and social activities of the Palouse. This thirty-year commemorative edition is a gem—Dick's articulate and interesting story of the diverse people who came to call the Palouse home and John Clement's striking images of an unusual land. An important, and powerfully told and illustrated, contribution to our understanding of the history of the Inland Pacific Northwest. As I heard a friend tell someone about *The Palouse Country* before the WSU Press came out with this anniversary edition: "If you can find it, buy it!" Sage advice. And now easier to find!

Steptoe Lupine

Steptoe Butte, Washington

Preface

"The fur trade is the principal branch of business at present in the country situated between the Rocky Mountains and the Pacific Ocean. On the banks of the Columbia river, however, where the soil and climate are favourable to cultivation, we are directing our attention to agriculture on a large scale, and there is every prospect that we shall soon be able to establish important branches of export trade from thence in the articles of wool, tallow, hides, tobacco, and grain of various kinds."

—Hudson's Bay Company Governor George Simpson, 1837

Agricultural opportunity in the Pacific Northwest was a frequent topic of consideration by Meriwether Lewis and William Clark and by the region's earliest nineteenth-century European-American explorers. Lewis and Clark's contemporaries David Thompson and Jacques Raphael ("Jaco") Finlay inaugurated transcontinental travel by canoe, foot, and horseback from Hudson's Bay in the East to the Pacific Ocean on what would become known as the Columbia Express, and the famed astronomer-geographer and his Chippewa Indian guide found time to plant cereal grains in 1808, although they did not thrive. That spring they established Kootenae House, the North West Company's first trading post west of the Rockies near present-day Invermere, British Columbia.

Within a quarter-century, intrepid American and British traders were operating a string of bustling frontier "Columbia Department" outposts stretching from Ft. St. James on Stuart Lake on the western slope of the Canadian Rockies, south to Ft. Nez Percés near the junction of the Columbia and Snake rivers, and west to Ft. Nisqually on Puget Sound. In these and other places, the early fur traders and their Indian hosts generally lived together amicably, as the two cultures had learned to coexist before the onslaught of settlers and soldiers. Furs and salmon were bartered for metal, cloth, and glass trade goods, and early in their experience together, residents of both the Columbia Plateau and Coastal Lowlands began cultivating the soil to give rise to Northwest farming culture.

My great-grandfather, Andrew Sunwold, provides a tenuous personal link to the West's frontier trading and farming past. After emigrating from Norway in 1881, he lived first along the Missouri River near old Ft. Mandan of Lewis and Clark fame in Dakota Territory. Hidden among the dense prairie grasses were countless buffalo bones, which could be sold in town for $5 a wagonload. He also procured seasonal but hazardous employment as a "woodhawk," cutting timber for steamboats that plied the river from Bismarck to the westernmost terminus of Missouri River traffic at Ft. Benton in Montana Territory. The American Fur Company

facing page

Dying 'n Drying

looking southeast
from Steptoe Butte

outpost was the eastern terminus for the fabled Mullan Road, the primary immigrant route to Washington Territory before the advent of the Northern Pacific Railroad along its course. This was the path he followed, as he eventually acquired land for his two sons to establish farms near the rural Palouse Country hamlet of Fairfield, close to the Washington-Idaho border.

About two miles west of my boyhood home north of Endicott, Washington, several clapboard houses remained clustered together at a remote location on the Palouse River known locally as the "Palouse Colony." My paternal grandfather, Karl Scheuerman, made sure we knew that this was the first home for our family group in the Pacific Northwest. His parents, Henry (H.B.) and Mary Scheuerman, were among the region's *Russland-Deutschen*, or Germans from Russia. They were people of the soil who for generations had sown their grain and gathered harvests in a progression that led from the Hessian countryside and Volga steppe to the Palouse prairies. H. B. and his family had arrived in 1891 and lived with earlier colonists on this fertile bottomland until arrangements could be made to acquire land nearby.

Some of our favorite family photographs depict the everyday scenes of Northwest pioneer farm life. One shows Great-Grandma Sunwold feeding her agitated flock of Plymouth Rock chickens; another casts Uncle Art Sunwold in a sea of stiff club wheat on his farm near Waverly. While the pioneering experiences of our first-generation relatives living on the Palouse were as varied as the foreign languages they spoke in my youth, a common theme framed the stories they told us children: The Northwest was a Promised Land and we should be grateful for our blessings here and work hard to ensure a secure future for our families. Having eked out a hardscrabble existence in the Colorado Rockies, on stony Norwegian slopes, and in politically unstable Russia; they seemed in a position to know the beneficial prospects of sacrifice.

Great-Grandma Sunwold, c. 1900.
Scheuerman Family Collection

Grandpa Scheuerman knew his land intimately. He and my father taught us to distinguish the swales, saddles, and other unique topographic features and soil conditions of the Palouse meaningful to a farmer. As with rural families everywhere, many features on the landscape hold special significance. We learned such names and locations as the Huvaluck (Hessian dialect for "Oathole"—a notoriously steep horseshoe basin), "Barley Hill," and "Three-Finger Draw." Grandpa would recount the experiences of the first Volga German immigrants to the region who had labored for years to turn the tawny, knee-high bunchgrass and plant the Turkey Red wheat that their Mennonite countrymen had brought from Russia. Grandpa knew of their exploits firsthand and understood that other groups had shared in these pioneering experiences. He spoke wistfully of the days his father had traded flour and fruit on the river in exchange for Indian salmon.

Our tiny half-section farm clung precariously to economic vitality by the thrift and uncanny ability of my father to keep second-hand machinery running indefinitely with sufficient supplies of baling wire, canvas, and "Rock-Hard"—a gritty, gray goop that turned to stone moments out of the can and was guaranteed to plug any hole in sheet metal. Grandpa loved to visit the ranch long after his retirement, especially during August's sweltering hot "thrashing weather," as he called it, a desire entirely lost on adolescent bondservants. We would sit in a black Ford grain truck that we had polished before harvest, perched for view as Dad reaped some of the finest crops around with a growling mechanical dinosaur of speckled red skin that slowly ate its way through rolling seas of wheat. The high yields produced year after year reflected an agrarian sense in both men that had been passed down over centuries.

Places like Ft. Benton and the Palouse Colony remain significant locations in the American West. Through able living history interpreters Ken Robinson at Ft. Benton and Ft. Nisqually's Mike McGuire, one can still experience the summertime atmosphere of bustling trade and colonist centers where five-point trade blankets and blue Russian cobalt trade beads were exchanged for beaver pelts and bear skins. We can only imagine the settings of other places like Ft. Colville, Ft. Okanogan, and Ft. Nez Perces that now rest beneath the reservoirs of Columbia River dams. Fortunately, the remarkable paintings of nineteenth-century American and Canadian artists like John Mix Stanley, Gustavus Sohon, John Alden, and Paul Kane vividly depict their original appearance.

I have long been drawn to the story of these places and the First Peoples and fur trade families who knew them in part because of what Kentucky folklorist Jay Anderson calls "living history time travel." The experience helps us to examine critically the value of technological change and to make choices to promote wisdom, healthy living, and respect among peoples. Without romanticizing previous lifestyles, there is something to be learned about the value of hard work and wholesome living of that era. Stories of Christmas and Harvest Home celebrations and gatherings devoid of commercialism offer insights into personal and social wellbeing that address the challenges of twenty-first century future shock through understandings akin to what T. S. Eliot terms "felt-truth," or the informed balance of knowledge, wonder, and empathy.

Change can be beneficial when living within the sustainable constraints of the natural world. The frontier era shows how conflict with other cultures has often arisen when such limitations are ignored in the name of short-term commercial gain or perceived higher needs. Northwest Plateau and Coastal Indian leaders like Kamiakin of the Yakamas and Nisqually leader Leschi welcomed Christian missionaries and adopted agricultural and pastoral innovations like the raising of grains, crop irrigation, and selective breeding of livestock. Spiritual leaders (*twáti* , "shamans," or "medicine men") like the Snake River Dreamer Thomash and teachers (*iyánča*) like the Wanapum prophet Smohalla spoke of the family of all mankind and accepted technological progress within the limits of moral obligations to the natural world. Appreciation and application of these lessons for healthier living can be fostered through understandings of the frontier experience.

This book is the result of efforts by individuals throughout the Palouse Country to better understand, celebrate, and perpetuate a special heritage. Palouse area communities evidence a vibrancy and pride in such annual events as Tekoa's Slippery Gulch Days, Pullman's National Lentil Festival, Endicott's Fourth of July Celebration, the St. John Fair and Horse Show, and the Coeur d' Alene Tribal Memorial Warriors Horse Ride from Plummer to Rosalia; active church fellowships, and support for local school sports teams, Future Farmers of America (FFA) programs, and marching bands. The "university cities" of Pullman, Moscow, and Cheney offer cultural and educational opportunities not often accessible to a rural populace and provide repositories for research by those interested in a deeper awareness of our legacy and responsibility as residents of the Palouse. Volunteers work throughout the year to perpetuate the region's cultural and natural heritage through the Palouse Empire Threshing Bee Association, Palouse Folklore Society, Palouse-Clearwater Environmental Institute, county fairs, and quilting circles. Listed in the bibliography are individuals from many of these places and organizations who have shared their stories with me over the years to make this book possible.

We thank John Brown of the WSU College of Agricultural, Human, and Natural Resource Sciences (CAHNRS) for organizing the 2010 E. Paul Catts Memorial Lecture, which provided an opportunity for us to gather and present information on Palouse Country history for the first time. We also thank Kristie Kirkpatrick, Cindy Wigen, and Peggy Bryan of the Whitman County Library in Colfax; and Steve Perisho and Cindy Strong of Seattle Pacific University Library. Useful materials were also made available through Charles Mutchler of Eastern Washington University's Kennedy Library; Charles Webbert at the University of Idaho (UI) Library; Ed Nelson and Doug Olson at the Eastern Washington State Historical Society, Spokane; and Laila Miletic-Vejzovic, Trevor Bond, and Patsy Tate at Washington State University's Holland Library.

The historical photographs featured in this work are from the R. Raymond Hutchison Studio Image Collection in Holland Library's Manuscripts, Archives, and Special Collections at WSU (HSIC, MASC). This remarkable assemblage of 200,000 images documents the visual history of the Palouse Country as recorded throughout the lifetime of pioneer photographer R. R. Hutchison (1887-1967) who established studios in Endicott, LaCrosse, and Pullman, Washington, and Moscow, Idaho. Hutchison's commercial interests were secondary to his lifelong passion for documenting the heritage and scenic beauty of the Palouse during the years of its transition from the homestead to early modern eras. While just a boy on the family farm near Endicott, he carried his first Brownie on recreational trips to the Palouse River and into the fields surrounding the Hutchison home to photograph men, women, and children working throughout the farm year—cultivating and harvesting, butchering, thinning apples and canning fruit, and countless other ordinary tasks that he understood to be significant in the life of rural families.

With growing expertise and improved equipment, he expanded his interests to portraiture and the enormous wide-framed pictures of Palouse Country threshing outfits, family reunions, church conferences, and other special events identified by the small, white-lettered epigraph "Photo by Hutchison" known to residents throughout the region. In the 1920s he founded the Inland Empire Professional Photographers Association and became an unofficial photographer of university events and personalities at both WSU and UI where his camera captured hundreds of sporting events, construction projects, and celebrity visits. Individuals with rare and fragile pictures taken across the Palouse in the settlement era would often turn to Hutchison for copies and restoration work and he would retain negatives for his own files. Given the length of his career in one area, the quality and prodigious output of his work that was safeguarded for decades, R. R. Hutchison bequeathed the people of the Palouse one of the finest regional photographic collections in existence anywhere.

Historians whose works have greatly benefited our research include Donald Meinig, David Stratton, Keith Petersen, Fr. Thomas Connolly, SJ, Jack Nisbet, Dennis Solbrack, and the late Walter Gary, Glen Adams, and Verle Kaiser. Special thanks go to Linda Bathgate, Editor-in-Chief at Washington State University Press, who first suggested this special edition, and to Director Ed Sala, Kerry Darnall, and Caryn Lawton for a most valued publishing partnership over the years.

Richard D. Scheuerman
Richland, Washington

R. Raymond Hutchison, 1936.
Hutchison Studio Photographs Collection, 1910–1973,
Manuscripts, Archives, and Special Collections,
Washington State University Libraries.

following page

Mader Farm Sunrise

east of
Uniontown,
Washington

Harvest Lines

Palouse Land Designs II   near LaCrosse, Washington

CHAPTER I

Place and First Peoples

Looming above the panoramic Palouse near the heart of the region stands a promontory revered by the region's First Peoples and known today as Steptoe Butte. To the native Snake River-Palouse Indians, it was *Yamústas* ("Elk Mountain"), a sacred high place of spirit quests and the home of mythic Elk. (The meaning of its ancient Coeur d'Alene Salish name, *S'y̓mtíte'*, is lost to antiquity.) An honored figure in tribal folklore, Elk was said to have found sanctuary during the time of the Animal People in the cleft of the butte's eastern face. In the ancient time, a great flood covered the land and Yámústas became an island. After the waters subsided, the Creator brought forth the animals, fishes, roots, and berries.[1] The area's first European-American explorers dubbed Steptoe Butte "Pyramid Peak" for its resemblance to Egypt's great monument to Cheops. The formation served like a mariner's landmark in a maelstrom of earthen waves that crested with wind-pulsed native wheatgrasses and fescues. Viewed from above, the undulating Palouse is a vast labyrinth of whorls and swirls that resemble a deific thumbprint.

Before the sextant and plow demarcated and denuded these fertile swells, they were seasonally transformed from soft springtime viridian hues with wildflowered splashes of bluebells, flaming Indian paintbrush, and bright yellow arrowleaf balsamroot into summer and fall's muted green-brown pastels mixed in the bunchgrass billows. The butte continues to serve as a landmark Palouse portal to Native Americans today. On several occasions while in the company of Palouse-Nez Perces returning to Lapwai from the Colville Reservation or with Coeur d'Alenes headed east from Warm Springs, I have heard elders say, "When I see Steptoe Butte, I know that I am home."

With its summit at 3,612 feet often shrouded in purling clouds, the butte is the highest and most ancient formation in the Palouse hills. Its ascendance preceded the plateau lava flows by eons and it is composed of billion-year-old sandpaper-orange quartzite related geologically to the eastern upland shore of Precambrian metamorphic strata twenty miles beyond in the foothills of northwestern Idaho's rugged cordillera. I still look with awe at a chip from the summit given to me as a paperweight. Formations similar to Steptoe Butte create an inland atoll within this restless sea of grains and grasses, of which Steptoe is the westernmost in a chain of prominents that includes Stratton, Granite, and Kamiak Buttes and Moscow and Tekoa Mountains. A timeless sentinel cloaked in beige and ochred beauty, Steptoe Butte's vista provides evidence of the surrounding terrain's geologic origins and a point from which to view the twisted course of the Palouse River that unites its varied landscapes.

The Palouse region covers that part of Eastern Washington and Northern Idaho in the Palouse River basin as well as adjacent lands characterized by a rolling terrain of fertile loess soils. This area covers approximately 4,000 square miles and

facing page

Big Sky Over Steptoe

lies largely in Washington's Whitman and Spokane Counties, substantial portions of Adams, Columbia, and Garfield Counties, and in Idaho's Latah and Benewah Counties. Nearly seventy percent of the land is arable, composed of deep deposits of rich but fragile topsoil. These cover immense layers of brown-black basalt, composed of fine-grained pyroxene and plagioclase. This bedrock shield is up to 10,000 feet thick, resulting from successive lava flows through fissures across the Columbia Plateau during the late Miocene Epoch between six and seventeen million years ago. Before the Cascade uplift, this vast area of land received as much as fifty inches of annual rainfall to host a mixed forest of conifers, maples, water tupelo, and oak similar to America's southeastern bald cypress swamps of today.

The Palouse Country is bounded by the Snake, Tucannon, and Clearwater Rivers on the south and Idaho's imposing Bitterroot and Clearwater Mountains to the east. The evergreen forests of these eastern uplands extend across the northern half of Spokane County along a line roughly

corresponding to the deepest penetration of the great Pleistocene glaciers to form the region's northern limit. The Cheney-Palouse lobe of the Channeled Scablands comprises the region's western boundary, which extends from the timber line near Tyler, Washington, south to the mouth of the Palouse River. Annual rainfall increases from an average of fourteen inches in the western Palouse prairies to eighteen inches in the central Palouse hills and up to twenty-two inches in the foothills of the eastern mountains. This pattern corresponds to a rise in elevation from 1,200 feet in the southwest corner of the Palouse prairie to the fringe of the Clearwater Palouse Range at 2,800 feet, almost exactly one inch of precipitation for every hundred feet of elevation. Variations in soil fertility, developed over ages due to increasing rainfall eastward, led to climax vegetation associated with the Palouse's three climatic life zones: Upper Sonoran in the western Palouse, Arid Transition across the central Palouse hills, and Canadian in the eastern mountain uplands.

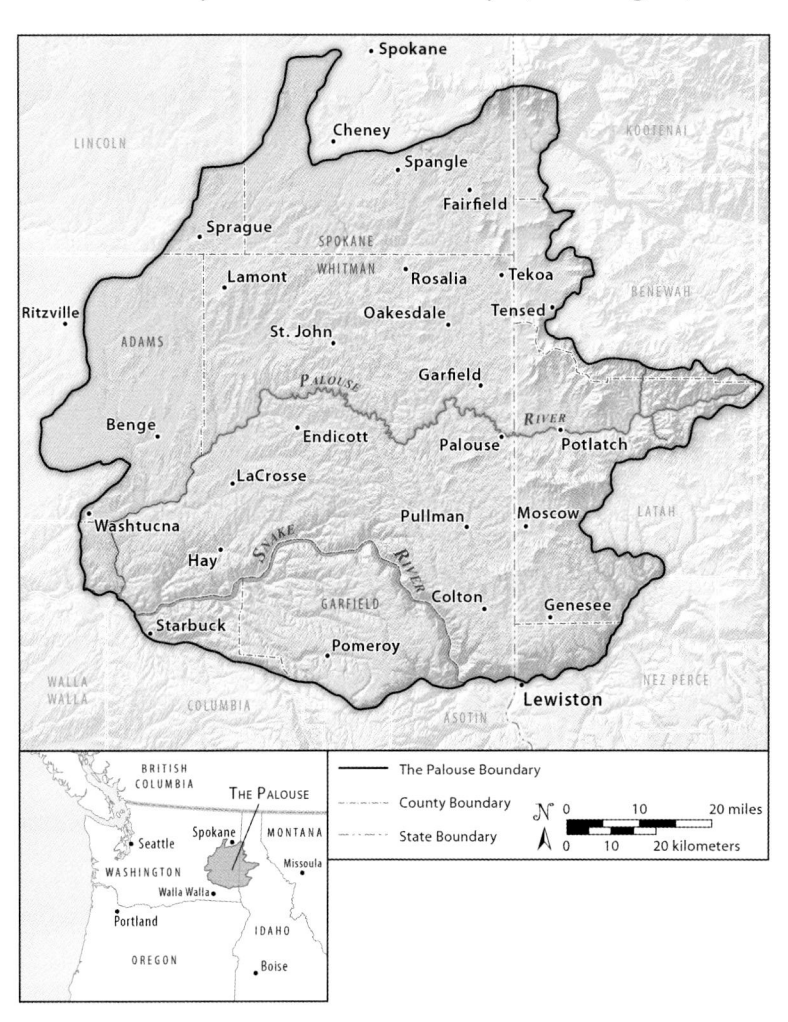

The Palouse Country Today

The name "Palouse" is likely from *Palús*, the Snake River-Palouse tribal Sahaptin word for the rock monolith prominent in regional mythology that was located near the confluence of the Palouse and Snake Rivers. The term combines the Palouse Sahaptin prefix *pa-* ("placed upright") with the root *–lú* ("be in water") which is combined with the diminutive suffix *–s*. "Palouse" in modern conventional spelling first appears in the 1855 Yakama Treaty, following references to "Peloose" in 1846 by Horatio Hale with Charles Wilkes' U. S. Exploring Expedition, and Isaac Stevens' "Pelouse" in an 1854 report to the Office of Indian Affairs. Early independent variations of the name may also be associated with the village of *Palótap* which was located on the northwest side of the Snake River west of present-day Colton. Although apparently unoccupied at the time of the Lewis & Clark Expedition, its

phonetic may relate to their use of the terms "Pallotepallows" and "Palloatpallah."

The commonly repeated notion that the word "Palouse" was derived from the French term *pelouse*, meaning "greensward or lawn," has no basis in nineteenth-century accounts describing the region. The idea probably first appeared in print as an editor's footnote to a 1904 edition of the Lewis and Clark journals. French-speaking fur traders with the North West Company and others who first spied the rolling hills of pulsing grasses would have likely referred to it with the same French word for such a landscape that was lent to the English language—prairie. An early description of the Palouse hills—an account of the 1846 Warre-Vavasour expedition published in French—describes the region as "*une vaste prairie ondulante*"—a vast undulating *prairie*.

The Eastern Palouse Uplands

The Palouse River headwaters are born in the clear stony brooks of Idaho's Hoodoo and Clearwater mountains and are fed by tributaries emerging from the Thatuna Range located between the river's north and south forks. These eastern uplands are composed of the western buttes' parent belt quartzites and argillites that rose with the Rocky Mountains when the Cascade Range had not yet emerged above the Pacific waters. In the formative processes of this early Mesozoic Age of explosive Rocky Mountain strato-volcanoes, hot magmatic fluids under great pressure penetrated this younger earth's crust and brought certain metals in gaseous state nearer the surface to form soluble compounds like gold chloride and aluminum-iron silicate. In places where water penetrated to great depth, these compounds dissolved, mixed with the magma, and were forced through fissures with other solubles like silicon dioxide, or quartz, to create veins containing precious metals and almandine garnet crystals.

Where this petrographic drama transpired under ancient, weathered surfaces, as in the Hoodoos, these deposits were worn by water until soft yellow flakes, larger nuggets, and violet-red gemstones fell out into streams which usually held these heavy particles near their sources. As in other high places along the Pacific Slope, indications of this placer gold in North Idaho resulted in nineteenth century regional rushes as prospectors flocked to the rumored El Dorados. Dodecahedron-faced garnets and rainbow-colored "harlequin" opals have also been sought in the eastern Palouse as the region's only semi-precious stones.

The eastern Palouse hosts a complex forest habitat that begins several miles east of Steptoe Butte where scattered ponderosa pine grows among the ubiquitous native grasses along the Palouse River with willow browse and brambles of wild rose and flowering shrubs. Spotted timber gradually becomes a mixed forest as the moister climate eastward brings forth stands of Western larch, or tamarack—a deciduous conifer—

and Douglas fir. Pines were dominant on the southern exposures. Thickets of black mountain huckleberry, serviceberry, and buckbrush flourish in sunlit meadows where their leaves and mountain bunchgrass have fed creatures of horn and hoof for centuries. Witness to a thousand years of whitened furies and springtime Chinooks were stands of giant red cedar on Kamiak Butte and Moscow Mountain. The tallest trees in these ancient forests rose to heights of 250 feet and some remain in threatened huddles as the oldest living things in the region.

The nation's largest white pine forest—mixed with larch, Engelmann spruce, and other conifers—commences at about 3,000 feet and covers the upper elevations of the Clearwater Mountains with old growth several hundred years old and often over two hundred feet high. These areas provide summer habitat to several songbird species including yellow warblers and red-breasted nuthatches as well as the smaller ruby-crowned kinglets, pine siskins, and black-capped chickadees. Beneath their flight patterns grow delicate orchid-like pink lady slippers and yellowbells that favor the canopy shade. Pioneer Palouse residents hunted these sylvan uplands for wild game and exploited the region's forests as sources of lumber and fuel unavailable on the bunchgrass prairies.

Mineral Mountain (Skyline Drive), 1945
Hutchison Studio Photographs of Washington State University and Pullman, WA., 1910-1973 (PC 70)
Manuscripts, Archives, and Special Collections, Washington State University Libraries, Pullman, WA.

The Palouse Hills

When the undulant verdure of the central Palouse emerges from winter's chill, the snowdrifts viewed from Steptoe Butte highlight barchan pattern of hills aligned northwest by southeast with recurrent concave headwalls of northeast-facing exposure. These features indicate hills of loess, or windblown silt, deposited by ancient winds from the Pasco Basin into gigantic earthen dunes connected by twisting benches, amphitheaters, and saddles. The fine-grained sediments far to the southwest had accumulated under prehistoric Lake Lewis after its appearance during the late Pliocene nearly a million years ago. These waters stretched across the lower Columbia Basin until the early Pleistocene when changes in weather and surface uplift reduced the lake to massive piles of desiccated silt.

The lower elevations of Steptoe Butte and its metamorphic neighbors as well as the Palouse's irregular basaltic overlay became inundated with these displaced particles along with periodic dustings from Cascade volcanic ashfalls. Wafted gusts of primordial winds patiently formed the textured tiers of the region's fertile hills and sculpted a curving labyrinth of swales, ridges, and slopes unique to the Palouse. The occasional dust storms that today reduce the late summer sun to a gossamer balloon invariably blow from the same direction as these ancestral currents and give some indication of the suffocating swirls that visited the region for ages. Further evidence of this peculiar earthen displacement is found in the size of particulate grains in the Palouse Hills that range from the heavy, coarse sands of the Juniper Dunes Wilderness Area southwest of Kahlotus to the fine yellow subsoil silts of the eastern Palouse.[2]

Large prehistoric mammals lumbered throughout the hills, seeking seasonal forage along grassy bottomlands during the later Pleistocene. Camel, giant sloth, antelope, mastodon, bison, and bighorn sheep have been excavated at a dozen sites along the western tier of the Palouse Hills from Washtucna to Rosalia, and many are displayed at WSU's Conner Museum of Natural History. Images of bison and sheep appear in the red and yellow pictographs and chipped petroglyphs at Buffalo Eddy near Lewiston, which are believed to be hundreds of years old. In 1876, a fascinating array of four mammoth skeletons, a human skull, spear point, and other artifacts were unearthed south of Latah by Henry Coplen and his five sons, from which was assembled the largest skeleton of the mammoth species ever found in North America. Standing thirteen feet high at the shoulder and with fossilized ivory tusks curving ten feet in length, the popular attraction was shown at circuses throughout the West until it was eventually acquired by Chicago's Field Museum, where it serves today as one of its most popular exhibits.

The protected northeast crescents of the hills are shielded from the prevailing southwesterlies and lie silently in shadow throughout most winter days, limiting evaporation and allowing deep drifts to form, which often remain into spring. This phenomenon reoccurred over millennia, penetrating the headwall soils with greater moister to foster banks of prodigious prairie and accumulations of enriching humus. Variations in biotic growth created a palette of topsoil browns across each hill's fertile patina, with the three microenvironments including a steeper leeward side-hill and draw of black earth and greatest fertility, an exposed ridge of intermediate chestnut soil, and the more gentle but drier and lighter southwest-facing slope. As precipitation increases across the central Palouse, three principal topsoil types of increasing fertility similarly characterize the hills from east to west that are known progressively as the Walla Walla, Athena, and Palouse associations.

Blue bunch wheatgrass, blue bunchgrass, ryegrass, and other mixed prairie perennials predominated on the legendary rolling Palouse Hills, providing luxurious forage for deer, bison, antelope, and in recent times, the Native peoples' vast horse herds that had descended from Spanish stock brought to New Mexico and New Spain in the sixteenth century. Several of these native grassland species are being reintroduced to the Palouse through the 1985 Conservation Reserve Program that has idled vast tracts of western Palouse farmland which were once in production. The Palouse Indians referred to the wild Gramineae species simply as *wasku*, or forage grass. In early summer, the prairie base was a tufted universe of slender stalks, emerging petioles, and curling leaves inhabited by herbivorous nations of crickets, beetles, and grasshoppers. Equipped with tiny, serrated sickle jaws, these species were integral to the grassland's ecological renewal by their ingestion of vegetative growth and subsequent deposition of organic forms essential to plant nutrition.

Biblical numbers of wraithlike mayflies, midges, and damselflies still appear with the first warm days of spring to feed neotropical creatures of larger wing that nest in the Palouse during seasonal migrations including shimmering calliope and Rufus hummingbirds. Birds of prey like the prairie falcon and sparrow hawk that reside in the Palouse throughout the year also capture dragonflies, moths, and other large insects flying against lucent summer skies. Underground, the patient labor of earthworms—one extinct species nearly a foot long (*D. ameriicanas*: Magascolecidae) being unique to the Palouse—work diligently in the fibrous darkness to transform soil minerals into organics also usable by prairie flora. Their infinite twisting tunnels together with the penetrations of decaying roots kept the ground open to aeration and percolation.[3]

The Palouse from Kamiak Butte, 1934.
Hutchison Studio Photographs of Washington State University and Pullman, WA., 1910-1973 (PC 70),
Manuscripts, Archives, and Special Collections, Washington State University Libraries, Pullman, WA.

facing page

Old Farm

east of
Colfax, Washington

Five large tribes of the grass family (Poaceae), representing at least eighty-five native species, once blanketed the Palouse in a rippling expanse of prodigious fecundity. These varieties were described by pioneer botanists Charles Piper and R. Kent Beattie, who assembled a comprehensive taxonomy of grasses that formed the woof and weft of the Palouse Country patina and described them in *Flora of the Palouse Region* (1901).[4] The seven principal native grass groupings below are distinguished by the number and arrangement of the miniscule spikelet flowers during inflorescence.

Native Palouse Grass Families

Panicae: Spikelets with one perfect flower or neutral and perfect flowers which fall with the seed—previously widespread on the sandy banks of the Snake River (e.g., *Panicum barbipulvinatum*).

Phalarideae: Spikelets with one perfect flower which does not fall with the seed—typically occurring in wet places, and often in shallow water as with reed canary grass.

Agrostideae: Spikelets with a staminate or neutral flower in addition to the perfect one—found in both dry and moist places; including *Calamagrostis rubescens*, the most abundant grass in the eastern Palouse pine forests.

Aveneae: Spikelets with a perfect and an imperfect flower which do not fall with the seed—including the once-abundant annual *Deschampsia calycina* and introduced members of the oats family.

Festuceae: Spikelets with two or more perfect flowers on a longer modified leaf (bract) —the widespread bromus (which later included foreign cheatgrass), *poa*, and *fescue* genera.

Chlorideae: Spikelets which do not fall with the seed and are crowded in two rows—coarse perennial grasses relatively rare in the Palouse.

Hordeae: Spikelets with two or more perfect flowers which do not fall with the seed and are arranged in opposite rows—including the Palouse Country's famed six native wheatgrass (*Agropyron*) and five ryegrass (*Elymus*) species.

In addition, some forty varieties of grass-like sedges, rushes, and reeds grew primarily in wetland areas. The sedge known as wool grass, however, preferred the drier areas of the western Palouse and would become a notorious pioneer plow-breaker. At least nine species of nutritious *Lomatium* were found along the Snake and Palouse rivers bluffs and on talus slopes. These plants intermixed with *Poaceae* members to create a complex Palouse prairie ecology of perennial, seed-producing, herbaceous mixtures. Several species had adapted to unique Palouse environmental conditions of soil moisture, alkalinity, chemistry, and climate. The flame-colored blossoms of sphaerostigma are found only in the vicinity of Sprague Lake while rare, orange-flowered balsam and purple Jacob's Ladder grow along Rock Lake. A unique pale-green rush (*J. confusus*) exists along the forest perimeter near present-day Spangle and a potentilla of yellow petals is restricted to moist meadows along central Rebel Flat Creek. White-flowered dogbane appears among tufted goldenrod only in the Albion lowlands. The Pullman area hosts the Palouse's only growth of leafy, white-flowered *Piperia elegans* and spiky-podded entanglings of the tall grass *Calamagrosis macouniana*.

The microenvironments of several regional geographic features also weave unique patterns of uncommon species into the region's botanical tapestry. The lower slopes of Steptoe Butte host a densely tufted fescue (*F. hallii*) and reed meadow grass in the surrounding lowlands. Multicolored beard-tongue and pink-petaled Claytonia are fleshy herbs found only to the south on the slopes of Kamiak Butte. The pine-covered ridges of the Thatuna Hills north of Moscow shelter the delicate, blue-blossomed bellflower amid one of the region's few stands of the bromegrass *B. eximius*. Clusters of scraggly hackberries grow on the basalt bluffs along the lower Palouse and Snake rivers while serviceberry bushes are found on the grassland bluffs east of Central Ferry. Copses of cinnamon-colored almond willow are located in the same areas where gentle springtime whirlwinds bring drowsy carousels of catkin and cattail cotton. A sea green sedge (*C. aristatus*) is found only at Almota and a densely tufted wheatgrass (*A. flexuosum*) and head-high ryegrass (*E. leckenbyi*) favored the sandy bars and lower hillsides near Wawawai.

Generations of wildlife browsing across slopes that were especially steep combined with the effect of annual frost heaves to create horizontal terracettes upon the hills. These natural stair-steps of mellow loam combined with the thick bunchgrass cover and rootlets to sponge up precipitation and deter any erosion. The waters of the Palouse River were clear throughout the year and while salmon were not found above Palouse Falls, trout, whitefish, and freshwater clams were plentiful in the upper river and its tributaries. Turtles were common along the water and, along with the mythical trickster Coyote, were often featured in tribal folktales to explain the origin of the natural world. According to Native elders, the Palouse Hills were formed by *Spilyái* (Coyote), who "outsmarted himself" in an attempt to be more clever than the other Animal People with whom he once shared the land. He scooped the earth into the distinctive pattern of undulating hills in a vain attempt to defeat Turtle and his brothers in a race from the Snake River to Spokane country. The story offered more than entertainment and explanation, for it taught Native youth the futility of deception and the value of persistence.

The serpentine Palouse River swims through the heart of the hills along a shallow western course beneath the base of Steptoe Butte, fed by quiet grassy streams that bore sibilant designations in the languages of the Native peoples: *Mocallisah* (North Palouse Fork), *Ingossamen* (Pine Creek), *Oraytayous* (Rock Creek), and *Cherana* (Cow Creek). These verdant bottomlands have hosted a more diverse flora with isolated pines and clumps of willow, black hawthorn, and cottonwood brightened by the seasonal blossoms of golden currant bushes and tangled honeysuckle vines with rows of fiery tubular flowers. An imminence of redolent meadow wildflower blossoms appear throughout spring and summer with bluebells, wild hyacinth, buttercups, purple iris, and yellow asters while sugar bowl clematis grows among riverbank conifers on southern exposures. The fuzzy purple heads of lupine were gathered by area Natives as grave decorations.

Low trees along Palouse streambeds provide habitat for the spherical twig and mudded mansions of magpies draped in their distinctive feathered robes of white and iridescent black, ever anxious to investigate and noisily render opinions in any riparian dispute. The magpie is the only bird with a greater length from beak to tail feather than its wingspan. Red-winged blackbirds also inhabit stream bank willows and nest several weeks earlier than their more aggressive yellow-tipped cousins who attempt similar songs of guttural prattle. Each spring clouds of delicate, white flowered ocean spray hang along the streambanks, held aloft on green stems that harden into brittle each fall. (The present-day riparian stands of poison hemlock are invaders.)

The sweet scent of pink roses emerges from thickets wands of osier dogwood along creeksides. Mourning doves and mergansers are common along the watery brambles while lumber along trails to their hillside burrows. Bobcats and coyotes pocket gophers, mice, ground squirrels, and other rodents that dwell in the adjacent rocky bluffs and surrounding hills. Birds, animals, and valley flora draw life daily from the river which can often be traced for miles from Steptoe's heights at dawn by tissues of fog rising from the waters to meet the spectral sun.

The Channeled Scablands

Appearing abruptly twenty miles west of Steptoe Butte is an alien landscape with evidence of unimaginable cataclysm. The same panorama that evokes Dantesque visions of wrath from some travelers has been extensively studied by NASA scientists investigating similar Martian features. The Cheney-Palouse channel of the scablands represents the western boundary of the Palouse region. But the term "scablands" is an unkind name obscuring the area's zephyred melodies and mysteries. These enchanted canyons are alive with complex biological diversity in spite of gargantuan prehistoric assaults. The terrain was formed after a collapse of a massive ice dam near the mouth of the Clark Fork River in northern Idaho that had created enormous glacial Lake Missoula some 15,000 years ago. The lake grew to cover 3,000 square miles across western Montana and contained approximately six hundred cubic miles of water—larger than Lake Erie.

When pressure and melting due to a warming trend caused the ice dam to break, the lake surged into an explosive flood, termed a "joekulhaup," that may have drained the lake in forty-eight hours releasing a volume of water larger than in any similar event indicated on the planet. Unable to contain such volume in the Columbia's ancient canyon course, the onslaught of Ice Age flooding tore across the soft rolling grasslands, which were violently "scabbed" or cut to bedrock, and formed three major drainages across the Columbia Plateau. The easternmost is the Cheney-Palouse lobe which contains mammoth boulders lying as ancient monuments carried from the Rockies, etched and shattered by mutilative force in areas up to about 2,400 feet in elevation. These ice-rafted erratics are above the shallow soil and glacial outwash on the vast prairies and mesas from Cheney to Kahlotus but are composed of granites, quartzites, and diorites from the metamorphic supergroup of the Montana-Idaho Rockies.

As the unimpeded waves sought declivities for escape, a peripheral branch of the eastern flow engorged what was likely an insequent streambed to form a torrential trench carving Hole-in-the-Ground's grandiose pavillioned walls, Rock Lake's incredible depth, and churned out the Rock Creek and lower Palouse River Canyons. The ancestral Palouse River ran through Washtucna and Esquatzel coulees to form several distinct Giant Current Ripple formations indicating wavelengths and heights of some two hundred feet. The torrid waters sped at seventy-five miles an hour to engorge the lower Columbia River at present-day Pasco and were temporarily impounded behind Wallula Gap. Here the waters backfilled the Pasco Basin to form 3,000 square mile Lake Lewis to a height of 900 feet.

The prehistoric lake's sediments are strikingly evident in the cream-colored cemented sandstones and chalky siltstones of the Ringold Formation some thousand feet thick which form the spectacular White Bluffs formation along the Hanford Reach. As the lake slowly evaporated each time, microscopic crystals of silicon dioxide bonded together into distillate amber and gray-brown nodules to form some of the continent's most spectacular chalcedony and banded agates. Lakes Lewis and Missoula may have filled and drained dozens of times over the last eight hundred millennia recurrently sending forth walls of water thundering southwest toward the lower Columbia and Pacific Ocean. About ten major glacial-interglacial cycles took place over the past million years with some fifty to one hundred floods across the region in each glaciations.[5]

Rock Lake in the western Palouse was known by some Natives as "Never Freezing Water" in which were confined the remains of a great reptilian monster that had terrorized both humans and animals long ago. In response to the people's prayers for deliverance from the pestilence, the Great Spirit slew the creature with a huge stone knife which then was used to tear the ground open for a grave. The dismembered creature was cast to the bottom and the chasm filled with water. Although tranquility to the region was restored, Native legend held that the monster's tail did not die and periodically thrashed to the surface in menacing fury. For this reason, Rock Lake was rarely fished by Natives, who deemed it a fearful place, and their stories of its creation may explain why pioneer travelers through the Palouse referred to it as "Specter Lake."

The same epochal forces that eroded the region's western loessal veneer and upper streambed strata penetrated at greater depth to fashion the lower Palouse River Canyon. Stretching from the confluence of the Palouse with the Snake River to

Rock Lake, northwest of St. John, Washington, 1931.
Hutchison Studio Photographs of Washington State University and Pullman, WA., 1910-1973 (PC 70), Manuscripts, Archives, and Special Collections, Washington State University Libraries, Pullman, WA.

Palouse Falls, the canyon stretches for five miles through a corporeal world of stair-stepped igneous solidity. Sparsely covered by clumps of scabland sagebrush, large-leaved forbs, scarlet native paintbrush, and bursts of ryegrass and bunchgrass, this Upper Sonoran zone of shrub steppe is home to coyotes and jackrabbits, marmots, rattlesnakes, and burrowing owls. Geese, canvasbacks, redhead ducks, and other migratory fowl find refuge on the many small lakes and in the sheltered river canyons of the western Palouse. These domains reveal austere clues to the mysteries of the land's creation in the lichen-painted sides of successive lava flows that lie in oppressive stacks.

Tens of thousands of years may have elapsed between these fissured Miocene outpourings giving rise to diverse prehistoric flora and fauna that was entombed beneath the flows. The average lava eruption resulted in a basaltic layer fifty to one hundred feet thick, and the several flows dramatically evident along the lower Palouse River constitute but a cap upon related formations nearly two miles thick. Each flow erupted through lengthy fissures from which the hot vicious swells oozed for dozens of miles or more. As the molten rock cooled inward from both surfaces, the bottom tier often formed basaltic colonnades of jointed columns which supported an upper entablature of downward radiating fans and irregular shapes. The exposed crowns of each level are porous, highly weathered, and overlook rocky talus slopes below Palouse Falls that cascade beyond the fractured cliffs toward the distant canyon floor.[6]

Located five miles above the river's mouth, Palouse Falls is a deafening cataract throughout the spring that pours down nearly two hundred feet into a spectacle of rainbowed spume. The falls pour over a basaltic layer some 15.5 million years old that divides the lower Grande Ronde Flows from the Wanapam and subsequent flows that substantially ended abruptly some fourteen million years ago. The Palouse Indians knew the lower river as a favored fishing area and had several seasonal camps amid the quiet copses of Osage orange and hackberry. The tribe's namesake, which was later given to the vast domain over which they ranged and knew intimately, was their principal village of *Palus* located on the right bank of the river at its confluence with the Snake. The site was at the historic crossroads where the ancient east-west river route from the Columbia to Nez Perce country met the main north-south Indian trail leading from the Walla Walla Valley to the land of the Spokanes. The word *Palus* referred to "Standing Rock," a basaltic monolith central to Palouse Indian cosmology located a short distance upstream.

According to tribal lore, in the time of the Animal People four Giant Brothers armed with spears attacked Beaver who peacefully resided near his lodge at present-day Hole-in-the-Ground. A terrific fight ensued during which Beaver clawed and chewed out the Rock Lake channel, one of the deepest lakes in the region with areas reaching down 325 feet. Beaver tore his way toward the Snake River and where he beat his tail along this route several times to form the smaller falls along the lower Palouse River. He was struck again at *Aput Aput* (Falling Water) where in his pain Beaver cut the castellated formations and sheer cliffs at Palouse Falls. The massive creature finally fell from his wounds where the rivers met and his heart was turned to stone. The Palouse people were said to have sprung from this part of Beaver and Indian youth were taught to affirm courage as one the tribe's most noble traits.[7]

Marmes Man and *Walsákwit*

In anticipation of lower canyon flooding to be caused by the completion of Lower Monumental Dam in 1965, WSU archaeologists led by Richard Daughtery, Roald Fryxell, and Carl Gustafson began excavations in the summer of 1962 at the mouth of a cavernous rock shelter on property along the Palouse River owned by Roland and Joanne Marmes (mar'-mus). Located near the west bank of the river approximately a mile from its confluence with the Snake, the scientists were encouraged by their initial findings of artifacts and prehistoric animal remains at what became known as the Marmes Rock shelter. By 1965 they had penetrated beneath the thick ash layer from the massive eruption of Mt. Mazama that formed Oregon's Crater Lake some 6,700 years ago.

In the summer of 1965 the first remains of Marmes Man were found at a depth of fourteen feet near the bones of an Arctic fox, pine marten, and other species associated with a significantly colder climate. Several weeks later two more individuals and artifacts were discovered including a delicately fashioned whalebone needle and coastal olivella necklace shells dating back ten millennia. The bones were determined to be from the burials of two young adults and a child about seven years old and were the oldest human remains ever recovered in the Western Hemisphere. In the words of American Archaeological Society president Hannah Worthington, the Marmes Rock shelter constituted America's foremost "calendar of the centuries," but soon fell victim to the backwaters of the dam.

Another discovery of major anthropological significance was made in July 1996 southwest of the Palouse periphery near the confluence of the Snake and Columbia rivers where the nearly complete skeleton of Kennewick Man was found. The remains, containing a Cascade Phase spearpoint embedded in the left hip bone, were dated approximately 7,400 years BC. These individuals are among those reverently referred to by Plateau peoples as the "Ancient Ones," and the tribal governments of the Inland Northwest's reservations became embroiled in protracted legal struggles in federal courts successfully fighting for their reburial as a sacred responsibility.[8]

Based in large part on Palouse and other Native oral traditions describing the massive floods, people, and creatures of these past ages, US Secretary of Interior Bruce Babbitt ruled in favor of the tribes in 1999. Though contested in court by scientists who contend that the cultural affinity of groups separated by such great time is unlikely, Babbitt's landmark decision affirmed that these stories, known to the Palouses as *walsákwit*, provide valid ancestral links between these prehistoric people of the Columbia Plateau and those living here today. The archaeological record does indicate that few humans probably lived in the region 10,000 years ago years ago but a thousand years later evidence of seasonal human occupation exits throughout the Columbia Plateau, from The Dalles to Hells Canyon and from the lower Palouse River Canyon to Kettle Falls.

These first residents ranged widely using travel routes along Pacific shorelines and inland waterways to gather plant foods, hunt small and large mammals, and to find favorable salmon fishing sites after the great ice sheets melted. The beginning of a significant warming trend some 7,500 years ago, continuing until approximately 2,000 BC, was accompanied by the appearance of fishnets and tackle assemblies along the Columbia and Snake rivers. The availability of salmon as a reliable staple of the Native people's diet brought about more seasonal and regional migration patterns with pit-house villages appearing on the lower Snake River around 3,000 BC. At that time King Menes united Upper and Lower Egypt to establish the first dynasty, the Sumerians were beginning to grow barley, and a thousand years remained before Abraham

Lower Palouse River Canyon, 1932
*Hutchison Studio Photographs of Washington State University
and Pullman, WA., 1910-1973 (PC 70)
Manuscripts, Archives, and Special Collections, Washington State University Libraries,
Pullman, WA.*

Palouse Falls, 1941
*Hutchison Studio Photographs of Washington State University
and Pullman, WA., 1910-1973 (PC 70)
Manuscripts, Archives, and Special Collections, Washington State University Libraries,
Pullman, WA.*

would leave Ur for the Promised Land.

An abundance of nephrite and diorite pestles along the lower Snake River and at the Marmes site dating from 3,000 BC suggests that the milling of roots and berries also came into widespread use at that time. Finely flaked projectile points show a gradual transition from use for hunting large prehistoric mammals with enormous Clovis spearpoints associated with the earliest occupation sites to those half the size for thrusting with an atlatl and finally, the beautifully crafted smaller arrowheads that came with the introduction of the bow around 500 AD. I recall occasionally spotting artifacts of the latter sort during hikes in my youth along the Palouse River and Union Flat Creek. Invariably they were knapped into exquisitely symmetrical shapes and made from the widely assorted colors of semiprecious crypto-crystallines—yellow opals, banded agates, milky chert, blood red jasper, obsidian, and transparent chalcedony.

Emily Peone, a descendant of both Kamiakin and Moses, told me that the people of her great-grandparents' generation were quick to adopt useful innovations from the first *Shuyapos* (Whites) who came to the Inland Northwest. (The name was likely derived from the hats worn by the early fur traders.) Raised to a great extent by her great aunt, Mary Owhi Moses, Emily recalled listening attentively in their cabin near Nespelem to her stories about times long ago. "Whenever we would take Mary with us to dig roots," Emily recalled, "whether toward the Yakima or Palouse, she could point out something special that had once happened on most any hill or in any valley. 'Here's where Chief Moses kept his horses in summer, there's where we traded with the King George's men [Hudson's Bay traders].'" Mary Owhi Moses served as an honored matriarch among the Columbia Plateau tribes during the nineteenth century, an especially venerated elder who survived the cataclysmic events that shaped the region's history during an unprecedented lifetime of change.

Born in 1829, Mary Moses (Sanclow) witnessed the arrival of the first fur traders and missionaries to the Inland Northwest. She was the daughter of the Yakama Chief Owhi and first cousin to Chief Kamiakin—principal leaders with whom Governor Stevens negotiated the Yakima Treaty of 1855. Her brother was the warrior Qualchan whom Col. George Wright hung at Smith's Ford near Spokane in 1858. As a young woman, Mary became the youngest wife of the Columbia-Sinkiuse leader Moses, whose political skills were instrumental in establishing the Colville Reservation in the 1880s. Emily Peone was one of dozens of Moses and Kamiakin descendants who lived on reservations throughout the Northwest. Passing away in 1937, Mary Moses lived to great age and spent her last years in Emily's household where she provided rare and unusually informative insight into events surrounding the wars of the 1850s and the tribes' transition to reservation life.[9]

Landscapes of Coyote and Beaver

At the dawn of the nineteenth century, perhaps 2,000 American Indians lived in the Palouse region for much of the year, frequenting various favored places to hunt, gather roots, pasture horses, and fish. Their numbers are difficult to estimate given the fluid nature of Plateau Indian culture; however numerous winter villages existed among the Sahaptin-speaking Snake River-Palouse and Nez Perce tribes along the lower Snake River while Coeur d'Alenes and Spokanes who spoke Interior Salish languages also made extensive use of the northern region. As with Native peoples throughout North America, the Columbia Plateau tribes had a close relationship with the natural world.

Snake River-Palouse elder Mary Jim Chapman related that "the land was our religion. We considered the earth to be our Mother because it provided us all food. The Great Spirit (*Imepship*) had placed us on our Earth Mother (*Imephsha*) who blessed us with her nutritious roots, berries, and vegetables. The Great Spirit had created the deer, antelope, and elk, and these animals shared the earth with the Indian people." Like other Natives on the Plateau, the world of Palouse area tribes revolved about a yearly cycle or seasonal round that covered an immense territory. Beginning in the spring of each year, salmon swam out of the Pacific Ocean, fought their way up the great current of the Columbia River, and followed its tributaries upstream until they reached their spawning grounds in the Inland Northwest. Conditions were most favorable for fishing in May and from July through October.

The Native peoples of the Palouse Country caught salmon by the thousands as these were part of the abundance given to them by the Creator. Both the physical and spiritual worlds were inseparable and both were derived from their relationship with the earth throughout the seasons. The spring renewal of life was strikingly evident in the resurgence of flow in the Snake and Spokane rivers and their tributaries. Fed by the melting waters of the Bitterroots and Blue Mountains, the Snake began to rise and carry with it a variety of debris from the high country. The animals felt the change as well, particularly the horses that still sported their heavy winter coats. Migration, trading, and raiding probably brought the first horses to the Inland Pacific Northwest by 1750. March was a time of much activity for the Natives who busied themselves in preparation for their journey onto the Columbia Plain. "We called this *Shai Tash*, 'Time to Move Out,'" recalled Mary Jim;

Palouse Regional Tribal Domains, c. 1850

"those horses that were to make the trip out of the canyon were cut out from the herds. Many of these animals had not been ridden in some time, so the men mounted the skittish ponies and rode them hard until they stopped bucking."

Men, women, and children alike then mounted the horses and began their jaunt to the root grounds while some family members remained along the rivers for the first salmon runs in May. For children like young Mary, traveling again and seeing the animals of the land was an exciting time. Linguistic indications of the Native People's intimacy with the natural world is evident in countless Sahaptin terms for plant species used for food, as medicine, or in fashioning baskets, mats, and other useful items. The Palouse and Nez Perce Sahaptin languages are among the most ancient spoken by Native Americans anywhere in the Western Hemisphere. Many Palouse names for birds were as much sung as spoken, in onomatopoetic mimicry of the creatures' calls—*áčak* (magpie), *mítalu* (mourning dove), *siwlalí* (trumpeter swan), *xwíɫxwɫ* (meadow lark), and a sentinel bird, *wawyik'k* (whip-poor-will). Others were known by their behavior or other distinct qualities including "dances together" (sage grouse), "traveler" (snow goose), and the prairie falcon, or "comes at you," America's only indigenous member of the Falconidae.[10]

Northern Sahaptin Palouse and Nez Perce are members of the Macro-Penutian super-language family and are more closely related to Coastal Chinookan and even Mesoamerican tongues than Spokane and Coeur d' Alene Salish. Linguistic analysis have led some anthropologists to postulate that Sahaptin speakers may have descended from some of the earliest American Indian populations that migrated southward along the western Rockies at least 15,000 years ago before dividing into groups that continued south and west. Others chose to remain in the vast realm of the Inland Pacific Northwest where, according to their traditions, humans were formed from the body of giant creature and the land was prepared for their occupation by the Animal People.

The "winged seed" Lomatium family includes such familiar greens as parsley, dill, and celery. The nine species native to the Palouse, nutritious staples of the native diet, favored the shallow lithosols among rocky outcroppings. The appearance of blossoming Canby's lomatium, known to the Palouse and Nez Perce as *lukš*, in late February and early March signaled the beginning of spring for Plateau rootdiggers. Early army topographers identified Union Flat Creek by the Interior Salish name *Skolkul* because of the four major rootgrounds found along its course (near present-day LaCrosse, Wilcox, Union Center, and Colton). Among the other eight important tuberous lomatiums that grew along the Snake River and in the western Palouse were Gray's lomatium, or "Indian celery," Hamblen's lomatium, and yellow-flowered kouse (*L. cous*).

Over twenty principal camas grounds covering up to several dozen acres each were located across the Palouse in vernal meadows at such places as Washtucna and Rock lakes, along Latah, Pine, and Union Flat creeks and the Palouse River, and in the fertile lowlands near present-day Colfax, the Pullman-Moscow area, and at the southeastern base of Steptoe Butte. Edible camas (*Q. quamash*) displays white or blue flowers and was gathered in vast quantities during early summer while the shunned death camas (*Z. venenosus*) presents yellow blossoms.

The rock rose, or bitterroot, also grew in the rocky soils of the western Palouse but was more abundant on the drier plains to the west. Along with the wild huckleberries that ripened in the fall on bushes clustered among the pines in the eastern Palouse, camas, kouse, and bitterroot were the four most important plant foods of the four Palouse Country tribes. Places favored by the Coeur d' Alenes and Spokanes for spring bitterroot and camas digging included the upper Palouse Country from *Nigualk'h* (Tensed) in the valley of the Palouse North Fork and northwesterly across the present-day Rockford, Spangle, and Cheney districts. Here the size of the roots and the ease of digging in the rich black loam attracted large tribal gatherings each spring.[11]

Palouse area Natives gathered roots during their spring journey onto the Columbia Plain and Palouse Hills until the salmon began their movement up the Columbia River. When the bands learned of the spring run of the salmon, they returned to their permanent villages and prepared for fishing. Many varieties of fish were taken from the Snake, Spokane, Clearwater rivers and streams tributary to them including trout, whitefish, squawfish, suckers, chubs, and eels. Snake River white sturgeon were also fished although when mature some could reach twelve feet in length and weigh a half-ton-making them virtually impossible to capture. Three genera of the Salmonidae family of fishes were native to the Snake River including the genus *Oncorhynchus* with five species of Pacific salmon (Chinook, silver, pink, sockeye, chum). *Salvelinus* members are the Dolly Varden, or bull trout, and brook trout, while the genus *Salmo* includes the anadromous steelhead and non-anadromous rainbow and cutthroat trout.

Historic Snake River-Palouse Salmon Species

Chinook (King) Salmon (*Oncorhynhus tshawytscha*) / Snake River-Palouse Sahaptin: *núsuҳ*
Freshwater lifetime: 2 to 5 years; ocean lifetime: 1 ½ to 5 years
Historic Snake River-Palouse spawning season: September to November
Distinguishing characteristics: black gums, spotted tail fin

Silver (Coho) Salmon (*O. kisutch*) / Snake River-Palouse Sahaptin: *sinúx*
Freshwater lifetime: 1 to 2 years; ocean lifetime: 1 to 2 years
Historic Snake River-Palouse spawning season: September to January
Distinguishing characteristics: white gums, upper tail fin spots

Pink (Humpback) Salmon (*O. gorbuscha*) / Snake River-Palouse Sahaptin: *wak'ya*
Freshwater lifetime: 6 months; ocean lifetime: 1 ½ years
Historic Snake River-Palouse spawning season: June to September
Distinguishing characteristics: dark oval spots on back and tail fin

Sockeye (Blueback) Salmon (*O. nerka*) / Snake River-Palouse Sahaptin: *k'halux*
Freshwater lifetime: 1 to 2 years; ocean lifetime: 1 to 4 years
Historic Snake River-Palouse spawning season: August to October
Distinguishing characteristics: small pupil, no tail fin spots

Chum (White, Dog) Salmon (*O. keta*) / Snake River-Palouse Sahaptin: *čilí*
Freshwater lifetime: 1 to 3 years; ocean lifetime: 1 to 3 years
Historic Snake River-Palouse spawning season: December-June
Distinguishing characteristics: large pupil, no tail fin spots

Steelhead Trout (*Salmo gairdneri*) / Snake River-Palouse Sahaptin: *šušáyš*
Freshwater lifetime: 1 to 3 years; ocean lifetime: 1 to 3 years
Historic Snake River-Palouse spawning season: January to June
Distinguishing characteristics: reddish horizontal side-band

Snake River-Palouse Fish Species.
(From top: Chinook, Steelhead, Cutthroat, Chum, Brook)
John H. Richard, Smithsonian Artist-in Residence
Reproduced from Isaac I. Stevens, *Report of Explorations for a
Route for the Pacific Railroad*, 1860.

With no major waterfalls for dip-netting on the lower Snake River, most salmon were taken by gill netting, weirs along small tributaries, or by gaffing spawning fish. Palouse area Natives also traveled to net fish at Celilo and Kettle falls, the two largest fisheries on the Columbia River. The annual catch of salmon and steelhead by Columbia Plateau tribes prior to White contact is conservatively estimated to have been 17,000,000 pounds. Fish accounted for approximately one-third of the Plateau Indian diet while roots and berries contributed about half. Game meat including venison and wild fowl substantially completed nutritional needs.[12]

Salmon, however, were by far the most important fish to the Natives of the region. Besides being one of the most important sources of food, they held a special significance in the cosmology of the Natives. Most Plateau tribes of the Northwest held a thanksgiving ceremony in honor of the salmon as soon as the first fish was caught. All fishing in the area stopped when a man brought in the first salmon. It was cooked, usually boiled, and became the center of the rites. Everyone was issued a portion of water, to fill horn spoons or wooden vessels, and after a prayer was said, the water was drunk by all present. Another prayer was sung thanking the Creator for the fish. Everyone then took a portion of the salmon, ate it, and then took another sip of water. A lengthy prayer was sung and the remaining skeleton of the fish was returned to the water facing upstream. Once proper religious rites were completed for the sacred salmon, fishing resumed. Thousands of salmon were taken from the river, and each year they returned.

Fishing was very much a part of Columbia Plateau Indian lifeway as well as that of virtually all other Natives of the Pacific Northwest. The Snake River-Palouse believed that the salmon runs began in the age of the Animal People. According to tribal oral histories Coyote (*Spilyái*) had challenged anyone to break an immense elk antler. Various creatures tried, including Eagle (*Xwayamayái*), Racoon (*Keekiya*), and

Cougar (*Kwayawiyai*), but it was not until Salmon (*Nusuxyái*) strained over the rack that it finally split with a thunderous clap. Burning with envy, the other competitors killed Salmon with their arrows but did not notice something fall from one of his wounds into the river. It was a silvery scale that was carried all the way to the ocean, where it eventually grew into another Salmon Man. He later ascended the river to learn his ancestral origin and this journey began the cycle of salmon runs to the Snake River and its tributaries. Coyote later taught the Snake River-Palouse how to catch the salmon by using nets made of milkweed hemp.[13]

After the spring and summer runs of salmon, many families left their villages to venture onto the Columbia Plateau or the lowland valleys in the Palouse Hills. They would travel to root grounds and camp to dig, hunt, and relax. Summers in the region were usually mild and dry. The children played games with a hoop and a pole or a bat and ball. Men and boys would practice and hone their skill as archers. One of the most enjoyable pursuits was horse racing. The Plateau Indians became great horse people soon after the introduction of these animals to the Plateau in the mid-eighteenth century, and men and women alike could care for and ride horses. They were well aware of the qualities that made a good horse, and they bred horses that were strong, fast, and smart. Although it is unlikely that they bred horses for color alone, some Indians prized the beautifully spotted Appaloosa horses and recognized their value as a medium of trade.

The late summer and fall were also important times to area Natives for hunting and digging, as well as for gatherings with neighboring tribes of the region. This time of the year also had a religious significance as the time when young people, boys and girls alike, were sent on their spirit quests. Youth from about the age of twelve went out alone to seek a spirit in remote places like the summit of Yámuštas (Steptoe Butte). Similar places were located along the foothills and in the meadows of the Blue Mountains where tribal bands frequented fall hunting and berry grounds. As the brisk autumn weather transformed the mountain slopes into fiery landscapes of red and yellow, young people might seek their guardian spirits on such peaks as *Paléyniwees* (Lost Mountain) east of present-day Tollgate, Oregon. *Tahámtaham* (Cloudy or Dark [Mountain]) to the southwest was avoided since the summit was a portal to the Spirit World which humans were forbidden to enter. Animal People sentries clad in blue feathers and white bear hides stood high upon its slopes to warn seekers not to continue further into the foggy heights.

During the quest, a guardian spirit might appear in a dream as a wolf, cloud, bear, eagle, hawk, or other animal or natural phenomenon like hail or thunder. Protection and guidance could then be summoned for a lifetime through a song imparted to the seeker. After the youths experienced a few days of solitude, they returned to camp or elders of the tribe went to gather and feed them. The old men of the tribes, those of great wisdom, heard from the children about their experiences and interpreted dreams for the children who had now come of age. Such visions were not deemed fantasies but a deeply revered spiritual experience revealed through the imagination. The Native peoples' specific knowledge of the regional landscape and its creatures informed their mythology and spirit quests. Human beings existed within a sacred circle of life that brought together past, present, and place in a nexus that transcended tense and tangibility.[14]

Late summer meshed subtly with early fall and the bands moved gradually into that part of the seasonal round that took them to favored hunting grounds. The men killed larger game animals like deer and elk as well as grouse and waterfowl. They prepared the meat for the coming winter while the women gathered berries and dug the last vestiges of camas and kouse. gooseberries, thornberries, service berries, and blackberries were among the favorites of Palouse area Natives. Two varieties of elderberries were also picked, one from the prairie and one from the higher mountains. As the Natives moved their camps into the mountains where there was better hunting, the other variety of elderberry was picked. Also found in the higher country was the serviceberry, huckleberry, snowberry, and fire berry which sometimes were mixed with dried meat. The fireberry was so small that the Natives devised a small comb to pick the tiny fruit. Pine moss or bear-hair lichen was also collected in the high mountains, cooked underground like camas, and pounded into a fine treat that is still prized for its licorice-like flavor.

As winter approached, the many bands of Natives packed up their belongings and started on their journey back across the gentle valleys and rolling hills to their permanent villages along the Snake, Clearwater, and Spokane rivers. They were heavy laden with the prepared meat, berries, and roots.

During the winter months family lodges became the center of much activity although the entire band usually gathered for the Guardian Spirit Dance. This was a sacred ceremony for Natives of the Columbia Plateau and demonstrated their affinity with their spirit guardians and the natural world. Because of inclement weather people spent much time inside or gathered around a communal fire along the river. While the women mended baskets and men repaired hunting and fishing gear or knapped new points, family elders shared their legends and tribal history with the children. Few could anticipate, however, the sweeping changes about to unfold as sailing vessels of exploration and trade from Europe and New England began appearing along the Pacific coastline. In September 1805 a group of three dozen intrepid Americans and French Canadians, Nez Perce guides, and young woman with her infant son crossed Lolo Pass from the east.

facing page

Kamiak Butte Sunrise

south of
Palouse, Washington

Building Storm

southern Palouse, looking north towards LaCrosse, Washington

CHAPTER II

Pathfinders and Traders

After an arduous trek across the Northern Rockies during which the Corps of Discovery was befriended by Nez Perces—a name attributed to them by the Shoshones—Lewis and Clark entered the lower Snake River Valley in October 1805. They named Potlatch Creek "Colter's Creek" for quick-witted John Colter, one of Lewis's "nine young men from Kentucky" who all made the entire trip. Colter would earn fame for his legendary escape from Blackfeet Indians four years later when he was stripped of his clothes and afforded a brief head-start before the Blackfeet gave chase. Lewis wrote admiringly of the Nez Perces' horses, which he described as "lofty, elegantly formed, active and durable." He also noted some were colored "with large spots of white irregularly scattered and intermixed with the black-brown bay or some other dark color."[1]

In March 1899, a surveyor found a Jefferson Peace Medal near the mouth of Potlatch Creek during railroad construction in the vicinity. One of the Corps of Discovery's Nez Perce guides through the region, Neeshnepark Keeook (Cut Nose), lived in a village near this place and was presented such a medal by the captains during their return trip in spring 1806. This rare silver treasure, one of only about three dozen carried by Lewis and Clark, is now owned by the Nez Perce Tribe and displayed at the Nez Perce National Historic Park Museum in Spalding, Idaho. The explorers followed the Clearwater to its mouth near present-day Lewiston, where they camped on October 10, 1805. William Clark's diary entries for the next three days provide the first written account of the southern Palouse borderlands. On the 10th, he described the setting at this historic confluence:

"We arrived at a large southerly fork [the Snake River] *which is the one we were on with the Snake* [Indian] *nation. The country about the forks is an open plain on either side. The water of the south fork is greenish blue, the north* [Clearwater River] *as clear as crystal. The Indians came down all the courses of this river on horses to view us as we were descending. The Pierced Nose Indians are stout, likely men, handsome women, and very dressy in their way. The dress of the men are a white buffalo robe or elk skin dressed with beads which are generally white, sea shells, and mother-of-pearl hung to their hair on a piece of otter skin. The women dress in a shirt of ibex* [mountain sheep] *skins which reach quite down to their ankles...ornamented with quilled brass, beads, shells, and curious bones."*

On the following day, the explorers continued on their quest to the Pacific: *"We set out early and...passed a rapid at two miles. At six miles we came to at some Indian lodges and took breakfast. We purchased all the fish we could and seven dogs... for stores of provisions down the river. At this place* [Almota] *I saw a curious sweat house underground; with a small hole at top to... throw in the hot stones, which threw on as much water as needed to create the temperature of heat they wished. The country on either side is an open plain and fertile after ascending a steep ascent of about 200 feet with not a tree of any to be seen on the river."* On October 12, 1805, the party canoed nearly thirty miles and camped near present-day Riparia. *"We passed several stony islands today. The country as yesterday [is] open plains, no timber of any kind, a few hackberry bushes and willows excepted, and but a few drift trees to be found so that firewood is very scarce. The hills or ascents from the water are faced with a dark rugged stone."*

On October 13th, the party passed the mouth of the Palouse River and Clark paid tribute to the useful presence of Sacagawea as a member of the epic expedition: *"The wife of Shabono [Charbonneau] our interpreter we find reconciles all the Indians as to our peaceful intentions. A woman with a party of men is a token of peace. We took all our canoes through this rapid without any injury. A little below passed another bad rapid [Texas Rapids]....Passed the mouth of a large creek [Tucannon River]. A little river [Palouse] in a starboard bend, immediately below a long bad rapid, in which the water is confined in a channel about twenty yards between rugged rocks for two miles above....Here is a great fishing place, the timbers of several houses piled up, and a number of wholes of fishes. The bottom appears to have been made as a place of deposit for their fish for ages past."*[2]

The explorers' field map shows a village of tule-mat "cabins" on the west side of the Palouse River's mouth and burial "vaults" on the east side. Three days later, the explorers reached the great intertribal campground at the confluence of the Snake and Columbia rivers near present-day Pasco. A large gathering of Native peoples greeted their arrival, and the captains presented three Jefferson medallions to the assembled chiefs. One recipient was Palouse leader Ke Pow Han. Lewis and Clark incorporated the Palouse into their estimate of 2,300 Nez Perce inhabiting the region below the Clearwater River. At that time of the year, many of the Palouse tribal members were likely encamped on their fall hunting grounds to the southeast. By peculiar coincidence, a third Jefferson medal, one of a handful found along the entire transcontinental route, was also found in the region near present-day Wallula. The captains presented Walla Walla Chief Yelleppit, a "handsome Indian with a dignified countenance," the silver "token of peace" near this place. This artifact is now exhibited at the Oregon Historical Society Museum in Portland.[3]

Lewis and Clark's Corps of Discovery included among its thirty-three members two French-Canadians who served as hunters and interpreters. George Drouillard was the most dependable of the hunters and behaved coolly under any crisis. Lewis and Clark named the Palouse River for their highly regarded companion, and it bears the name "Drewyer's River" on their remarkably accurate 1806 map. The first person associated with the North West Company to reach the Pacific Slope was Corps' interpreter and the husband of Sacagawea, Toussaint Charbonneau. The verbose trader had apparently won the young Hidatsa woman in a gambling game several years after she had been kidnapped by Minnitaree raiders at the age of twelve. She was sixteen when Charbonneau took her as one of his several wives. Sacagawea gave birth to their son, Jean Baptiste, on February 11, 1805, while Lewis and Clark wintered among the Mandan Indians in present-day North Dakota. During the Corps' epic westward trek, she came to be highly regarded by the men for her kindness, occasional recognition of vital landmarks, and reassuring presence among the Native tribes which the group encountered.

In September 1995, our Endicott-St. John Middle School received its annual visit from the regional representative for our communities' annual magazine sale fundraiser. I had worked with affable Tom Sharbono for years, as his territory covered Whitman County schools, and on that 1995 visit I listened to his presentation and spoke with him afterwards. When I inquired about his previous life before helping supply us with *The Atlantic Monthly* and *Harper's Magazine*, he mentioned teaching near Mandan, North Dakota. Given that intelligence and the sound of his last name, I ventured to ask. "Yes, I am," he replied with a soft smile. "My great-grandfather was Sacagawea's grandson, Joseph Charbonneau." I was stunned at the significance of such a heritage and proceeded to learn much about Tom's efforts years earlier to help establish the Fort Mandan State Historic Site.

I had always wondered about the fate of the expedition's youngest member, tiny Jean Baptiste Charbonneau, and what the family thought of the popular story that Sacagawea might have lived almost to the century mark on the Wind River Reservation in Wyoming. "I wish it were true," Tom sighed, "but Clark's records and our family accounts agree that she probably died from sickness in 1812. Her son, however, went on to have a long and incredible life." Clark had asked permission from the boy's parents to adopt the boy, which they allowed, and he attended school in St. Louis. While still in his teens, Jean Baptiste guided Duke Paul Wilhelm of Germany on an excursion up the Platte River and was invited to join the duke's family to study in Europe, which he did from 1824 to 1829. During that time, the young American also toured North Africa, where he likely saw the original "Pompey's Pillar" in Alexandria, Egypt, for which Clark had named a promontory in Montana and which was the basis of the nickname "Pomp" that he gave the boy. Jean Baptiste then returned to the Western frontier, where he trapped with the likes of Jim Bridger and James Beckwourth. From time to time he would return to visit relatives in Montreal, where he met and married Tom's great-grandmother, Charlotte Guery.

Jean Baptiste Charbonneau was the only member of the Corps of Discovery who ever returned to the Pacific Northwest. "He was heading from California to the Montana gold strikes in the spring of 1866 when he took ill and died in southeastern Oregon," Tom explained. "He's buried in the Jordan Valley at a place called Inskip's Ranch. I visit the place from time to time." When Tom returned to the school a month later to deliver his regular sales orientation to the students, we made arrangements for him to extend his stay and share his remarkable story and family memorabilia with all our middle-school classes. The setting was our new school library, with Tom standing directly beneath a massive ivory colored bas-relief we had salvaged from the old Endicott School. Such three-dimensional works depicting pivotal moments in American history were once found in schools throughout the country, and this one gave the contractor fits getting it properly mounted in the wall of the new building. The image shows two buckskin-clad men with one pointing to crashing waves visible in the distance. Nearby stands a woman with a child carried in a sling on her back. Tom pointed to them to begin his presentation.

The romanticized scene is titled "Lewis and Clark Reach the Pacific" and alludes to lines from Elmer Harper Sims's epic poem commemorating the 100th anniversary of the expedition, *Sacajawea and the Lewis and Clark Expedition*. The saga moves to the iambic rhythm of *Hiawatha*:

Swift they glided to the westward, down the Snake to the Columbia.

Here a wise and learned chieftain, very learned Yakima head chief,

Like the Nez Perce made an outline, of the country round about them.

Like the friendly Nez Perce tewat, *marked the rivers and the trails,*

Marked each mountain and each village, foot–prints pointed out the trails.

Again they floated down the river, down the deep and blue Columbia....

Here they heard the mighty breakers, only forty miles to seaward,

Roaring, surging, dashing, breakers, of the deep and briny ocean.

There upon a towering headland, when the sky was bright and pleasant,

They beheld the wondrous ocean, saw the open road to China,

Saw that vast expanse of water, stretching far away to westward.

Caproni Brothers, *Lewis and Clark Reach the Pacific* (bas relief), cast c. 1910.
Courtesy Endicott-St. John Cooperative Schools

Seeder Lines   near Mica, Washington

facing page

Aeolian Hills

south-central Palouse Hills aerial view

Nor'Westers, Astorians, and "The Honorable Company"

Amiable relations continued between the Palouse Tribe and the European-Americans through 1811, when the Palouse "forced a gift of 8 horses" on British explorer-trader David Thompson, who visited the village of Palus in August. En route to the North West Company's Spokane House, he found the Palouse tribal members frenetic over his arrival and eager to trade. The diminutive yet irrepressible Thompson was assiduous in his efforts to accurately map the regions he explored for the Hudson's Bay Company (HBC) before he entered the employ of the North West Company, founded in 1783 by Montreal merchants of Scottish ancestry. Known to the Native peoples as "Star Man" for the measurements he regularly made to determine locations precisely, Thompson's early years in the wilderness rendered him nearly blind in one eye. He attributed this condition to excessive smoke exposure while reading by candlelight about surveying techniques while he convalesced for almost a year after a near-fatal fall east of the Canadian Rockies when he was still in his teens. The seriously broken leg left him lame for the rest of his life but did not deter him from eventually crossing the mountains and opening the Pacific Northwest to company interests.

In a successful effort to find the source of the Columbia River, Thompson had crossed the Continental Divide in 1807 and established Kootenae House near present-day Golden, British Columbia, the first Nor'Wester outpost in the region. In April of the following year, Thompson planted a small experimental garden and scattered a few kernels of barley, which, he reported in August, had flourished. Under his direction, Finan McDonald and Jaco Finlay founded Spokane House at the junction of the Spokane and Little Spokane rivers in 1810. In the summer of 1811, Thompson ventured up from the lower Columbia and Snake rivers, heading to Spokane House. He reached the mouth of the Palouse River in August. On the way

he noted the peculiar basalt formations of the Snake River cliffs, some appearing "like flutes of an organ at a distance" and others "broken or cracked by a violent blow." At Palus village the intrepid geographer found dozens of Indians delighted with his arrival. They danced in his honor and gave Thompson eight horses and a leather war garment. He tried to repay their kindness with trade goods, but the Snake River-Palouses declined any compensation for their highly valued gifts.

Thompson then turned north and became the first explorer to traverse the western fringes of the central Palouse using the ancient route that frontiersmen dubbed the Palouse Trail. As usual, he kept detailed field notes on his travels, in which he described an open country where "there is often a few aspens, alder, a very rare fir along the brook, with much wild cherry and three sorts of currants." Thompson likely rode from the mouth of Cow Creek along the Palouse River and Rock Creek to the foot of Rock Lake. He then veered north and followed the main trail that led to Spokane House. (Incidentally, Cow Creek is one of the area's few waterways that is still identified today with the name given it by fur traders.) Some years after Thompson traversed the region, trappers spotted the curious sight of what appeared to be a cowhide hanging from a post near the stream's mouth.[4]

Among the American responses to economic opportunities on the Pacific Slope was the organization of the American Fur Company by New York financier John Jacob Astor in 1808. After months of planning, Astor dispatched an overland expedition that included Donald McKenzie, a 300-pound giant whose determination matched his size, and sent by sea a rancorous group that reached the mouth of the Columbia River after a voyage around Cape Horn. The Americans built Fort Astoria in 1811, and Fort Okanogan, near present-day Brewster, was established the same year. Fort Spokane was built in 1812 and, in August of that year, Astorians McKenzie, John Clarke, Ross Cox, and others traveled up from the lower Columbia and Snake rivers to the village of Palus, at that time consisting of forty large tule mat-covered lodges, where they were welcomed by the "small and friendly tribe." The group divided at the mouth of the Palouse River, with Clarke and most of the others continuing north to Spokane country to trade, while McKenzie pressed farther eastward along the Snake River to establish a post among the Nez Perces.

Eighteen-year-old Ross Cox remained with the main party, but became separated from them soon after they departed Palus on August 15. The account he wrote later of "the greatest ordeal" of his life portrays days of wandering along what came to be known as the Colvile Trail. He later noted, "The country to the westward was chiefly plains covered with parched grass, and occasionally enlivened by savannahs of refreshing green, full of wildflowers and aromatic herbs, among which the bee and hummingbird banqueted." On August 24, Cox pressed on through a "thinly wooded country," probably along Cow Creek. Here he camped near what "must have been an extraordinary nursery of wolves"—more likely coyotes—that sounded such "loud and dreadful howling…I never expected to leave the place alive." He used rocks and a stick to ward off a night attack and hurried along for several more days, only to encounter a lynx, a bear, and "a murderous brood" of rattlesnakes. Near present-day Reardan, he finally stumbled into a camp of Indians, who directed him to Fort Spokane where he rejoined his companions. The young trader's vivid account of his perilous foray through the western Palouse appeared in his 1832 book, *Adventures on the Columbia River.*[5]

Donald McKenzie reached the mouth of the Clearwater River at about the same time that Clarke reached his destination, and built the company's short-lived Clearwater Post across from present-day Lewiston. In the fall of 1812, McKenzie then journeyed northward on the Lapwai Trail to Fort Spo-kane to consult with his associates. He became the first European-American to explore the eastern Palouse, but he did not leave a record of this journey along the base of the Clearwater Mountains' Thatuna Range. The first recorded foray through this area was penned by the eminent Scottish naturalist David Douglas, who spent several days of early August 1826 in the company of Hudson's Bay trader John Work and the seventy-nine horses he was driving from Fort Vancouver to Fort Spokane via McKenzie's old post.

The meticulous Douglas described the Palouse's ubiquitous hawthorn (later named in his honor), the exclusive habitat of certain warblers and vireos, as well as eighteen distinct stem and blossom structures of lupine in the inland Pacific Northwest. Such variation within a single species led Douglas and other prominent scientists of the era to find explanations as to how such diversity through natural mutation could take place. Traditional church interpretations of the Bible's book of Genesis held that fruits, flowers, and animals had remained fixed "after their kind" since the time of their creation.

The summer heat was stifling along the eastern Palouse trace, exceeding 100 degrees F each day and leaving Douglas "parched like a cinder," but the scientist with flowing white hair also pronounced "the undulating woodless country of good soil." This judgment was in stark contrast to his later descriptions of the barren landscapes along the Columbia River, which he compared to Arabian deserts. Later, at Fort Vancouver, Douglas would read in the Royal Geological Society's *Proceedings* that his fellow countryman Charles Lyell proposed the earth was far older than the 6,000 years ascribed by many conservative theologians. Petrological evidence suggested to Lyell fewer indications of diluvial "catastrophism" than of a gradual "uniformitarianism" requiring millions of years to deposit fossil and mineral layers. Douglas would have seen exceptional evidence of both in the Palouse, where he rode and strolled with his gold-headed cane collecting botanical samples a short distance between some of

The Colvile Trail west of Benge, Washington, 1990.
Author's photo

Nez Perce Indians near Lapwai, c. 1920.
Hutchison Studio Photographs of Washington State University and Pullman, WA., 1910-1973 (PC 70), Manuscripts, Archives, and Special Collections, Washington State University Libraries, Pullman, WA.

the continent's most ancient Eocene and more recent Pliocene formations—geologic terms coined by Lyell.

Primordial Steptoe Butte, surrounded by the loessal hills deposited but moments ago in geologic time and sheared off by catastrophic flooding to the west, would soon give its name to world science. In the twentieth century, "steptoe" entered geological nomenclature as any ancient remnant surrounded by substantially more recent soil or rock formations. Unlike some others of his and later generations, Douglas, who had never been an especially religious person, actually found in the growing debate on the earth's origins and his own discoveries reasons to hold in greater awe the work of "that Being, in whom all truth finds its proper lasting place."[6]

Early Palouse Country traders and explorers like McKenzie and Douglas often fed on the abundant wild fowl in this haven of sharp-tailed grouse that gracefully glided in formations on extended dihedral wings. The early settlers would soon hunt these birds, known to them as prairie chickens, to extinction. Later efforts to introduce the ringneck pheasant and Hun-

garian partridge—both European species— as well as Asia's chukar partridge, the American bobwhite quail, and other Galliformes were successful. Less welcome foreigners were the starling, English sparrow, and rock dove, or pigeon.

Much of the botanical diversity experienced by the Native peoples and explorers of the eastern Palouse Hills can still be found at 800-acre Smoot Hill Ecological Preserve, owned by Washington State University, and at Rose Creek Nature Preserve, a National Natural Landmark owned by the Palouse-Clearwater Environmental Institute, both located about ten miles north of Pullman. The latter's twelve acres of fertile Palouse loam have never felt the plow and host over 300 native species of plants and animals. Self-reliant stands of aspen and red osier appear amid clusters of hawthorn and wild rose brambles to offer sanctuary to Western meadowlarks and red-winged blackbirds. Other original inhabitants like mourning doves and killdeers sing plaintive tunes to smaller audiences of purple shooting stars and yellowbells as if celebrating the prairie solitude.[7]

The belligerence of some American traders contributed to the geographic challenges of viable regional trade with the Native peoples. In late June 1813, a party of fur traders led by the ill-tempered Astorian John Clarke arrived at the mouth of the Palouse River, en route to Fort Astoria from the Spokane River. In customary fashion, the traders were warmly received by their hosts at the village of Palus. While encamped there, Clarke displayed two small silver goblets to the Snake River-Palouse tribal members and invited their chief, Kahlotus, to share some liquor. The next morning Clarke discovered that one of the vessels was missing. He immediately threatened "ven-geance upon the whole tribe" if the article were not promptly returned. The chief called his villagers together and after a brief council the goblet was handed back to Clarke. But the traders immediately bound the arms and legs of the accused man and, to the shock of the assembled Snake River-Palouses, proceeded to hang him from a crude gallows quickly fashioned from his own lodge poles. Such arbitrary brutality elicited outrage, and several Indians hastily rode off to circulate the news. This first killing of a Native by Whites in the Inland Northwest would cast a pall over relations between the two groups that would culminate in a series of armed conflicts later in the century.[8]

Genesis of Northwest Grains

The entry of the British Hudson's Bay Company (HBC) into the Northwest fur trade marked the genesis of an endur-ing Euro-American presence and agriculture on both sides of the Cascade Mountains. After its merger with the North West Company in 1821, the company's leadership worked with monopolistic power to form "regular establishments" that would serve as more than exchange points for beaver and other peltries. Sir George Simpson, "The Honorable Company's" autocratic governor at York Factory on Hudson's Bay, was as interested in grain and growing seasons as in furs and supply routes. Following his first trip to the region in the fall of 1825—an epic three-month overland trek commencing in August—Simpson directed the construction of Fort Vancouver on a ver-dant plain north of the Columbia River. He appointed Dr. John McLoughlin to serve as the fort's chief factor and to super-vise company affairs throughout the newly formed Columbia Department. Within two years, the ambitious McLoughlin undertook to transform the region's mismanaged chain of thir-teen posts into an expanded and profitable operation of twen-ty-two and diligently worked to attain Simpson's goal of agri-cultural self-sufficiency.

Simpson supplied McLoughlin with barley seed from York Factory in 1825 and the following spring a small plot of Fort Vancouver bottomland was sown to yield two bushels of wheat. The next year barley, oats, Indian corn, peas, and pota-toes were also planted. The grain seed was likely sent over-land from York Factory, as shipments by sea to Fort Vancouver were irregular until after 1830. The wheat yields were initially low, which McLoughlin attributed to poor seed sown in the spring and fall, but what did ripen he reported as being "the finest I ever saw in any country." Within ten years, approxi-mately a thousand acres near the fort were in production, with frequent reference in period accounts to "Hudson Bay" White Lammas wheat.

White and red seed wheat and barley came by ship in 1827 from the prominent British nursery Gordon, Forsyth & Company, which also supplied the post with a variety of European vegetable seed for Welsh and Strasbourg onions, Dutch and Swedish turnips, French and Hungarian beans, melons, squash, and herbs. The company was among the first seed nurseries established in Europe due to economic pressures from industrialization and emerging techniques of "improved" plant types through selections by farmers and crop scientists for specific characteristics.[9] The principal British wheats of the period were red and white Lammas landraces (*T. s. vulgare*) from Scotland and England. Early references to Red River production mention "bald spring wheats." The most widely grown British barleys of the period were the two-row late maturing Archer and stiff-strawed Spratt landraces, and the hardy Viking six-row remnant Scotch Bere. A Suffolk farmer's selection about 1820 from a field of Archer gave rise to English Chevalier, an excellent malt grain that became widely raised in England and in the United States later in the century.[10]

British Fort Colvile (distinct from later Fort Colville, a nearby U.S. military post) replaced Spokane House in 1825 as a center of trading activity on the middle Columbia. Following a tour of the region in 1824–25, Simpson recommended the location near scenic and strategic Kettle Falls, the greatest Indian fishery in the area and uppermost on the river, as a better place for trade and farming. After its construction under the supervision of John Work, another Canadian of Scottish descent, Andrew McDonald, was placed in charge of local operations. Although many of the traders did not share Simpson's exuberance for farming, McDonald persevered, and by the end of the next decade, Fort Colvile had grown to employ twenty men as laborers on a 400-acre farm and for local company operations.

The first grain substantially grown in the Inland Northwest—fifteen bushels of barley—was raised at Fort Colvile in 1826 with seed from McLoughlin. Horses, cattle, and hogs from Fort Vancouver and abandoned Spokane House also flourished on Big Prairie near the fort. Wheat was likely planted the following year, as grain production rose to 200 bushels in 1827. Hand-milling equipment was used to produce the first flour until a water-powered gristmill was built in 1830, several miles south of the fort at Myers Falls on the Colville River. Larger areas were soon under cultivation at two nearby company farms, yielding nearly 3,000 bushels of wheat, corn, barley, oats, buckwheat, and peas in 1832. A grist mill was also built near Fort Vancouver on Mill Creek in 1832 and wheat came to be considered the company's dominant commercial as well as subsistence crop.

"Hudson Bay" White Lammas Wheat
Palouse Colony Farm, Endicott, Washington

McLoughlin entered into an agreement in the late 1830s with the Russian-American Company to supply their fur trading posts in Alaska with flour and grain from the HBC's Puget Sound Agricultural Company's operations at Cowlitz Farm and Fort Nisqually. Wheat soon became legal tender to British authorities in the Northwest, with one bushel the equivalent of one dollar. A second, more efficient gristmill was constructed near the original Fort Colvile structure in the late 1840s and became operational in 1850 under Chief Factor Alexander C. Anderson. This new mill enabled distribution of company flour from New Caledonia to the Snake River country. "White" and "yellow" wheat was also imported in 1842 from Russian America for use in the Columbia Department, probably in response to a drought that had ruined much of the year's harvest at Fort Vancouver and Fort Nisqually.[11]

Canola Sky

east of Palouse, Washington

 **PACIFIC NORTHWEST HERITAGE GRAINS**

WHEATS

Northern European (*T. s. vulgare*):
White Lammas (1700s) > White Australian (1820s) > Pacific Bluestem (1850s) > Hybrid 128[a]
Red Lammas (1700s) > (Colonial) Red May (1700s) > (Northwest) Red Spring, Red May (1820s)

Southern European (*T. s. compactum*):
Mediterranean (1700s) > (Mexican) Little Club (1700s) > (NW) Little Club (1800s) > Hybrid 128[a]
Black Sea (1700s) > Ukrainian/Red (Scotch) Fife (1830s) > Federation and Marquis (1890s)[b]

South American (*T. s. compactum*):
Chili (Chile) Club (1600s-1700s) > Chili Wheat, Oregon Club? (1850s) > Big Club (1870s)

BARLEYS (*Hordeum vulgare*)

North Africa and Spanish Mediterranean
North African (Atlas?) Coast (to Mexico, six-row, 1500s) > California Coast (1840s) > Coast (1890s)

European
Scotch Bere, Common Bere? (six-row, 1600s) > Scotch Barley (1800s)
English Archer (two-row, 1700s) > Chevalier (1820) > Hallett's (1860s) > California Chevalier (1880s)
German Moravia (six-row, 1700s) > Hanna (1800s) > Bethge (Viktoria, 1900s)

Manchuria-Russian Amur River
Manchuria (6-row, 1700s) > Manshury, New Manchuria (1870s-'80s) > Golden Queen, Silver King

[a]Hybrid 128 was developed in 1899 by William Spillman at Pullman's Washington State College by crossing Little Club and Jones Fife.

[b]The spring hybrid Federation was developed in the 1890s by Australian breeder William Farrer who crossed Improved Fife with Australian Purple Straw and Yandilla; Marquis was developed in Ontario, Canada by crossing Red Fife and hard red Calcutta, a variety that emerged in India for the short growing season between monsoons.

[c]Common pot barley for human consumption, regardless of variety, has also been termed "Scotch barley." Scotch Bere was likely introduced to Britain by the Vikings and its name perpetuates the ancient northern European Latin term bar for bearded grain, or barley, from which the English words barb, beer, and barn are also derived. Bere is the only European landrace still raised commercially, though relic landraces still survive in remote areas of Italy, Serbia, Russia, Ukraine, and Turkey. Trebi barley, named for the ancient Black Sea coast city of Trabzon (Trebizond), was widely grown in the Pacific Northwest in the 1920s and descended from a northern Turkish landrace.

facing page

Heaven's Light Palouse

looking west from
Steptoe Butte

A boatload of "Ukrainian wheat," probably spring Galician Halychanka from western Ukraine, was shipped in 1842 from Danzig (Gdansk) via Glasgow to David Fife in Ontario, Canada, to become the progenitor of Red ("Scotch") Fife, the Northern Plains' premier nineteenth-century hard red spring wheat, widely grown in the Northwest by the 1880s. White Lammas, which came to dominate Australian wheat production in the 1840s as Australian White, was brought to the Pacific Northwest around 1852 and developed into the widely grown Pacific Bluestem. Red May, a soft red winter wheat popular since colonial times, was derived from Red Lammas, the ancient Celtic grain of the Roman era originally from the Fertile Cresent region of the Middle East.[12]

The popular Northwest hard red winter wheat Little Club arrived around 1859 from California and was derived from a southern European variety of Mediterranean (*T. s. compactum*) which may have been introduced to American growers from Genoa in 1819 by Delaware importer John Gordon. South American Chili (Chile) Club, a soft yellow winter wheat also probably of southern European origin, was introduced along the Duwamish River on Puget Sound by Hudson's Bay Company workers as early as 1854 and was reported on Crab Creek in the 1870s. Chili soon became known across the Palouse as Big Club.[13]

In an age before area land-grant college agronomy stations and genetics, Northwest farmers depended on experimentation, fortuitous accidental crosses, and international connections to provide wheat strains adapted to the region's environmental conditions. Palouse Country pathfinder Joseph DeLong tended small plots near the orchard he planted by the Kentuck Trail on his Palouse River homestead, using varieties supplied by the nurseries of prominent Walla Walla developer Phillip Ritz. In the 1880s, Tacoma "experimenter" William Reed imported grains from the Midwest and from the French firm Vilmorin, one of Europe's most prominent wheat breeders and suppliers, to identify strains most adaptable to eastern Washington.[14]

At Fort Vancouver, John McLoughlin took great pains to build up a cattle herd which probably numbered about 100 head in 1825. Most of the animals were from Spanish stock obtained in California, although McLoughlin also imported some Durham bulls from England to improve the breed. The two bulls and two cows McLoughlin parted with in 1825 for

Colfax Threshing Bee

Colfax, Washington

Fort Colvile bastion and barns, c. 1880.
Courtesy Northwest Museum of Arts & Culture, Spokane

Fort Colvile grew to a herd of some 200 by 1841. Even languid Fort Nez Perces, founded by Nor'Westers in 1818 near present-day Wallula on the lower Columbia River, began to show signs of prosperity under McLoughlin's attentive guidance. Since the drier climate there did not foster agricultural development, the post came to specialize in horse breeding. In the 1820s, there were usually between fifty to a hundred head at the fort and almost all had been obtained from the neighboring Cayuse Indians, likely giving rise to the frontier synonym for a horse. A small cattle herd was begun around 1830 but these animals never numbered more than fifty at the fort. However, Chief Trader Pierre Pambrum, a mixed-blood French and Indian native of Vaudreuil, Canada, did raise corn, potatoes, carrots, and other vegetables on fifty acres along the banks of the Walla Walla River for consumption by his family and a half-dozen employees.[15]

Most company workers were unmarried *engagés* from Canada who had transferred voluntarily to new assignments in the Columbia Department. The chief factors and officers were usually of Scottish background and nominal members of the Anglican Church. French-Canadian ancestry predominated among the regular employees; most of them were *Métis*, or individuals with European-American fathers and Native mothers, and virtually all were Catholic. Although many did not consider themselves settlers, their labor first tilled the Inland Northwest's soil and built its earliest frontier outposts. When the British were forced to forfeit their claims south of the present-day U.S.-Canadian border under the terms of the Oregon Treaty of 1846, some residents of the interior posts, like the Pambrum and McDonald families, chose to remain in the region and continue similar operations among the Indians and growing European-American presence. Fort Nez Perces then came to be known as Fort Walla Walla. A military post of the same name would be established twenty miles farther east and give rise to the frontier town of Walla Walla.[16]

The principal fur-bearing animals actively sought by the traders were not native to the grassy hills of the Palouse area. However, the region was located between the three dominant points of early fur trading activity—the Hudson's Bay Company's Fort Nez Perces near the mouth of the Walla Walla River, Astorian McKenzie's post at the mouth of the Clearwater, and Spokane House located at the junction of the Spokane and Little Spokane rivers. The natural triangular boundaries of the Palouse Hills were marked in ancient times by well-worn Native trails embroidered with the imprint of horse hooves connecting these three points. The trails were used extensively by the fur traders to reach their posts. Native people's exposure to the European-Americans resulted in devastating epidemics of smallpox and measles that took a heavy toll among all Northwest Indians, reducing the Columbia Plateau's Native population by as much as two-thirds by 1850. In one village near Wawawai, the 1847 measles epidemic took all but one boy. Never a large tribe, the Palouse numbered about 500 in 1853 when Governor Isaac Stevens arrived in Washington Territory. At that time, the Coeur d' Alenes numbered approximately 450, some 600 fewer than in 1780.

Blackrobes, Protestants, and the Star Brothers

The first Catholic missionaries, or "Blackrobes," entered the region in 1841, led by the Jesuit Father Pierre-Jean De Smet, following four visits to St. Louis in the 1830s by Nez Perces and Flatheads seeking the "white man's book of heaven." Father De Smet's humility was matched with an uncanny ability to engender the cordiality of Natives and Whites alike. Few persons have received such widespread acclaim amidst the trials of conflict between such widely divergent cultures. "No white man knows the Indians as does Father De Smet," President Lincoln was told when introduced to the Belgian priest by Thurlow Weed, "nor has any man their confidence in the same degree." Catholic missionaries responding to the "Macedonian Cry" for spiritual help led to peripatetic Father De Smet's founding of the Coeur d' Alene's Sacred Heart Mission in 1842. He was followed by such equally dedicated Jesuits as Joseph Joset, Nicholas Point, and Joseph Cataldo.

Subsequent work by members of the Oblate Order including Fathers Eugene Chirouse and Charles Pandosy at the request of the Yakama-Palouse Chief Kamiakin led to the building of St. Joseph's Mission in 1847 adjacent to his camp along Ahtanum Creek in the Yakima Valley. Unlike most Protestant missionaries, the Catholics generally believed that Christian conversion need not be accompanied by significant changes in the hunting and gathering patterns pursued for countless generations by the Native tribes. They did, however, insist on monogamy before baptizing an adult convert, which was an unacceptable condition to some Natives on the Plateau.

Sororal polygamy was not uncommon among men with sufficient means to care for more than one wife. Kamiakin's first wife, for example, was his second cousin, Sunkayee, and upon taking another wife, Kemeeyowah, daughter of a Klickitat chief, he also chose to become the husband of her three younger sisters. To Kamiakin, the celibacy of the priests seemed more peculiar than plural marriage. Yet Kamiakin welcomed the Blackrobes and had all his children baptized. His marital obligations remained a sacred bond, however, and the chief refused baptism until the hours preceding his death in the Palouse Country many years later.[17]

Kamiakin had been born about 1800 to a Palouse father famed for horse racing, Tsiyiak, who had married Commusni, the daughter of the prominent Upper Yakama (Kittitas) Chief Owhi, patriarch of the Weowicht family clan. Although he was raised primarily among his mother's people in the Yakima Valley, Kamiakin often traveled to the Palouse and camped at one of his family's four traditional campsites, which included "Tsiyiak's Place" on a small lake some two miles west of Sprague Lake and on "Kamiak's Flat" at the foot of Rock Lake. Both bodies of water and the many pothole lakes in the western Palouse were seasonal homes to the now rare white pelican, trumpeter swan, whooping crane, and other migratory fowl. Narrow ledges tucked into mysterious Rock Lake's immense western cliffs provided one of the Northwest's few nesting sites for turkey vultures, which could be seen for great distances circling high on vagrant currents of air, joined occasionally by the *khwama'* ("high above"), or golden eagle.

The Kamiakins also camped on the Palouse River north of present-day Endicott ("Kamiak's Crossing"), where native trout, whitetail deer, great blue herons, and other wildlife abounded, and at the village of Penawawa on the Snake River. (Although not a family campsite, Kamiak Butte was later named in the chief's honor by Colfax founder James Perkins, who thought the patriot chief should have a landmark bearing his name if Colonel Steptoe was entitled to one.) Though Kamiakin directed some of his children to the "power mountain" *Yámuštas* —"Elk's Abode" (Steptoe Butte), for their vision quests, he acquired his *wyak* from the power of a buffalo seen a dream while taking his quest on the majestic but dangerous slopes of *Takhuma*, the "Mighty One," Mount Rainier. He would sing the song taught to him in the dream to summon strength needed in the battles that lay ahead in a life that witnessed nearly a century of cataclysmic cultural change.[18]

As a member of the Weowicht clan, Kamiakin was treated with a deference that bespoke the family's unique ancestral ties to the two Star Brothers. Whether living near the mission or camping on the Palouse, he could point out *Khaslou*, the Evening Star, to his children and tell how Khaslou's human wife gave birth in the ancient time to their ancestor at the foot of Chief Mountain, *Miyowax*, known today as Cowiche Mountain. Kamiakin was held in great esteem by both Native peoples and Whites throughout the Northwest and was described in regal terms by frontiersman Theodore Winthrop in his popular frontier memoir, *The Canoe and Saddle*. He was introduced to the legendary chief in 1853 by Father Pandosy after Kamiakin rode up to the men on a white stallion wearing a long green "robe of ceremony" with fine cloth patches "of all shapes and sizes….He had an imposing presence and bearing, and above all a good face, a well-lighted Pharos at the top of his colossal frame." He was, Winthrop concluded, "every inch a king."[19]

Consistent with the Protestant policy of the American Board of Commissioners for Foreign Missions (1810–60), which was a joint creation of Congregational, Presbyterian, and Dutch Reformed denominations from the East, missionary couples were recruited in the 1830s to evangelize the Indians of the Pacific Northwest as the nation itself expanded westward. Most of those responding were conservative and Calvinistic in their theology, believing that progressive change among the tribes could best be undertaken through the proclamation of the Gospel, instruction in farming and animal husbandry, and opposition to "foreign influences" like Catholicism.

Walker Family Reunion, c. 1900.
Standing left to right: Rev. Joseph Walker, John Walker, Cyrus Walker, Marcus W. Walker, Mrs. Abigail Walker Karr, Levi Walker, Samuel Walker, . Seated in front is Mary Walker.
Manuscripts, Archives, and Special Collections, Washington State University Libraries, Pullman, WA.

The American Board's first efforts in the Northwest were led by Presbyterians Dr. Marcus and Narcissa Whitman, who founded the Waiilatpu Mission in 1836 among the Cayuses near present-day Walla Walla. The site's Cayuse name meant "Place of the Rye Grass" and it was a scenic location that afforded good forage for the livestock and fertile land for the fruit and grain Dr. Whitman hoped to raise at the mission. The Whitmans were accompanied by their close friends Henry H. and Eliza Spalding, who established the Clearwater or Nez Perces Mission of Lapwai on the north bank of the Clearwater River, just above its confluence with the Snake. The two couples' children, Clarissa Whitman and Eliza and Henry Hart Spalding, were the first three White American children born in America's Far West.

In 1838 the nascent Protestant presence was reinforced by the arrival of Congregationalists Elkanah and Mary Walker and Myron and Myra Eells, who were all directed northward where they launched Tshimikain Mission among the Spokanes near the mouth of the Spokane River. In the spring of 1838 Methodist Episcopal missionary Daniel Lee came from the Willamette Valley to build the Wascopam Mission on the tableland south of the Columbia River at The Dalles. The following year, Lee reported that five acres were under cultivation, yielding a considerable crop of potatoes and other vegetables as well as twenty-five bushels of wheat. At each of these points the Protestant missionaries planted gardens and grain in order to lessen their dependence on the British Hudson's Bay Company for supplying provisions.[20]

A fertile tract of about sixteen acres at Waiilatpu yielded an abundance of corn and vegetables in 1837 and Whitman planted some of the ground to wheat in the fall. The next year's harvest produced about ninety bushels of wheat, three hundred of corn, and a thousand bushels of potatoes. A small herd of cattle, oxen, and horses were maintained in 1838, with Indian help. By 1842 the mission of the industrious Whitmans had grown to include two large adobe houses for use as a residence, school, and chapel, a sawmill, and two gristmills. The school was attended by young Cayuse, Walla Walla, and Palouse Indians. The Spaldings were essentially self-sufficient by 1843. But Whitman expressed another priority for the Americans' presence. "Our greatest work is to be to aid the white settlement of this country," he wrote to his parents in 1844, "and help to found its religious institutions."

facing page

Palouse Pastels

north of
Albion, Washington

Leonard's Barn Sunset

East of Pullman, Washington

CHAPTER III

Immigrants and Exiles

When immigrant travel commenced over the Oregon Trail to the Willamette Valley in 1841, American travelers found Waiilatpu to be an oasis on the vast dryland prairie after the strenuous trek through the Rockies. Many were as notably impressed with the mission's crops as with the Whitmans' hospitality and must have wondered what opportunities the surrounding landscape held. A number of the overlanders who finally reached the Willamette only to find the best lands already claimed may have recalled how the Whitmans spoke in most favorable terms of settlement opportunities in the fertile lowlands and hills to the north. Whitman and Spalding had explored this area in March 1839 while examining a possible mission site at the mouth of the Palouse River.[1]

One future Palouse settler who lived with the Whitmans overcame a series of unimaginable tragedies during her earliest years in the West. Matilda Jane Sager was just five years old when her parents, Henry and Naomi Sager, decided to leave Missouri in the spring of 1844 to seek a new life in the Oregon Country. The Sagers had six children under fourteen years of age, with Naomi carrying their seventh, when they set out from St. Joseph in a large wagon train in May. She gave birth to a girl within two weeks of their departure and struggled for months to recover her strength. Shortly before reaching Fort Laramie in late July, the couple's nine-year-old daughter Catherine fell from the wagon and suffered a severe

bone fracture when the rear wheel rolled over her left leg. The family continued on after a brief rest at the fort but when crossing South Pass in August, Henry Sager contracted "camp fever" and died several days later.

Naomi's health continued to decline the following week as she struggled to contend with her sorrow, the stifling heat, and suffocating clouds of dust. Sixteen days after her husband's passing, Naomi Sager died on the trail near present-day Twin Falls, Idaho. When the wagons finally reached Waiilatpu in late October 1845, the captain of the wagon train informed the Whitmans that nobody with him could properly care for the seven children and that their father's final wish had been for them to remain together. In spite of their reluctance to take on such new responsibilities given the small community already existing at the mission, the Whitmans agreed to raise the children. The missionary couple had lost their only child, Clarissa, in 1839, when at age two she had drowned.

In July 1847, the Whitmans hosted Canadian artist Paul Kane, who painted a spectacular view of Palouse Falls, a sublime object to other Western artists including Henry Warre, Gustavus Sohon, John Mix Stanley, and John Alden. Kane described his travels in the book *Wanderings of an Artist among the Indians of North America* (1859). Kane and Warre, both from Europe, provided vivid accounts of their visits to the falls sounding as mystical as an encounter with Celtic runes. "At

facing page

A Private Garden

north of
Potlatch, Idaho

one place the strata assumed the circular form," Kane noted, "and somewhat the appearance of the Colosseum at Rome." Kane was guided to the falls by a Palouse chief "through one of the most sublime passes the eye ever beheld…The water falls in one perpendicular sheet…from rocks of a grayish-yellow color, which rise to about 400 feet above the summit of the fall.

Kane continued upstream to also sketch Little Palouse Falls, feasting on "delicious wild currants" and "much gratified with the surrounding magnificent scenes." But traveling in the July heat, the artist "never met with an animal or bird—not even a mosquito or a snake." In one of the first descriptions of the Palouse Hills, which Henry Warre saw from a high vantage point enroute to the falls in March 1846, he described "a vast undulating prairie, from whence the view was magnificent extending far into the distance & bounded by the Blue Mountains which were covered to the base with snow. The apparently rolling prairie is intersected by vast gullies of greater or less breadth & through one of these the Peloos River has its almost subterranean course."[2]

Had Kane or Warre visited the falls during a frigid, clear February day, they might have witnessed one of nature's rarest phenomena. The month bore the Sahaptin name for the appearance of the year's first wildflower blossoms, "Buttercup Blooming Time." Sagebrush buttercups were known to the Palouse as "Coyote's eyes," an important element in tribal myth. The position of the sun in February was such that it shot brilliant rays at midday up the lower canyon sanctum, striking the falls at hallowed moments, as if the cenotaph deep inside the ancient Temple of Abu-Simbel. The combination of this light under distinctive climatic conditions at the head of the imposing basaltic colonnade created a mesmerizing display of colors. Deep reds and greens and yellows were refracted by rime ice clinging to the basalt cliffs flanking the falls and by prismatic mists arising from the pool beneath the narrow cascade of late winter. These spectral rays merged fantastically to create a shimmering rainbow halo suspended above the falls against February skies of lucent blue.

In 1845, relations between the Whitmans and the Cayuse became increasingly strained. The Indians looked with suspicion upon the many wagonloads of Whites traveling through their lands likes bits of flotsam across the marine-like swells of grass. But these White families were carrying more than wooden trunks and cooking supplies. They unwittingly introduced another series of communicable diseases that ravaged the area's tribes. When a measles outbreak in the fall of 1847 brought death to many Cayuse, despite Dr. Whitman's efforts to inoculate them, some Indians believed the missionaries were deliberately acting to harm them.

In a macabre scene on November 29, 1847, witnessed by Matilda Sager, her sisters, young Eliza Spalding and others, a group of Cayuse men visiting the Whitmans suddenly brandished guns and hatchets and began killing the men who were working outside as well as some of the women. Marcus and Narcissa were struck down in the kitchen of their residence, where Matilda watched helplessly as her two brothers were shot to death. Fourteen mission residents were murdered during the chaos. The survivors were held captive at the mission for a harrowing month of terror before a ransom of Hudson's Bay trade goods from Fort Walla Walla purchased their freedom. Casualties from disease and exposure during the captivity included six-year-old Hannah Sager, Helen Meek, eight, daughter of famed mountain man Joe Meek and his Nez Perce wife, and Mary Ann Bridger, the eleven-year-old daughter of Jim Bridger.

The murders created a sensation in the Willamette Valley. A volunteer army was raised to bring the perpetrators to justice and this response led to the Cayuse War of 1848–49 and the eventual destruction of the tribe. On June 3, 1850, five Cayuses accused of the Whitman killings were hung in

Oregon City. The Sager sisters, the Spaldings, and others were relocated to the Willamette Valley where many remained for the rest of their lives. However, following Matilda Sager's subsequent marriage to Matthew Fultz in the 1870s, the couple moved to Farmington in the Palouse Country. She then wrote *A Survivor's Recollections of the Whitman Massacre* (1920), one of the few eyewitness accounts of her family's tragic experiences on the Oregon Trail and the Whitman massacre, with an explicit description of the survivors' Indian captivity. Eliza Spalding went on to marry James Warren, son of frontiersman Hugh Warren; they later lived in Almota where she authored *Memoirs of the West* (1916). But the notion that the Whitmans knowingly sought to destroy the Indians by spreading disease lingered long with some Indian families.[3]

The Interior Wars of the 1850s

With the extension of U.S. sovereignty over the Oregon Country in 1846, renewed interest was expressed by many Americans in the lands north of the Columbia River. The so-called Great Migration of 1843 had brought nearly 900 immigrants across the Oregon Trail to the sparsely settled Willamette Valley. Like the majority of later overland travelers, most were from America's heartland, and some who ventured West on the historic 1843 trek, like young J. A. Stoughton, would later find their home on the Palouse. This first surge of immigration tapped the states from New York, Pennsylvania, and Virginia across to Iowa and Missouri. Most were descendants of European colonists who had come to America a century or two earlier. They came from rural areas and honored the values of faith, family, and farm. Some of the men also possessed skills as carpenters, livestock raisers, promoters, and businessmen, and most couples tended to be active in church, local politics, and fraternal societies.

The women provided stability under frequently primitive conditions and filled the more private roles of mother, wife, physician, and moral guardian. These complementary functions were joined to create a culture centered on the family which often could number a half-dozen or more children. The Stoughtons were natives of Massachusetts who had relocated to Alabama in 1836. Dissatisfied with conditions in the South, they joined others in Missouri to undertake the six-month journey to the Willamette Valley. Like many others there, however, the Stoughtons would eventually relocate to the Palouse in order to settle on unclaimed farmland.

European-Americans were attracted to the Pacific Northwest in unprecedented numbers during the 1850s on a quest for land, gold, and business opportunities. As early as 1850, disgruntled miners who had headed for the California gold strikes a year or two earlier were moving north again in their search for the precious metal. In the summer of 1850, Henry Spalding, having moved to the Willamette Valley after the Whitman Massacre, wrote that "Great numbers went from country last June to explore the Spokane and Nez Perce countries for gold." Further incentive for travel to the region came in the fall of 1850 when Congress passed the Oregon Donation Land Law—three years before treaties extinguished tribal land titles—in order to "provide for the survey, and make donations to settlers of the said public lands." This legislation granted a half-section (320 acres) of land to every eligible citizen who had settled prior to 1852, while those occupying lands between 1852 and 1855 were able to obtain quarter sections. News of these liberal settlement provisions led to a homesteader exodus over the Oregon Trail, and in five years the territorial population rose from approximately 8,000 in 1850 to nearly 30,000. This dramatic increase led to the creation of a separate Washington Territory in 1853 and the appointment of General Isaac I. Stevens as its governor. President Franklin Pierce also named Stevens Superintendent of Indian Affairs for the new territory and directed him to undertake an extensive survey for the proposed northern transcontinental railroad.

Beginning in 1853, survey teams under the direction of Governor Stevens were dispatched throughout the region to locate possible routes for the northern transcontinental railroad that would link Washington Territory with Minnesota and the East. A final determination was later made for the main line to enter Washington near Spokane and head southwest to the mouth of the Snake River, thereby skirting the northwestern Palouse. However, information gathered through the surveys was used for the construction of the Northern Military Road, or "Mullan Trail," in the late 1850s and for subsequent railroad branch lines that tapped the Palouse grain district and eastern forests. Stevens himself traveled from Fort Colvile to the mouth of the Palouse River in October 1853.

While riding along the Snake guided by Chief Spokane Garry en route to Olympia, Stevens met the Palouse Chief Witimyhoyshe who "exhibited a medal of Thomas Jefferson dated 1801, given to his grandfather…by Lewis and Clark." Despite the efforts of officials like Stevens and Catholic and Protestant missionaries to reconcile fundamental cultural differences, the surveys aroused concern among the Native peoples over control of their lands, and American zeal for development broke into open hostilities in the Pacific Northwest in the 1850s. Pivotal events during this decade of the "Interior Indian Wars" took place in the Palouse, which served as the principal theater for the Edward Steptoe and George Wright expeditions in the latter years of the decade. Territorial Governor Isaac Stevens and topographical engineer Lt. John Mullan directed the first thorough explorations of the Palouse Country from 1855 to 1859.

An unexpected consequence of the railroad surveys was the discovery of gold in 1853 by the group working in the Yakima Valley. In the same year similar finds were made by Stevens's own party in the Bitterroot Valley of Montana. To avert an impending disaster caused by the anticipated flood of miners and in an effort to abolish Native claims to interior lands sought for the railroad and settlers, Stevens called a grand treaty council near Waiilatpu in the Walla Walla Valley in the spring of 1855. Attended by some 5,000 Nez Perce, Walla Wallas, Yakamas, and others, the Palouse were noticeably absent. A messenger was dispatched to their principal village at the mouth of the Palouse River but was told by their elderly Chief Kahlotus that "his people were indifferent to the matter." The chief alone accepted the invitation to participate. During these meetings, the Yakama-Palouse Chief Kamiakin, appearing "as a great sphinx," and other tribal leaders seemed unyielding when informed of Stevens' proposals.

The governor aggressively pressed the Native tribal leaders to accept payments and designated homelands in return for signing away most of their Plateau and mountain domains including the Palouse Country. To the assembled chiefs, however, the issue was spiritual, not economic. "I wonder if the ground is listening to what is said," challenged Young Chief of the Cayuse. Yakama Chief Owhi responded, "Shall I say that I will give you my lands? I cannot…I am afraid of the Almighty." Stevens was stunned and angered at what he had assumed would be a simple business transaction. He needed his railroad and the Native tribes were in the way. After several weeks of apparent stalemate, however, the chiefs were induced to sign away over 45,000 square miles of their land in return for three reservations in the Yakama, Nez Perce, and Umatilla areas and the promise of extended time to make the transition. Kamiakin stoically signed, as did Kahlotus, primarily because they were threatened that they would "walk in blood knee deep" if they did not. The leaders likely realized further negotiations were futile and may have signed only to gain time to prepare for war. Yakama Chief Owhi, Kamiakin's father-in-law, later stated that "the war commenced from that moment."

That Stevens and his party did not grasp the extent of tribal objections to the treaty proceedings is evident in the governor's written account and travels immediately following the council. On June 16, 1855, Stevens headed north from the Walla Walla Valley on the Nez Perce Trail with his son, Hazard, secretary James Doty, Gustavus Sohon, seventeen packers, and others. They were led by Joseph, a Coeur d'Alene guide. Stevens' next objective was the Clark Fork River near present-day Missoula in western Montana, where he sought to secure a similar agreement with the Blackfoot tribes. The group traversed across "remarkably fine grazing and wheat country" and in two days reached the Tucannon River and found the residence of "very experienced and kind-hearted mountaineer" Louis "Maringouin" Raboin where the hamlet of Marengo in present-day Columbia County would be established two decades later. A French-Canadian native of Illinois, Raboin was a legendary American Fur Company veteran turned farmer. After fleeing hostilities among the Blackfoot in the 1850s, he had settled in the vicinity with his Flathead Indian wife and six children.

Stevens noted that the hospitable Raboins raised wheat and potatoes on four acres as well as keeping horses, cattle, and chickens. They also fished for salmon from the cottonwood and willow-lined banks of

the Tucannon and hunted deer and elk. The next day, Stevens met Nez Perce headmen Lawyer and Red Wolf at the latter's Snake River camp near present-day Clarkston. Here Stevens noted "a fine field of corn" on twenty irrigated acres that was also "tolerably well set out with fruit trees." On June 19, the expedition crossed the Snake River and continued north across the virgin prairies of the eastern Palouse. The governor described the surroundings as "a luxuriance of grass [and] richness of soil" and that "the whole view presents to the eye a vast bed of flowers in all their varied beauty." This portion of the trip east of Pyramid Peak (now Steptoe Butte) likely provided Sohon's historic vista, *Source of the Peluse*, showing the earliest depiction of the Palouse Hills as a color lithograph in Stevens' 1860 Pacific Railroad Surveys Senate report.[4]

Gustavus Sohon, *Source of the Peluse*, c. 1855.
Image from Isaac Stevens, Report of Explorations for a Route for the Pacific Railroad (1860).

Soon after Stevens' Walla Walla negotiations, a group of Yakama women gathering roots was assaulted by a party of miners headed to the gold strikes. Retaliation for the attack led to the murder of two White offenders, followed by a number of skirmishes between the U.S. Army and civilian volunteers against the Columbia Plateau tribes. When the elder Yakama chiefs Owhi and Teias sought peace on the military's terms in 1856, Kamiakin defiantly relocated to the Palouse Country. Gold strikes made in 1858 in the Colville Valley and on the Fraser River in Canada had complicated the situation by renewing the onslaught of miners across restricted lands long before Stevens's treaties were ratified by Congress. Some Palouses reacted by killing two miners headed north from the Snake on the Colvile Trail in the spring, and on the night of April 12, 1858, raided livestock near Fort Walla Walla. After hearing that the hostile Palouse were near Alpowa on the Snake River, Colonel Edward Steptoe and five companies departed Fort Walla Walla in an effort "to stop this thieving" and to reassure the Colville miners with a personal visit and show of strength. Finding only friendly Nez Perce there, Steptoe proceeded north, to a point about eight miles northwest of present-day Rosalia.

On May 16, 1858, several miles south of present-day Cheney, Steptoe's detachment camped where they met a force of some six hundred mounted Palouses under Tilcoax, Chief Polatkin's Lower Spokanes, Coeur d' Alenes with Chief Vincent, and the Yakama firebrand Qualchan with other middle Columbia Indians. Kamiakin was probably not aware of the Army's incursion until after the fighting had commenced. Two days later, the Native combatants forced the U.S. Army to retreat to a small hill, where they were assailed throughout the day at what became known to the Palouse as the "*Hngwsuum* (Rope Making Place) Battle," and to military historians as the "Steptoe Disaster."

The Palouse warriors may have helped start the fight, for they were very hostile toward the Army. The Palouse Chief Tilcoax was present from the beginning of the battle, but Kamiakin probably did not arrive until the Army troops had been surrounded. Although seven of Steptoe's men were killed and thirteen others wounded, the command managed to escape at night and return to Fort Walla Walla. One of the casualties, Private Victor DeMoy, had served in the French army and fought in the Crimean War. After sustaining mortal wounds early in the battle, DeMoy cried words that became synonymous with one of the Army's few defeats in the era of the Indian wars: "My God, my God, for a saber!" He asked to be left on the battlefield during the retreat, armed with a fully loaded revolver.

The hatred felt by the Americans after their losses in the Cayuse War of 1848 was minor compared to what arose after the Steptoe Battle. The Palouse soldiers were not only defiant and insulting but also had participated in attacks on the Steptoe command and killed American soldiers. The Army set out to punish the Palouse tribe and their allies.

Colonel George Wright organized a well-equipped expedition throughout the summer of 1858 and in mid-August departed Fort Walla Walla with some 570 well-armed troops. The Army had been embarrassed by the Steptoe defeat, and Colonel Wright set out to avenge the death of Steptoe's men. The colonel crossed the Snake River near the mouth of the Palouse on August 25, but the Indians usually residing there had moved north. They kept their huge herds of horses ahead of the military column, trying to reach the relative security of the mountainous areas of the Coeur d' Alenes.

A series of battles took place in which the Native tribes, led again by Owhi, Kamiakin, and others, were utterly defeated by the soldiers' newer long-range rifles and howitzer artillery at the Battle of Four Lakes on September 1, 1858, near present-day Cheney. Chief Kamiakin and his warrior-woman wife

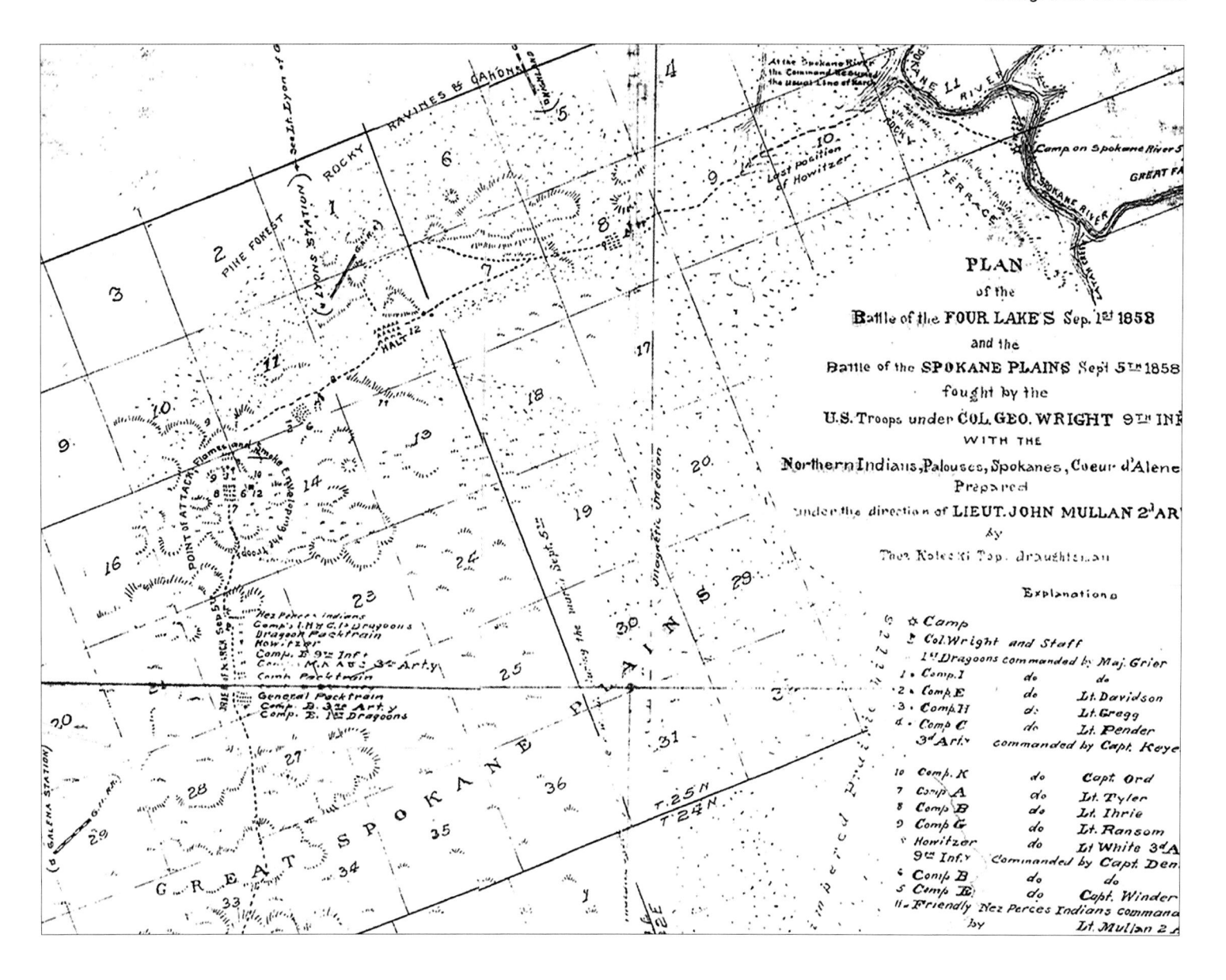

Spokane Plains Battle Map (1858)
superimposed on a modern quadrangle grid.
Courtesy Spokane Public Library

Colestah, clad in battle dress with her scarlet headscarf, fought together at Four Lakes until a cannon shell shattered a tree under which they were sheltering. A falling limb broke Kamiakin's shoulder, and he was taken to a camp near the mouth of the Spokane River for safe haven.

Four days later, the Battle of Spokane Plains (near today's Fairchild Air Force Base) also ended disastrously for the Indians. Then, on September 8, Wright overtook a herd of about a thousand Palouse horses along the Spokane River, near what is now the Washington-Idaho state line, and shot virtually all of them. Wright continued eastward and forced a treaty upon the Coeur d' Alenes at the Cataldo Mission, then swung around Lake Coeur d' Alene to Latah Creek. Chief Owhi approached Wright's camp under a flag of truce to discuss terms of peace. He was immediately seized and shackled. Messengers were sent out demanding the surrender of his son, the notorious warrior Qualchan, and Kamiakin.

Chief Kamiakin could not be moved, due to his injury, but Qualchan, while still recovering from serious wounds inflicted at a recent skirmish on the Columbia River, boldly rode into Wright's bivouac with his wife, Whistalks, to seek his father's welfare. He was also summarily taken into custody, although the effort required several soldiers. Fifteen minutes later, Qualchan was hung, as were several other Indians Wright had captured. Whistalks defiantly flung a beaded lance at Wright's tent and rode back to the Spokane River camp. The quiet stream would henceforth bear the name "Hangman Creek."

Chief Owhi's daughter, Mary Owhi Moses, retold these traumatic events to her great-granddaughter Emily Peone in 1918: "About ten days after Qualchan was hanged and we were told the soldiers had left the camp... my sisters and I ventured over to the campground. We found where they had buried Qualchan in a shallow grave covered with dust, grass, and sticks. The soldiers had taken his war bonnet and clothes.

Gustavus Sohon, *Battle on the Spokane Plain*, 1858.
From the Sohon Collection, Smithsonian Institution

My sisters dug a deeper grave, took the body and wrapped it in a blanket, put moccasins on the feet and buried it again with some shells in the grave." The site is about sixteen miles southeast of Spokane near Smith's Ford.[5]

On his return trip to Fort Walla Walla, Wright hastily called a "Palouse Council" on the Palouse River at the mouth of Willow Creek, in order to hang several more Indians, and threatened the annihilation of the tribe should they make any further trouble. The column then crossed the Snake River near Palus, and as they continued on the south side of the river toward to Fort Walla Walla, two soldiers shot Owhi to death as he rode chained to a horse. Chief Kamiakin and his family managed to escape to the Blue Mountains, where they found sanctuary with Chief Victor's Flathead band. They returned to the Palouse Country in 1860 to live on the Palouse River at Kamiakin's Crossing. Here they had sufficient root grounds, wild game, and space to raise gardens and feed themselves, and for his young sons to race their horses.

Father Joseph Joset visited the chief and his family in November 1861, near present-day Desmet, and baptized five of Kamiakin's children. Kamiakin remained in the Palouse until his death at Rock Lake in April 1877, in spite of later government offers to handsomely reward him for returning to the Yakima Valley to establish order on the newly organized Yakama Indian Reservation. He steadfastly refused all such requests, once even baring his ragged sleeves and telling the visiting agent he had never accepted anything in exchange for his lands and would never be poor enough to do so.[6]

The Northern Pacific Railroad Survey

When Governor Stevens first entered the territory in 1853, he was surveying the northern route for a railroad that would link the eastern portion of the United States with the Pacific Ocean. His dream of a Northern Pacific line was shared by many visionaries and as settlers of the Oregon Country. Yet long before the eventual completion of the Northern Pacific Railroad in 1883, significant immigrant movement to the Palouse was taking place. Indian trails extensively crisscrossed the region and the major north-south routes had been known by trappers and traders for some time. Apart from the ancient paths along both banks of the Snake River, most Indian trails tended to lie on a northeasterly axis to expedite travel between the lower Snake and the domain of the Spokane and Coeur d'Alene tribes.

A route known to the frontiersmen as the Colvile Trail had been used for centuries by the Indians as the principal path from the Walla Walla Valley to the Colville area. Because it crossed the Snake River a short distance below the mouth of the Palouse River, Whites frequently encountered the Indians encamped at Palus. The first ferry on the Snake River began operating at this famous crossing after the Washington Territorial Legislature granted the rights to Edward L. Massey in 1858. A year later, the trail developed into a "road" as a crew under the command of Major Pinkney Lugenbeel at Fort Colville graded parts of it to improve transportation to and from Fort Walla Walla.[7]

Stretching along the foothills of the Bitterroots in the eastern Palouse was the Lapwai Trail, which led from Nez Perce country to the western shores of Lake Coeur d'Alene. The major route through the central Palouse was known to the settlers as the Spokane Trail. It was formed where paths along Penawawa Creek, Almota Creek, and other tributary streams to the Snake in that area converged on Smokle (Union Flat) Creek. From there it led northward to the land of the Spokanes, crossing the Palouse River near its northernmost point between present-day Endicott and St. John at the ancestral campsite of the Kamiakin family and skirted the base of Pyramid Peak, later renamed Steptoe Butte.

In his negotiations with the Indians in the 1850s, Colonel Wright had insisted that Americans be permitted to cross through Indian lands unmolested, and the tribes, under duress, consented. Trails that had been used for centuries by Indians were now thrown open to the Americans and soon developed into roads carrying the newcomers to "the land of milk and honey." Lieutenant John Mullan had been commissioned in 1858 to begin the first surveys for a military wagon road to link Fort Walla Walla with Fort Benton, Montana, which marked the head of Missouri River steamboat traffic. His work having been stalled by the war with the Indians, the ambitious young officer dispatched three advance parties in the summer of 1859 to explore the region ahead of his main column. Their objective was to locate the most practical route across the Palouse Country.

In the first recorded exploration of the central Palouse, Gustavus Sohon, in his capacity as explorer, interpreter, and artist for the surveyors, traversed the course of Union Flat Creek in June 1859 with topographers Theodore Kolecki and frontiersman Donald McKay. Their Indian guide was Slo-wiarchy, compliant headman at Palus. Kolecki noted in his journal that there was a plentiful supply of grass along lower Union Flat Creek and ten miles above its mouth grew large stands of cottonwood, aspen, birch, pine, and brushwood. The view from Pyramid Peak he described as "rolling prairie, very much resembling a stormy sea" and densely wooded in the spurs of the Bitterroots. The abundance of these pioneer necessities—water, grass, and timber—interested many readers of Mullan's official report, which described his road, arcing northeasterly across the Palouse region from present-day Benge and Lamont to the Spokane Valley at Dishman. The book describing the journey was published by the government in 1860 and widely distributed throughout the

East, necessitating a second edition. Both publications and Mullan's *Miners and Travelers' Guide* (1865) served to spark renewed interest in Northwest settlement opportunities, now that the Indians had been pacified.[8]

Gustavus Sohon, Sketch of John Mullan, Sohon, and Theodore Kolecki, c. 1859.
The Mullan Collection, National Archives

Stevens' official railroad survey report to Congress contained a wealth of information about the Inland Northwest's landscape, natural history, flora, and fauna. The extensive document also noted the presence of seven Indian farms along the Snake River from Palus to Alpowa, "amounting to from 300 to 400 acres." At these places, on sandy riverbanks and some islands, the Palouses and Nez Perces raised "wheat, corn, ... and vegetables of different kinds, and gained sufficient crops to encourage them in their labors." Also notable were the higher plateaus on both sides of the river that "offered magnificent pasture grounds" and several "Indian farms" along the lower Palouse River that "bespeak its agricultural bounty." The government's publication of the transcontinental railroad survey reports was illustrated with a series of rare color lithographs.[9]

Coeur d'Alene Relocation to Desmet

By the early 1860s, Sacred Heart Mission on the St. Joe River had emerged as the center of Jesuit activity among the Coeur d' Alenes, and in the fall of 1866 Father Cataldo established the mission of St. Michael's on Peone Prairie near Spokane Falls. With each passing year of that decade both missionaries and tribal leaders became increasingly concerned about the level of immigrant traffic westward on the Mullan Road. The priests warned of the corrupting influences brought by whiskey peddlers and also noted that the best farmlands would be the first to be taken in the rich Palouse region while the fields adjacent to the mission were stony and subject to recurrent flooding. The priests advocated the tribe's transition to a more settled agrarian existence, and as early as 1863 Father Joset raised the question of resettling to the fertile and more sheltered Palouse River Valley.

The periodic festival gatherings at the mission in later years provided opportunities to enunciate this advice to the entire tribe. "Those who are farming know by now," Andrew Seltice remembered Joset preaching in 1864, "that the Palouse soil is the richest in all this land of yours. It is not only the best you own, but it is better than any land I know of. That is saying a lot, because I have been in many countries. Even on the other side of the ocean, I have never seen better soil anywhere than you have right here in the Palouse." Given their ancestral ties to the Coeur d' Alene Lake area, the tribe's initial response to the priests' advice was cool. The Jesuits did not force the issue, however, and over several years tribal leaders came to share the view that relocation of their homes and the mission would be in their best interest.

Several Coeur d'Alene families had been living for some time at traditional family campsites near present-day Oakesdale, Colfax, Plummer, Potlatch, and Tensed where the proposed mission site near present-day Desmet, Idaho was located. The scenic place had been a popular summer encampment for generations of *Schitsumsh,* who found fish plentiful in the river, abundant game in the timbered slopes nearby, and an ongoing supply of nutritious roots. Although some members of the tribe began resettling southward in the late 1860s, the first significant relocation began in the spring of 1870. At that time, the Andrew Seltice family built a cabin at the fork of Latah and Lovell creeks (present-day Tekoa). Others moving that year included Ignace Timothy (to present-day Plummer), Peter Wildshoe (to Tilma), and Massisla (near Worley). The families of See-mo Chimineme, Steptoe Battle veteran Andrew Youmas, Krato Nickodemus, and others went to the Moctelme Valley near the new Palouse River mission site.[10]

The severity of the first winter tested the group's resolve to remain in the Palouse region, but the following years brought a new prosperity to the tribe. Their devotion to the church came to the Holy See's attention and the felicitous response from Pope Pius IX in 1871 is believed to be the only papal brief ever addressed to an Indian tribe. By 1876 most Coeur d'Alenes who had remained in the vicinity of the old mission joined the others in the Palouse Valley. A new Sacred Heart Mission Church was completed there in 1877 and in the following year a school began operation under the direction of a group of Sisters of Providence recruited from Vancouver, Washington. The cluster of buildings soon developed into the small community of Desmet, which was surrounded by farmsteads spread across the verdant lowland. Sacred Heart Mission developed into a model mission under the supervision of Fathers Alexander Diomedi and Joseph Giorda. The mission also came to serve as the center of Catholic ministry to settlers throughout the Palouse Country. The priests in residence made frequent visits to congregations in Sprague, Oakesdale, Cheney, Uniontown, Colton, and Lewiston, since the enormous area could not be adequately covered by the nearest diocesan priests in the Walla Walla parish.

New Trails and the Palouse Reserve

Kamiakin family members continued to reside at Rock Lake for several years after the chief's passing in 1877. His four sister-widows maintained busy households, tending the younger children and following the old trails to customary root and berry grounds and fishing sites. A schoolteacher visiting White families at Rock Lake in June 1878 encountered "a company of Indians… driving a band of cayuse ponies," who may well have been the chief's sons still tending their substantial herds in the area.[11]

In time the Kamiakins adjusted their seasonal travel patterns to the new realities of life in a region undergoing unprecedented change. The seasonal spring root grounds to the east were being rapidly claimed and fenced by farmers, which also complicated travel to autumn berry picking areas in the Bitterroot foothills. Like other non-reservation families in the area, the Kamiakins shifted to more westward destinations on their annual journeys. They gathered camas and bitterroot with Moses and their relatives in his bands on the lowlands of the Big Bend country and trapped deer in group drives up the coulees to the north.

Grand tribal gatherings were held each year at places like *Nt'palnwt* ("Rock on the Hillside") at the ancient crossing on Rocky Ford Creek between Moses Lake and the tiny White settlement of Ephrata. A main north-south trail crossed the stream at this site, where enormous encampments of Plateau tribes had been held for generations and continued into the twentieth century. The Kamiakins joined relatives and friends among the Palouses, Nez Perces, and Spokanes on the east side of the creek while others they knew among the Columbia-Sinkiuse, Yakamas, and Umatillas resided along the west bank. An enormous racetrack was located near Moses' camp to the west and, following in the footsteps of their Grandfather T'siyiyak, the Kamiakin sons could compete as he had

for piles of valued buffalo hides, bags of root flour, and other highly prized items wagered on the outcome.

Before moving on to catch salmon in the Columbia and Snake rivers, the Kamiakins also fished and gathered the eggs of migratory waterfowl at Moses Lake. Here the chief's son, T'si-yiyak, died while camped in the vicinity, leaving two sons and a daughter to grieve his unexpected loss. The girl, Ka-mosh-nite—named for Chief Kamiakin's mother, eventually married Hay-hay-tah (Smith L. George), and the couple chose to remain at Palus where they were among its last residents.[12]

As a result of the older Kamiakin sons' marriages into prominent non-reservation Palouse and Nez Perce families and the successful entry of land claims, the extended family began spending more time along the Snake River. In the absence of their guardian father, the late chief's wives and children sought protection and fellowship among relatives and friends. Tesh Palouse came to frequently reside at Palus and married Me-a-tu-kin-ma, sister of Waughaskie (Chief Bones), the Cayuse refugee who would live to be one of the last permanent residents of the ancient village. Perhaps about the time of the Spokane Council with Howard and Ferry, We-yet-que-yet, son-in-law of Chief Húsis Moxmox, also relocated to Palus, where he and his brothers maintained the family's substantial horse herds.[13]

The Palouses came to have high regard for prominent Snake River rancher George Hunter, consulting him about land policies. Hunter had served as a volunteer army soldier during the Yakama and Nez Perce wars but, after making his home near Grange City, he became a friend of Chief Big Thunder and the residents of Palus. At the outbreak of the Bannock-Paiute hostilities in 1878, General Howard held a council with the villagers at which Hunter served as interpreter, and both men learned of the Indians' desire to remain in the area by taking up lands in severalty. As he did at the Spokane Falls Council in 1879, Howard encouraged them to do so and Big Thunder later asked Hunter "to go with him and others of the tribe to find the 'corner' and 'lines' and generally assist them in locating and entering their lands in severalty at the local land office in Colfax." About 1884, Hunter traveled with Big Thunder and Bones to Colfax and helped them file claims on their ancestral lands.[14]

John Pettyjohn, a Touchet Valley settler of 1859, and Dan Lyons also joined Hunter as unofficial spokesmen for area Indians and advocates for Indian homesteads, which strained relations with some of their White neighbors. With the help of these three White men, the Kamiakin brothers We-yet-que-yet and T'siyiyak, their nephew Kah-yee-wach (Pete Bones), We-yet-que-wit's father-in-law Chief Húsis Moxmox, Yosyos Tulikecíin (Sam Fisher), and other Palouses filed claims for Indian homesites. By carefully arranging their entries on unsettled lands, Pettyjohn, Lyons, and Hunter helped the Palouses claim quarter-sections totaling some 1,600 contiguous acres along the entire course of the lower Palouse River from its mouth to Palouse Falls. Although the canyon area was semi-arid and rocky, it was also the sacred landscape of the Palouse people's origin. Now they now held legal title to prevent its occupation by settlers.

Young Skolumkee assumed new responsibilities in managing the Kamiakin family's vast remuda. The family's herds never again approached the numbers owned before the war, but their distinctive "S" brand could again be seen on dozens of animals grazing in the western Palouse. Skolumkee's reticent ways and slight hunchback belied his knowledge and wisdom, which remained unknown to those who might find his silence and appearance somewhat peculiar. Throughout his youth, Skolumkee spent weeks on end tending the family herds on the bunchgrass prairies of the western Palouse. He came to be utterly self-reliant and could subsist at length in any season by his wits and nature's provision, even in the desolate places

of the sand hill and coulee districts southwest of the lower Palouse River. Skolumkee came to prefer the solitude of open spaces and companionship of the horses and other animals who understood his whispers. In time he excelled at horsemanship and became renowned for his deft skills at taming animals most others found unmanageable.

The Kamiakins' wayfaring brother often appeared without notice after an extended absence, only to vanish just as mysteriously. But Skolumkee seemed to have an uncanny sense of coming when needed by the family to encourage a sick child or mend gear needed for the livestock. He comprehended the messages brought to him in the howls of coyotes and knew of their dire warnings. In this way he was able to keep the herds in shielded coulees and other safe havens when fierce storms brought by the fearsome weather-changer suddenly struck the prairie.

Skolumkee was also among the first to hear and report announcements by the colorful *wawshukla* of spring's arrival. Such long anticipated news by northern orioles was generally far more important than meadowlark and magpie gossip that he also comprehended. Skolumkee eventually married Pemalks, a woman from the coast. Although the couple remained childless, Skolumkee's many nieces and nephews greatly looked forward to periodic visits by their beloved trickster uncle. He delighted in the children's company and kept them entertained with his storytelling and such antics as pretending to hide tiny creatures inside his head.[15]

In time the lives of the Kamiakins meshed with other Indians on the reservation where they lived out their lives far from the winding rivers and rolling hills of the Palouse country. They also visited relatives and their old homelands to the southeast during periodic treks between the Colville and Nez Perce reservations. The route led along ancient trails that were now being graded for long stretches for motor traffic. Travel by horse from Nespelem to Lapwai took at least one week. The long procession of riders would ford the Columbia River at Moses Crossing (Barry) or three miles downstream on Seaton's Ferry near the mouth of Spring Canyon.

Often traveling in groups of more than one hundred, they would then camp where pioneer hamlets had emerged at *Telahats* (Wilbur), *Sumki-Ilpilp* (Harrington), and *Elatsaywitsun* (Sprague) before reaching the Kamiakins' old home at the foot of *Tax'líit* (Rock Lake). Following a night's respite near the lakeshore and visits to nearby family gravesites, they would continue on to camp near present-day St. John, Colfax, Pullman, and Lewiston. Ben Owhi also recalled a pilgrimage with Moses to Qualchan's execution and burial site near the Kentuck Trail Ford, where the men paid homage to their martyred relative.[16]

The Kamiakin's Paween and Poyakin relatives from the *Pinawáwih-Wawáwih* area were also in the throes of difficult decisions about their future in the last years of the nineteenth century. Chief Húsis Paween had dispatched his nephews Wayayentutpik and namesake Húsis Paween (Tom Paween) to consult with Moses, where they had been favorably received. As with the Tilcoax-Wolf family farther down the Snake, the matter of relocation to the reservation for the Paweens was complicated by their enormous horse herds that ranged along the river.

Several factors conspired early in the next decade to force that decision. A smallpox epidemic in 1890–91 drove more Indians from the Snake River to area reservations. Among those who died about 1890 was Húsis Paween, who had recently come to the reluctant conclusion that his family should move their herd to the Colville Reservation. But before

The Charley Kamiakin Williams, Willie Redstar, and Smith L. George families at the Wilbur Fair, c. 1913.
Darryl Barr Collection

he could act, the "hi-yu fire" exacted a merciless toll, especially among the children, and the disease spread wherever they were taken. In April 1891, Ah-kis-kis, son of Chief Húsis Paween, reported the recent loss of his son along with seventeen other children. Parents and elders were left to mourn and despair.[17]

One outbreak began after several Palouse women washed clothing belonging to residents of Dayton, Washington, who had been infected. Disease and deprivation drove others to area reservations, where the Indian bureau provided limited relief. Even the forces of nature seemed displeased with the newcomers' decisions to move, as the camas harvest and salmon runs along the Columbia and Snake rivers were far below normal levels in 1891. The few families who stubbornly clung to their ancient homesites from *Alamōtin* to *Pinawáwih* where they also grew corn and melons faced the pain of separation from relatives who had died or moved away as well as other challenges. White settlers claimed the choicest lands along the river and planted vast acreages to orchards and gardens. Heavy snows in late 1893 led to flooding, which scattered the remaining Indian horse herds.

Relocation and Resilience

These circumstances led the Paweens and Poyakins, including the Jim Billy Andrews family, to move to Nespelem in 1892 and 1893. Members returned seasonally to their homeland for some years to work as farm laborers in the Dayton and Touchet districts before settling back in the Nespelem area or on the Nez Perce Reservation. For similar reasons, Chief Tilcoax's son, Wolf Necklace (Peter Wolf) also moved substantial numbers from his massive herd to the Colville Reservation in 1893 and sold some 3,000 head in Ephrata after a celebrated round-up led by his nephew Harry Jim with thirty-four riders.[18]

At the turn of the century, only about seventy-five Indians lived at Palus, including the remnants of bands once led by Hahtalekin, Big Thunder, and Húsis Moxmox. These Palouses continued "to cling tenaciously to this barren spot where their children were born and their mothers and fathers have died." Events had moved rapidly in their lives, but their feelings about the land had not changed. However, they seemed powerless to stop the removal policies of the United States.

Yakima Agent Lewis Irwin visited Palus in the spring of 1897 to survey the land and the condition of the Indians. Lewis reported that the Indians cultivated ten acres but lived primarily from their fishing. Their root grounds had been destroyed by settlers' plows, and the Indians had difficulty eking out a living from fishing due to the intense salmon harvests at the mouth of the Columbia River. The agent wrote about the Palouses with respect, but he recommended to the commissioner of Indian affairs "that they be forcibly removed to the Nez Perce, Umatilla, or Yakama Reservations." Indian agents and White settlers alike agreed with Irwin's suggestion to remove them. The Indian bureau soon acted upon this recommendation.[19]

Kay-yee-wach Kamiakin (Pete Bones) near Palouse Falls, c. 1915.
Robert Eddy Collection

In the spring of 1905, a steamboat arrived at Palus loaded with American soldiers, who ordered the Indians to gather their belongings and get aboard. Most of the families complied, and after boarding, they congregated at the stern of the boat, from which they looked back at their homes and the graves of their loved ones, and watched Standing Rock pass from their view. One Palouse Indian, a small boy at the time, recalled the entire scene which appeared in his mind "like a vision of the way things were." Andrew George remembered the removal of his family like a dream or an event which occurred outside the confines of his mind. When Andrew grew older, he asked tribal elders about that spring but found that "they never wanted to talk about it much." The memory of their removal was too painful for them to discuss even with younger members of their own families—a barrier to fuller understandings that remains today. George recalled that when the elders were asked about the event, the men and women grew silent and often wept.[20]

Only a small number of Indian families remained on the lower Snake River in 1910, and within two decades most would move to Northwest reservations. Tragedies sometimes befell the remaining stalwarts, stemming from mutual distrust that per-

sisted between Indians and Whites. Stories abounded among the Snake River-Palouse tribe about Natives being forced off farmers' property at gunpoint, or worse. In the early spring of 1914, a group of five Palouses was traveling along the Palouse River about one mile above the mouth of Rock Creek, when they were caught in a sudden and ferocious March blizzard. A large barn was nearby, but the group sought refuge in a small cove near the river. By daybreak three had frozen to death, but the rancher who rescued the two survivors found the adults had huddled to protect a boy who barely survived the ordeal. The lad was young Carter Slouthier, a nephew of Sam Fisher, who was then adopted by Fisher and his wife, Helen. The Fishers were allotted property on area reservations but continued to live seasonally at Palus.[21]

By 1920, a few Native American families like those of the Fishhook Jim family stubbornly clung to a few final outposts on the lower Snake River. Mary Jim remained with her family on the Snake River near Page until the construction of the Ice Harbor Dam in the 1960s forced her to relocate the family to the Yakama Reservation. Today the original people of the Palouse Country remain dispersed throughout Northwest reservations. The Kamiakins, Poweens, and Felixes are on the Colville; the Jim, George, and Jack families on the Yakama; and the descendants of Wolf Necklace (Tilcoax) and the Johnleys on the Umatilla. Other Palouse and Nez Perce families whose ancestors once lived on the Snake reside today on the Nez Perce, Warm Springs, Coeur d'Alene, and Spokane reservations where elders like the Jims, Fishers, and Sijohns work to keep tribal traditions alive through their teachings, story-telling, and periodic visits to the old homeland.

For decades, members of the Coeur d'Alene tribe have commemorated the 1858 Steptoe Battle with the annual Memorial Warriors Horse Ride from Plummer, Idaho, to Rosalia, Washington. As has been customary for generations, participants in the May 2000 Hngwsuum Ride witnessed a descendant of a Coeur d'Alene combatant raise a time-honored talisman from an exquisitely beaded sheath: the steel scabbard of an officer who fell during the fight. The memorial revisits an age when the Native peoples of the Palouse Country were masters of a vast domain that safeguarded the bones of their ancestors. The land remains home to the descendants of the Animal People, whose expressions can still be heard in a magpie's complaining call and read in the second glance of a loping coyote.

A remarkable series of Palouse and Nez Perce portraits are among those painted by Worth D. Griffin, who was hired in 1924 to teach art at Washington State College (WSC; now WSU) in Pullman and became the principal organizer of the summer Nespelem Art Colony in the 1930s. Griffin also painted a series of Palouse Country "historic characters," including frontiersman Felix Warren, Garfield businessman Winchester Oliphant, Hooper rancher Peter McGregor, and Jenny Kenny, an early settler and wife of a veteran of the 1858 Steptoe campaign. Griffin was critically commended for his

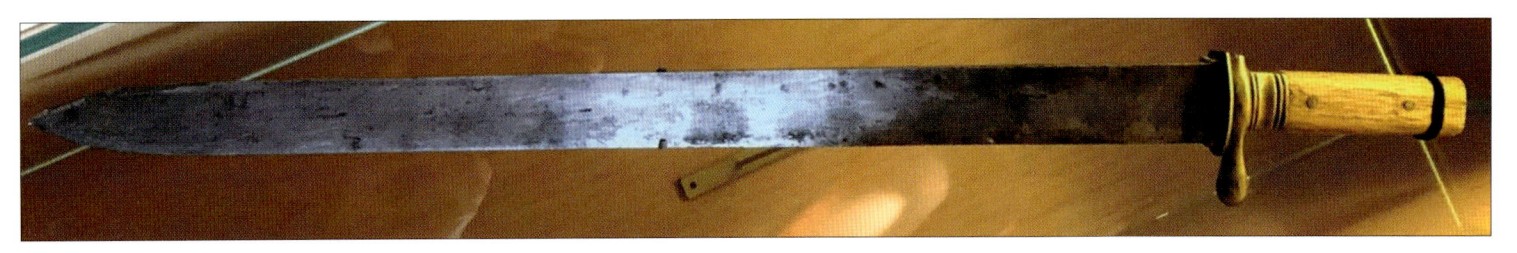

Steptoe Battle Army Officer's Sword
Coeur d'Alene Casino Tribal Heritage Exhibit, Worley, Idaho

works that depicted both the documentary and inherent creative values of his subjects. His orange ocher and olive green earth tones—shades of dawn and dusk—were favored colors of the Native Americans, whose arrows and sallie gags were decorated as uniquely as ancient cartouches.

Some of the most expressive images painted at that time were by colony member and Adams County native Anne Harder MacKenzie Wyatt, who was majoring in art at WSC. Her mother, Annine, remembered the days when some 200 Snake River-Palouses pitched their tipis near the Harder home east of Ritzville. Harder Wyatt's portraits were characterized by Nicolai Fechin-like splashes of bright cadmium yellow and vermillion. Griffin's portraits of Cleveland Kamiakin, Pemalks (Mrs. Skolumkee) Kamiakin, Agnes Andrews, and

other Nespelem area residents are safeguarded today by the WSU Department of Art, while those by other colony artist like Harder Wyatt are found in the Northwest Museum of Arts & Culture (NWMAC) in Spokane and in the Ritzville Public Library.

In 1956, at one of the last public appearances by Chief Kamiakin's last surviving son, Chief Cleveland Kamiakin told an Ephrata audience of Columbia Basin farmers, "We are gathering here at a special place and it still holds it sacredness (*ahtow*). ...[W]e must live together on the same land; one people to another, face to face. We have families, communities, in friendship on this land. I will not tell [you] how to manage the land, but my food is also here and I hope we can continue to gather it. You use this land for your needs as we have ours.

Worth D. Griffin, *Chief Cleveland Kamiakin* (left) and *Pemalks Kamiakin*, 1935. *Courtesy of the Jordan Schnitzer Museum of Art WSU.*

May we live together.... I have already shared what is important about maintaining a sacred relationship with the land, and all the creatures, so all of us can dwell here."

In the context of his parting words, Cleveland did not tell others how to work the land, but he asked for respect of the Native peoples' recognition that the land's natural resources are to be protected as a sacred obligation in order to sustain humanity. Elder Carrie Jim Schuster observes that the word *ahtow´* "suggests a sacred trust" with environmental consequences if selfishly broken. "The desire to get something more than we need and are provided leads persons, families, and even nations to do things that are harmful to the land and to life. This is what Cleveland and our elders meant when they spoke about the 'law' to [Governor] Stevens and others who

wanted to make the treaties. For the sake of our children and in accordance with these sacred ways we must respect the land and water and not pollute it as is happening now."[22]

On Cleveland's excursions to the family's traditional Palouse camps and elsewhere in the region, he would often point out landmarks of mythical and historical significance and tell of the great changes in the landscape he had witnessed in his lifetime. On his last trip to the old homeland not long before his passing in 1959, Cleveland ventured back to the Palouse Country to visit the graves of his parents and relatives. At Rock Lake where his legendary father was buried, Cleveland wistfully informed his younger companions that it was the last time he would see his ancestral homeland. "Always remember who you are, and where you came from," he told them.[23]

facing page

Palouse River Sunset

north of
Endicott, Washington

Bales

west of Genesee, Idaho

CHAPTER IV

Settlers and Ranchers

After spending months and hundreds of thousands of dollars to garrison the chain of interior forts during the 1850s Indian wars, the Army's Pacific Command found it necessary in the early 1860s to divert its resources of men and materials to the East. In late December 1860 South Carolina seceded from the Union and within weeks the country was embroiled in a national nightmare, the American Civil War. Officers who had fought together against the Snake River-Palouse, Yakama, and other Plateau tribes now found their loyalties divided between the Union and the Confederacy. In the fall of 1862, Washington Territory mourned the loss of General Isaac Stevens, who was killed while leading his men in a dramatic attack at the Second Battle of Bull Run.

As the War Between the States put a tremendous strain on the resources of the Army's Oregon Department, its command found increasing difficulties in dealing with disputes between Indians and settlers of the Inland Northwest. Wherever the two groups mixed, trouble seemingly ensued. The alarming loss of promised Indian lands to settlers in the Colville district was brought to the attention of the Superintendent of Indian Affairs in 1862; in the same year, Fort Lapwai, east of present-day Lewiston, was built to keep the peace. The Palouse region seemed to be encircled by brush fires of conflict; yet, at the beginning of the decade, not a single settler lived in the region between the Snake and Spokane rivers.

The Mullan Road and way-station marker near Benge, Washington, c. 2000.
Author's photograph.

facing page

Palouse River Spring

near
Hooper, Washington

The area's first White settlers selected homesites located in the western Palouse region at strategic crossroads near sources of fresh water. In 1861 William Newman, a Canadian immigrant, built a cabin near the head of Sprague Lake at the junction of the Colvile and White Bluffs roads. The latter was heavily promoted by the Oregon Steam Navigation Company (OSN) as its link between the Columbia River and the mines of western Montana and the Kootenai district. Newman's home served as a way-station for freighters and mail riders. In 1865 Henry Wind opened another roadhouse on the Colville Trail-Mullan Road, located on the lower end of Cow Creek below present-day Benge, Washington. The rock corrals and stone foundation built in the shadow of the steep basalt cliff are still clearly visible from the roadside. In 1866 stockman Jack McElroy moved into the area and began raising cattle in the grassy coulees south of Newman's cabin. He was soon followed by fellow immigrants Russell Bacon, Robert Potts, and William "Hoodoo Billy" Burrow.

The first settler in the Palouse Hills was George Pangburn, a 27-year-old bachelor from Walla Walla who had visited the area as early as 1862. He later squatted on unsurveyed land along lower Union Flat Creek, south of present-day Endicott. Pangburn wintered in Walla Walla but returned periodically to farm, plant a small orchard, and raise hogs for markets in the mining boomtown Lewiston. According to fellow settler J. B. Holt, Pangburn settled permanently in the area in 1865. He first lived in an earthen dugout and in 1867 was raising wheat, corn, and oats on the flat. He built a 12' x 14' log cabin in 1870, the site of which today holds a bronze plaque mounted on a basalt slab that commemorates "the first known farm in the Palouse."

About that same time, Joseph "Kentuck" Ruark and his Native wife settled near the mouth of Union Flat Creek. A native of Pennsylvania, "Kentuck" had also resided temporarily in Walla Walla before establishing his Palouse ranch. A settler named Knight squatted in 1864 on land near present-day Mica, southeast of Spokane. This site eventually developed into the famed "California Ranch" way-station operated in the 1870s by the colorful proprietor-brothers, Maxime and Peter Mulouin.[1]

Snake River Landings and Orchard Communities

The newly established hamlets that appeared on the north side of the Snake River at the early ferry crossing sites in the 1860s and 70s—places like Palouse Landing (Perry), Penawawa, Almota, and Wawawai—became the Palouse Country's "ports of entry" for many of the region's earliest settlers. In 1859 Edward Massey began operating the "Palouse Ferry" a mile below the mouth of the Palouse River, where the Colvile Road crossed the Snake River. Massey sold his interest in the ferry to brothers William and Cyrus McWhirt in 1864, but in the following year John Silcott and John Harding purchased the operation. Business was brisk for Silcott and Harding, who ferried Army and civilian traffic traveling on the Colvile Road from Walla Walla to destinations north of the river. Palouse Landing also became a principal destination of the OR&N Co.'s sternwheeler fleet that plied the fast waters of the lower Snake and Columbia rivers from Portland, Oregon to points east.

The Palouse Indians who resolutely remained at the mouth of the Palouse River were likely bewildered by the sudden surge in immigrant traffic across the land. The second ferry landing established on the Snake River was located about four miles upstream from Palouse Landing, near the mouth of the Tucannon (*Tukwenenma*) River. Rights for the business were first secured by Isaac Kellogg in January 1864 and operations began the following spring, in partnership with Samuel Caldwell and James McAuliff. Soon afterward, however, Kellogg was killed in a gunfight near the Spokane River, and, while the ferry was under repair, Caldwell drowned with two other men after upsetting his canoe.

Four more miles upstream Michael Tormey established the Taksas Ferry in 1865, near the massive woodyard opposite Riparia at which Lewiston steamers loaded fuel. The service came to be known as the Texas Ferry and its connecting trail dubbed the Texas Road, which continued northward through present-day LaCrosse, Washington, past Texas Lake, and skirted Rock Lake on the west to connect with the Mullan Road. The ferry and road's true namesake was the Palouse village of *Teksaspa*, or "Debouchement Place," located where the narrow Tucannon Valley opens into the majestic canyon of the Snake. By the late 1860s, this popular ferry had come under the management of Jesse Thompson, Thomas Newlon, and T. M. Slocum.[2]

Thousands of miners, described as "a restless, shifting crowd," began redirecting their paths when in 1865 reports of new strikes on the Little Blackfoot River in western Montana led them to travel the recently charted roads across the Palouse. In that year, Ruark joined Thomas W. Davidson in operating Angell Ferry six miles upstream from Texas Ferry. In an effort to capitalize on the burgeoning traffic to the Montana gold placers, they renamed their site "Blackfoot Ferry" which linked Angell Ferry Road from Walla Walla with what they advertised as "the nearest route to the mines." The path crossed the heart of the Palouse region along portions of the old Spokane Trail and soon became known as the Kentuck Trail.

Moving in 1865 to the vicinity of present-day Central Ferry was Joseph DeLong, a bachelor originally from the Midwest, and ferry service was operating at that point in the following decade. He had crossed the plains in 1862 and settled on the Tucannon River above Walla Walla, where he farmed and raised livestock. He joined George Pangburn on Union Flat in 1867, but relocated in 1869 to the scenic bottomland where the Kentuck Trail crossed the Palouse River after finding his missing cow grazing contently near the water. DeLong built a log cabin on a knoll of wild sunflowers that protruded from the northern bluffs, then raised apples, peaches, and apricots, and sold provisions to immigrants traveling along the trail. For protection from any unfriendly area Indians he also fashioned a wall of talus in a rock shelter overlooking the river's bend.

Steam navigation on the Snake River was inaugurated in 1859 by two Army supply runners who had sailed the waters from Celilo to Fort Walla Walla during the Indian wars using small scows. Entrepreneurs R. R. Thompson and L. W. Coe decided that the Idaho gold strikes made that year would justify their investment in building a steamer. They had the shallow draft sternwheeler *Colonel Wright* built at the mouth of the Deschutes River that year, which Master Leonard White then nudged fifty miles up the Snake on her first test run in 1860, during the spring runoff. Business soon boomed in response to all the mining excitement above Lewiston. The ship brought in as much as $2,500 per run on passenger fares alone for the weekly two-day trip from Celilo.

Freight was shipped during the first decade at rates varying from $60 to $80 per ton. Over the next twenty years, a fleet of ships like the gleaming white *Okanogan* and *Spray* were acquired and built by the OR&N Co. and did a brisk business in upriver traffic. They returned with ever increasing loads of grain each summer and fall. With the completion of the company's rail line from Walla Walla to the Snake River opposite Riparia in 1881, the vessels were needed only to run upriver from the south shore railhead. Vessels belching forth billowy clouds of black were seen almost daily from Riparia to Lewiston during the spring and summer, carrying loads of immigrants and supplies.[3]

Of the seventeen rapids between Lewiston and the river's mouth, Snake River rafters and riverboat pilots found the most daunting to be the Palouse Rapids. Beginning four miles above the mouth of the Palouse River, a series of basaltic outcroppings stood like a monstrous spine that created a watery obstacle course leading to the "chute." Here the channel narrowed for the river to descend six feet in a three-quarter mile stretch of billowy foam. In 1861, fifteen-year-old William Polk Gray accompanied his father, missionary William H. Gray, on a grueling 40-day rafting expedition upriver, using a capstan and rope to pull a load of merchandise from Wallula to Lewiston. That same year Samuel Clemens was serving as a cub pilot on the Mississippi, gaining experience that would culminate in the writing of *Huckleberry Finn* two decades later. Young Gray met first-hand the perils of life on the river, but the efforts of father and son confirmed the viability of river commerce despite the hazards.

While floating a skiff and raft of lumber downstream from Lewiston on a September return trip, Gray encountered Palouse Rapids with all its force. "I sent the raft into the center. The current was so swift it sent us into the eddy. The forward part of the raft went under water. The skiff ... started to float off but I caught the painter and got aboard. About a half-mile below the rapids our skiff was suddenly lifted out of the water by the reappearance of the raft." The party was surprised at the sight of both burden and raft that "had gone with the current and, oddly enough, had appeared directly under us." The boy's experiences on the Snake left him with the resolve that "no combination of wood, iron, or water" would ever scare him again. Gray went on to serve as a cub pilot on the sternwheeler *Yakima* and eventually made a career on the Snake River where he regularly visited landings from Riparia to Lewiston—the Hannibal, Missouri of the Inland Pacific Northwest.[4]

John Silcott relocated from Palouse Landing to a crossing eight miles west of Lewiston in 1861 to establish a ferry at historic Red Wolf's Crossing and another at Lewiston the following year. He married the daughter of the noted Nez Perce leader, Chief Timothy, whose people lived in the vicinity. Silcott sold his interest in Palouse Ferry to Daniel Lyons, a 43-year-old native of Limerick, Ireland, in 1872. Lyons had immigrated to the United States in 1847 and, following his marriage to Anna Wright in 1854, the couple moved west in a series of peregrinations that led from California and British Columbia to Walla Walla and Palouse Landing. The site came to be known as Lyons Ferry and, following Daniel's death in 1893, their son, Perry, established a small community nearby and continued to operate the ferry for over thirty years.[5]

In 1870, two dozen miles upstream from Lyons Ferry in the vicinity of Penawawa, homesteading stockmen began grazing vast herds of cattle on the steep grassy slopes of the Snake River canyon. Two years later, C. C. and Sarah Cram moved to Penawawa from the Walla Walla Valley and with the help of their son, William, established the Penawawa Ferry, which the

Lyons Ferry on the Snake River, c. 1950.
Courtesy Franklin County Historical Society Museum,
Pasco, Washington.

family operated into the 1880s. Cram, a veteran of the Interior Indian Wars, became an active promoter of Palouse Country settlement and built a substantial portion of the Territorial Road from Pataha to Penawawa and northward to Union Flat in the 1870s. This route became one of the primary arteries for travel from Walla Walla and Dayton to Colfax and Spokane. A fellow veteran of the Indian campaigns, Iowa native Alexander Canutt also settled in Penawawa with his wife, Sallie, and their family in 1872, as did George and Nancy Smith. In the following year, Emsley and Mary Fincher arrived in the fledgling settlement to begin a large sheep-raising operation. Like most of the Snake River ferry landings, Penawawa in the 1870s boasted several saloons, a hotel, and freight warehouses. Area homesteaders credited Canutt with the introduction of irrigated orcharding to the valley, and the family's holdings expanded when sons John and Joseph obtained property adjacent to the original ranch.

Fourteen miles upstream from Penawawa was the river settlement of Almota, where Civil War veteran L. M. Ringer settled in 1872 (though rancher Edward Johnson was raising cattle and horses in the vicinity a year earlier). In 1873 Ringer was joined by his wife, Sophia, and their children, and the family established a general mercantile business. Located at the northernmost point of the Snake River, Almota was soon transformed into a bustling community with OR&N Co. warehouses, two hotels, a saloon, gristmill, and another cable ferry service across the river. Joining the Ringer family in 1872 was Henry Hart Spalding, son of Henry Harmon and Eliza Spalding, the Congregational missionaries to the Nez Perce.

Following the 1846 Whitman massacre, Spalding and his parents moved to Oregon's Willamette Valley. Henry Hart missed the land of his youth, however, and decided to return east of the Cascades in the 1860s to settle in the Walla Walla Valley before moving to Almota. He acquired 1,200 acres of land adjacent to the Snake River and established one of the largest orchards in the valley, with vast plantings of apple, pear, peach, and other fruit trees as well as wine grapes and grain. His parents and the Whitmans had planted the first fruit trees between the Rockies and Cascades at their Clearwater and Walla Walla missions in the spring of 1837, and remnants of the neglected orchards were still producing four decades later.

Area orchardists like the Spaldings, Canutts, and others formed a horticultural society to better raise and market their fruit, and these efforts contributed to the successful promotion of the "Palouse Apple." The origin and name of this Red Bellflower variety was attributed to Joseph and Susanna Arrasmith, natives of Indiana, who in 1874 settled on the Palouse River several miles west of present-day Palouse. The succulent fruit's red skin with lemon yellow stripes was popular for its taste as sauce, in pies, and for cider. Also a hardy survivor of Northwest winters, the Palouse Apple became the most widely raised variety in area orchards, including those of the Arrasmiths' neighbors to the north, Lewis and Mary Love, who emigrated from Missouri in 1881 to homestead south of Garfield. Love was an innovator who tried his hand at raising numerous varieties of fruit and grain.

Nearby Elberton boasted the world's largest fruit dryer in the 1890s, with a daily capacity of 1,800 bushels of fresh fruit. An enormous dryer for prunes was built in the tiny settlement of Diamond and another large facility that took a variety of fruit was built in Colfax. Large orchards also flourished from 1890 to 1910 in the eastern Palouse region from Potlatch to Kendrick. The Palouse Country held approximately 300,000 fruit trees in 1910 but subsequent severe winters and the economic challenges of fruit production led to a gradual decline in production. Within two decades most large orchards in the Palouse Hills had been removed and planted to grains.[6]

In 1877 Almota witnessed the alliance of two of the Palouse Country's most colorful and prominent families as Henry Hart Spalding married Mary C. Warren. The Hugh Warren family had journeyed westward over the Oregon Trail in 1865 to settle in the Prescott, Washington area. Mary Spalding's brother, Felix Warren, became a legendary stagecoach driver for the Northwestern Stage Company on the Territorial Road from Walla Walla and Dayton via Pomeroy and Almota to Colfax. This route was an important company spur penetrating the Inland Northwest from its main route between Kelton, Utah and Portland, Oregon via Pendleton.

Felix Warren had an abrupt introduction to his life's work at age twelve. The boy's father, who served as wagon-master for the Missouri emigrants, fell gravely ill in the Rocky Mountains. Young Felix took over the reins and continued leading the wagon train all the way to Walla Walla. In later years Warren frequently overnighted at the Spaldings' palatial home—later known as Almota House—after a long day's run at the reins atop his Concord coach. In the evenings he often regaled passengers, relatives, and friends with stories of battles against the elements, wild animals, and notorious outlaws. Clad in fringed western garb and broad-brimmed hat with a neatly trimmed moustache and goatee, Warren was a gifted teller of tales and looked every bit the part he played in Palouse Country lore.

Taber Family Home and Orchard at Almota, 1889.
Courtesy Whitman County Library, Colfax, Washington

In the 1870s, the OR&N Co.'s only other north shore landing below Lewiston was located at Wawawai, eight miles southeast of Almota. The community was named for the ancient Indian village of the same name, near which homesteads for raising livestock were established by William Winter, John Gould, James Root, and others in 1875. The first apple and soft fruit trees were likely planted by Isaiah Matheny the same year, with large orchards planted soon afterward on both sides of the Snake by Sewell Truax. A large warehouse for fruit, sacked grain, and other commodities was constructed in 1877 by Matheny and Colfax businessman and miller John Davenport. Ferry service at Wawawai was inaugurated by John Kanawyer in 1885. Stone was quarried from the Miocene fissure at Granite Point, several miles upstream, and hauled to such burgeoning townsites as Colton, Pullman, and Moscow, where it was used for foundations and facades in many commercial buildings.[7]

Grain trader Aaron Kuhn built a second warehouse in the 1880s and began seeking a better transportation solution for his clients. At that time, they had to transport their wheat by wagon down the steep grade of winding Canyon Road that led from the grain districts east of Colton to the Snake. The entrepreneur eventually financed construction of the mile-long Interior Grain Tramway, an immense project that had the peculiar appearance of a gravity-powered ski lift carrying sacked grain down the slope on wooden benches. At the lower warehouse, the sacks were unloaded and stacked to await steamship transport to the railhead at Riparia for shipment to the Coast. When working properly, some 2,000 sacks of Palouse grain took the twenty-minute ride down the tramway each day. In an average year, as many as 150,000 sacks were transported to Wawawai warehouses using this method.

The 1880s also witnessed the first biweekly runs of the *Annie Faxon*, *Almota*, *Harvest Queen*, and other OR & N Co. steamers that could reach speeds of eighteen miles per hour on upstream runs and return with eighty or more tons of grain and freight. Their daring pilots continued to navigate the seventeen areas of dangerous rapids between Lewiston and Riparia. Eventually an OR & N Co. demolition crew began working from the steamer *Wallowa* to remove the most treacherous outcroppings in the river, and the thunder of downstream blasting eventually came within earshot of the remaining villagers at Palus. Inexorably the crewmen approached Palouse Rapids, and after several days of blasting, the crew moved four more miles upstream to tame Texas Rapids using the same method.

Colfax's *Palouse Gazette* reported in 1885 that farmers were rapidly fencing their lands to control damage from roaming livestock. In doing so, they cut across miles of trails that had been freely used by Native peoples to reach root grounds and traditional hunting areas since time immemorial. While most farmers tolerated the diminishing travel by Natives through the area along the few routes still open to them, and often traded their produce for salmon, others did not. They greatly objected to "Indian trespassing" and brandished weapons to impose the new order of the day.

In the late 1890s William and Mary LaFollette, Palouse settlers of 1877 who also farmed near Ewartsville, acquired several hundred acres of land adjacent to the river and divided by Wawawai Creek. The LaFollettes built a sawmill along the creek and devised an extensive irrigation system on their property. They planted vast tracts to orchard fruit, principally shipped to Portland for distribution, as well as strawberries, grapes, rhubarb, asparagus, and melons which were marketed to communities above the river bluffs. As the LaFollettes' enterprises prospered, William acquired adjacent properties and was later elected to Congress.

For the next seven decades, families throughout the Palouse region made festive outings in late summer or early fall to the Snake River orchard communities to spend a day picking tree-ripened fruit for home-canning to meet winter needs. Provisioned with picnic lunches, young and old would join together to gather the finest produce in a harvest sequence beginning in June with Mount Morincy pie cherries, Bings, and Royal Anns for canning. Apricots, nectarines, and Hale peaches ripened in July, followed by pears in August. Midsummer apples were also picked at this time including green Transparents for applesauce and Rome Beauties, a dessert favorite of railroad chefs on the region's early lines. Smaller crabapples—excellent for jelly—and pears were also picked in August. Fall apples included Jonathans and Red Delicious. Ripening last of all were the Winesaps and Winter Bananas, two of the finest baking apples. Friendships between orchard and farm families were renewed annually as boxes and baskets were weighed at wholesale prices on ponderous iron scales and then carefully loaded for the return home.[8]

Settlers in the Hills

Blacksmith James Hall obtained backing from Lapwai businessman W. A. Caldwell in 1868 to establish a cattle ranch near the head of Hatwai Creek north of Lewiston, and later constructed a cabin of hand-sawed planks. That same year twenty-year-old Riley Knight hauled lumber from Dayton to build a cabin on Thorn Creek northwest of Steptoe Butte. After three years on the isolated prairie, Hall had second thoughts about continuing his operation, as a fellow with his smithing skills could find employment almost anywhere. He decided to leave, and the place was acquired about 1870 by Michael and Elizabeth Ruddy, immigrants from eastern Canada. The Ruddy family built onto the house, which later served as a stagecoach and mail station until it passed into the hands of Orville Collins. The original home has remained in the family ever since and is likely the oldest residence in the southeastern Palouse.

In 1869 T. A. E. "Doc" Philleo established a ranch several miles northwest of present-day Spangle, where he found ample open rangeland and access to a small lake later named for him. Several miles due east of the lake was a wooded flat surrounded by small lakes, which was chosen by Cyrus Turnbull for his home. In the 1930s the original ranch was acquired by the federal government to form the nucleus of the Turnbull National Wildlife Refuge for migrating Canada and snow geese, swans, ducks, golden eagles, and other migratory fowl. The area has grown to cover 15,500 acres and also serves as an important sanctuary for beaver, river otter, the Palouse Country's largest elk herd, and ten species of bats, including nocturnal big browns and the long-eared myotis.[9]

A September 1869 issue of Portland's *Morning Oregonian* reported that the Palouse Country was "finally attracting the attention of settlers." The first significant surge of immigration to the area took place between that year and 1871, when settlers like James and Jennie Ewart located homes on Union Flat Creek in what later became known as the Ewartsville district. Most of these early settlers were Americans from the upper Midwest and Northeast, although nine were Irish immigrants, like the McNeilly brothers, who had come to the northeastern United States in the 1840s and moved on to pursue the western gold strikes. As was the case with Ewart, a Civil War captain in the Illinois Volunteer Cavalry, their loyalties had been with the North and the stream was dubbed "Union Flat Creek" accordingly. The 1870 federal census listed 116 settlers residing on Union Flat, and at the time of Whitman County's creation in 1871, about 200 were living within its boundaries.

Natives of South Carolina and Georgia, including the Alfred Holt family, settled along the neighboring stream north near Plainville (the present-day Palouse Empire Fairgrounds west of Colfax) in 1872, which resulted in it being named Rebel Flat Creek. Soon veterans who had fought against each other in the Wilderness Campaign, Chickamauga, and other Civil War battles found themselves neighbors in the Palouse. An immigrant presence also had emerged along Paradise Valley by 1870, in the vicinity of present-day Moscow. On a foray through the area in August of that year, census-taker C. P. Coburn encountered two prospectors, William Powers and Frank Points, as well as Kentucky native John Buchanan. Buchanan had begun raising livestock, to the consternation of local Indians, who prized the unspoiled root grounds of the verdant valley. In 1872, Civil War veteran "Major" R. H. Wimpy and his wife became the first settlers on Hangman Creek when they established a farm about seven miles southeast of present-day Waverly.[10]

Other Palouse homesteaders came in search of peace and possibility after experiencing nineteenth century American tragedies every bit as disturbing as the Whitman Massacre and Civil War atrocities. An old photograph of Rock Lake City shows blacksmith Joseph Lee standing behind his anvil and clutching a white-hot horseshoe with long-handled pliers. His thick apron and debris-laded floor portray the life of hard labor known to men of his trade. Lee's parents had joined the Latter-Day Saints in 1832, just two years after the church was founded, and the family witnessed the murder of Joseph and Hyrum Smith in Nauvoo, Illinois, in June 1844. The Lees had crossed the Great Plains in 1849 bound for Utah, but Joseph and his wife, Mary Ann, relocated to the Palouse region where they raised a family of thirteen children in the Rock Lake area. The Lees soon became acquainted with neighbors who had overcome unimaginable horrors at about the same time they had lived in Utah.

Georgia Donner Babcock was five years old in April 1846 when she set out with her family from Independence, Missouri in a California-bound wagon train led by her father and uncle, George and Jacob Donner. At Fort Bridger their group of ninety decided to take the little-known Hasting's Cutoff south of Salt Lake, but rather than saving precious time, the desert heat considerably slowed their progress, and the group did not reach the foot of the Sierra Nevada Mountains until late fall. An abnormally early winter struck as they began climbing the range, and they became snowbound near the shores of a lake, enduring frigid weather and famine. Fully half of the party perished in the mountains, and many of those who survived did so only after resorting to cannibalism. But the others, including members of Georgia's family, displayed bravery of the highest order and were eventually rescued. In later years Georgia moved from California to the Palouse region where she took an active part in managing one of the largest ranches in the Rock Lake area in partnership with her son, Frank B. Babcock.[11]

Many of these immigrants had initially lived for a time in the bustling settlement of Lewiston, where land seekers and freighters made connections to travel northward on John Silcott's ferry. His landing a short distance downriver became the beachhead for the impending European-American invasion onto the Palouse prairies and eastern mining districts. Following the boomtown excitement of the previous decade, which had brought recurrent waves of miners to its muddy streets, Lewiston at the dawn of the 1870s was experiencing an awkward adolescence. Its population had stabilized at about four hundred, though civic pride foreshadowed steady growth and was reflected in the replacement of false fronts and canvas roofs with substantial frame structures. Saloons and hotels still predominated along Main Street, but the town now also boasted a doctor's office, drug store, and school.

Although most Lewiston residents were native-born Americans from the East, fully one-third were foreign-born, with Chinese, Germans, Irish, and Canadians predominating. Lewiston in 1870 was home to a much more ethnically diverse population than other inland Northwest communities, with its citizenry also including natives of Sweden, France, Mexico, Chile, and the Philippines. Within months, some would

ascend the imposing bunchgrass-covered bluffs north of the river and join the handful of others to make a lifelong home in the Palouse. William Ewing, a Lewiston butcher from Pennsylvania, would soon establish a ferry crossing near the future site of Palouse City; drayman Michael Leitch founded the settlement of Leitchville at an important stage stop southeast of present-day Pullman; and Hungarian-born Jacob Kambitch was considering a homestead in Paradise Valley near present-day Moscow, to which he moved in 1872.

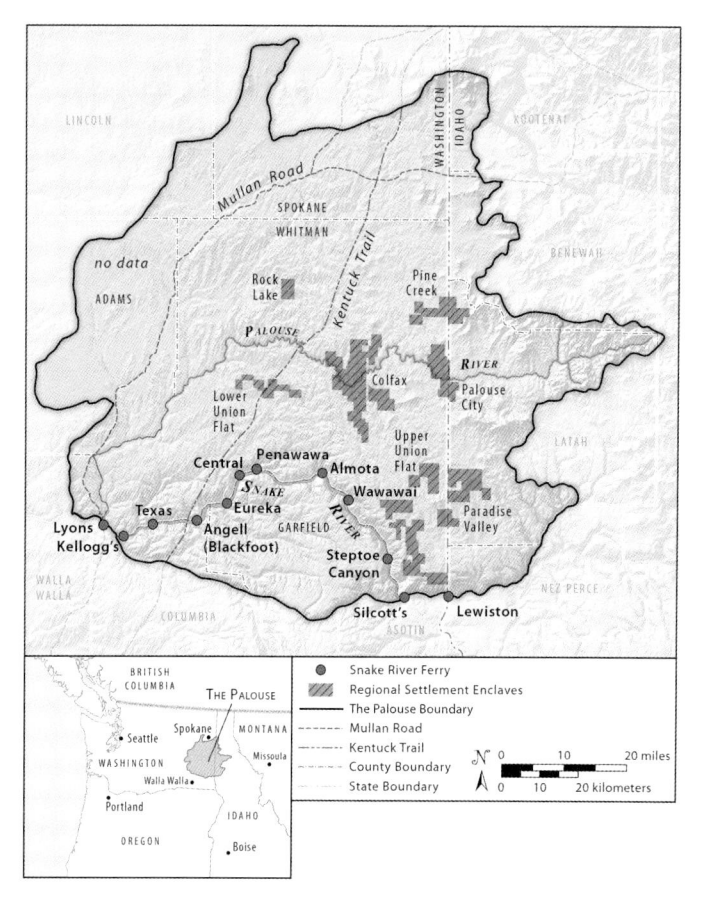

Palouse Regional Settlement Enclaves, c. 1872, and 19th Century Snake River Ferry Crossings

Belleville, Paradise Valley, and Three Forks

In 1870 settlement began at what is now Colfax, where James Perkins and Thomas Smith built a 24 foot by 16 foot log cabin at the base of a bluff near the confluence of the Palouse River's North and South forks. A testament to construction methods of the time, the building remains as the oldest structure in the Palouse Country and is on the grounds of the Perkins House National Historic Site. First known as Belleville, the name "Colfax" was suggested by Perkins to honor U.S. Vice President Schuyler Colfax, serving with President Ulysses S. Grant. Settlement also began at Farmington in 1870 and the following year saw families establish homes in what became the towns of Moscow, Palouse, and Rosalia. Growth was steady (if not rapid) between 1870 and 1872 as settlement expanded along Union Flat Creek and the Palouse River at Colfax. Other pioneers located during this time along Rebel Flat Creek, Pine Creek, Four Mile Creek (near present-day Viola), near what is now Genesee, Idaho, at the foot of Rock Lake, and at present-day St. John and Spangle.

The majority of these families were native-born European-Americans who had journeyed to the Oregon Country after the Civil War but shared the experience of one immigrant group that "found all the land taken up in the Willamette Valley and … heard there was still plenty of good land in the Palouse Country." Immigrant traffic to the region through Walla Walla was observed by the editor of the *Walla Walla Union*, who noted in April 1871 that the "country between the Snake and Spokane Rivers seems now to be the favorite region with stockraisers, and the valleys that skirt the small streams in that section are fast filling up with this class of settlers. We are told that no less than 500 head of cattle have been taken across the Snake River at the different ferries since last fall."[12]

In the summer of 1871, brothers Almon and Noah Lieuallen, natives of Tennessee who had crossed the Plains to Oregon in 1867, brought a herd of cattle from Lewiston to Paradise Valley and built cabins for their families about three miles northeast of present-day Moscow. The area was also dubbed "Hog Heaven," since razorbacks delighted in rooting up the camas fields and other native tubers. The Nez Perce name for the area was *Taxt Hinma*, or "Deer Fawn Place." Within a year, the Lieuallens were followed to the area by George Tomer, Thomas Tierney, John Russell, and enough other families to justify the creation of the Paradise Post Office. A school was erected in 1872, near Almon Lieuallen's home and adjacent fields of flax.

Farther down the valley and later in the decade, a small enclave of settlers clustered near the confluence of the Palouse River and Dry Fork and Missouri Flat creeks. Named "Three Forks" by its residents, the land that would later become the Pullman townsite was first claimed by Daniel G. McKenzie in 1877. Arriving in the vicinity a year later was Indiana native Daniel W. Boone, named for his famed frontiersman ancestor, who came with his wife, Amelia, after a brief sojourn in Oregon. A general mercantile was built in 1881 by Orville Stewart and M. D. Lee, and in the following year Northern Pacific Railroad surveyors laid out the town on property acquired from McKenzie.

Most homesteaders during the first decade of settlement lived next to streams or good springs in order to supply domestic needs and to maintain their livestock. Wood was needed not only for fuel and building material but also as fence rails, since barbed wire was not invented until 1873. Western yellow pine provided the best lumber, but large stands were found only in the mountainous eastern uplands, along both Palouse River forks and Union Flat Creek, and near the scabland

previous spread

Genesee Lutheran Church

north of Genesee, Idaho

channel northeast from Rock Lake. Many families camped for weeks or even months in tents until they obtained enough lumber to build a home. Some primitive habitations were little more than holes dug into leeward hillsides with crude shelters erected over them.

When sufficient preparations had been made for construction, the typical house in the Palouse hinterlands resembled the small box-house, measuring between twelve by four- teen feet to sixteen by twenty feet. Often a "lean-to" was added to one side to extend the sleeping area. Glass windows were a luxury and many families waited weeks for floorboards, since the demand for lumber usually exceeded the supply from local mills. Well-drilling equipment was operating in the Palouse region by 1878, to expand the possibilities for locating home- sites, and the silhouettes of windmills soon appeared across the Palouse horizon.

Country Living and Trade Centers

The journals and account books kept by Joseph DeLong at his Palouse River ranch and store provide a rare glimpse of life on the Palouse Country during its earliest years of settlement. Journal entries record information essential to self-sufficiency under such scribbled headlines as "Smallpox Cure" (a concoction of sugar, foxtail, and zinc sulfate), "Recipe for Preserving Green Fruit," and "Grasshopper Poison." Related knowledge of value clipped from early issues of the *Walla Walla Statesman* and *Palouse Gazette* was safeguarded between the small, lined pages of his hardboard bound books, providing the mathematical formula "To Measure Hay in Ricks," stories about Lincoln and Grant, and favored verse: "Let live for- ever grow, and banish wrath and strife; So shall we witness here below, the joys of social life." Perhaps to advance social relations with the travelers and neighbors who frequented his place, DeLong also found time to jot down riddles. One favorite of this thinly bearded soul with kindly mien was in rhyme: "I went to walk through a field of wheat, and there found something good to eat. It was neither fat, lean or bone, I kept it till it ran home. (An egg.)"

Most folks with whom DeLong most often shared such wit and practical knowledge were families of those who later settled near him on the pine-covered slopes of the Palouse River Val- ley. Names frequently appearing in his account books include Ben Davis, Frank Smith, Steve Cutler, Link Ballaine, and E. E. Huntley. These families came to DeLong's store to visit, col- lect mail, and procure staples, often on credit. His inventory included eggs, onions, coffee, sugar, baking powder, soap, sarsaparilla, and tobacco. He also stocked hardware sup- plies like nails and wire, and such curatives as oil of anise, oil of bergamot, and sulfu- ric of ether. DeLong and his neighbors spent considerable time building and repairing split-rail fences to hold in their livestock and also exper- imented with grains and fruits to determine which varieties were best suited to Palouse soils and climate.

Venerable Joseph DeLong, c. 1895.
Joe DeLong Collection

Palouse Winter Farm

north of Pullman, Washington

Beef Line

west of St. John, Washington

The Palouse River bachelor planted hundreds of apples and peach trees along the river obtained from Walla Walla nurseries as well as pear, cherry, plum, prune stock, grape vines, and currant bushes. Summer visitors to his store could always expect a good supply of Tall Pippins, Yellow Bells, and Northern Spy as well as soft fruit and vegetables. He sometimes traded these for salmon with Indians who seasonally passed along the old trails along the river. Ben Sissom, who settled two miles upstream from DeLong in 1867, is credited with seeding the first wheat along the river. Sisson sold his property to pioneer orchardist George Ruedy in 1872.[13]

The early American and Canadian settlers were primarily subsistence farmers and stockmen who raised cattle, sheep, and hogs. The virgin sod of dense bunchgrass crowning a fibrous root system was broken in the heavy, wet bottom lands by long-sheared breaking plows, primitive disks, and harrows with wooden teeth or fashioned from bushes. A two-horse team pulling a single shear plow could turn a half-acre per day, while a larger three-horse triple shear gang could cover two acres in the same time. The laborious task of breaking virgin sod, however, almost always required a single shear plow, steady strong hands, and a cooperative horse. Stands of hawthorn and wild rose were widespread along some draw bottoms and stubbornly resisted the settlers' attempts to burn them out and plow through the roots and sod.

The region's first farmers experimented with flax, rye, and spelt, a primitive grain used for livestock feed. Sufficient moisture in the bottomlands usually allowed two cuttings of alfalfa and grasses such as clover and meadow fescue in June and September. Small, cleared patches were seeded in the spring by hand broadcast to oats, barley, and wheat. The crops were usually cut with a scythe or cradle to hold the cuttings. The grain was trampled out by horses or flailed in the ancient manner and often yielded sixty bushels per acre in the early 1870s when not frostbitten. The settlers planted orchards and large

gardens and gathered wild currants, huckleberries, gooseberries, and serviceberries for canning. Trout were abundant in the clear waters of the Palouse River where the new residents also hunted doves, grouse, and waterfowl.

Meeting the physical needs of large Palouse-area families was a substantial undertaking in the homesteading era that required considerable planning, planting, and processing. Provisions stored for winter and spring were substantially home-grown or traded locally, since trips to Colfax or Oakesdale for bulk foods meant paying premium prices that many families could not afford. A family with six children commonly required butchering five hogs in the fall and canning or smoking the pork, along with five hundred pounds of flour and a ton of potatoes—about twenty gunny sacks or the product of one to two acres. At least a hundred pounds of sugar was needed for canning hundreds of jars with fruit and vegetables, another hundred pounds of dry beans and peas, and in some cases a substantial amount of popcorn.

Two coffee grinders were commonly stored in late nineteenth-century Palouse-area households. Since coffee beans were usually green when purchased, they were oven-roasted for grinding. Those for whom coffee was a luxury sometimes roasted wheat or barley kernels until dark brown to brew an acceptable substitute. The other machine was for crushing wheat berries to be mixed with rolled oats or dried fruit for a boiled breakfast "mush." To immigrant English, the variable mixture was called porridge, while my Germans forebearers knew it as *Hirsche*, from the German word for millet. They sometimes joked that it was "*nicht fuer essen aber fressen!*" (not for eating but for grazing).

From the earliest days of settlement, women pickled a variety of garden and orchard produce with a medley of spices in earthenware crockery, ranging in size from five to ten gallons. Cucumbers were crocked with salt and dill, tomatoes in water with herbs, and peaches with sugar and cloves. Potatoes,

previous page

Winter Rake

Moscow, Idaho

carrots, and beets were stored in root cellars, often dug into an adjacent side-hill and connected to the house by a porch. Milk, cream, and butter were made throughout the year and, if they were raised, chickens and eggs were readily available. These needs required farmyards with barns, chicken houses, hog sheds, vegetable cellars, smokehouses, granaries, and other out-buildings in order to substantially maintain self-sufficiency. Most families also pastured one or two dairy cows to supply milk, cream, and butter.

Land was claimed through several means. The liberal provisions of the 1862 Homestead Act promised 160 acres of public land to qualified adults who lived on their property for five years and improved it. Others purchased relinquishments from those who came as speculators or who wanted to leave after laboring under the difficult conditions. Land prices in the early 1870s ranged from $1 to $2 per acre. Timber cultures provided a quarter-section to those who wanted to plant ten acres of trees, few of which, however, survived the dry climate. Preemption claims involved a substitute payment to the government of $2.50 per acre for the five-year residence requirement.

Many early settlers merely "squatted" on the parcel they desired until compelled to gain legal title to the property. This became possible only after the 1871–73 federal land surveys were completed in the Palouse region by teams bearing chains, rods, stakes, and brass optical instruments. The work was directed by L. P. Beach, David Clark, Henry Meldrum,

and others who labored from spring to fall to measure and mark and section lines. A vast checkerboard grid was inexorably imposed upon the compliant Palouse region like a net cast on a slumbering creature, and without regard to the region's unique topography.

Colfax, Washington, 1889. *Courtesy Whitman County Library, Colfax, Washington.*

The first trading centers emerged in the Palouse Country in the early 1870s to provide lumber and milled wheat for flour. Those who settled on lower Union Flat Creek found little quality timber in native groves of cottonwood and willow and even eastern Palouse settlers lacked facilities to process their stands of higher-grade timber. Promotional material sent out at the time by a Portland immigration bureau had warned of the absence of timber in the Palouse, but advised that pine, fir, and tamarack could be obtained in the eastern slopes of the Bitterroots.

In October 1871, the first sawmill in the Palouse Country was built at the fork of the Palouse River near present-day Colfax by former Midwesterners James Perkins, Hezekiah Hollingsworth, and Anderson Cox. The scenic place was known to the Coeur d'Alenes as *Hnch'laqhemn* ("Canyon") while Sahaptin speakers knew this sheltered fishing campsite as *Tinatpolmat*, a name also used for the river's South Fork that abounded with trout and whitefish. Over 60,000 bushels of wheat were raised in the Palouse region in 1872 but the *Portland Oregonian* lamented the fact that "this amount will not any more than supply the settlers with seed for this year and yet, strange to relate, they have no thriving mill between the Snake and Spokane Rivers, a vast area of country, uninhabited four years ago but now dotted all over with the improvement of energetic farmers and some of the land already in a high state of cultivation."

In 1873 Joseph W. Davenport arrived from the Willamette Valley to construct a flour mill in Colfax, and the local farmers warmly responded by pledging 5,000 bushels of wheat for processing. By 1877, additional flour mills were operating in the town of Palouse, where James "Modoc" Smith had settled in 1873, and at Almota. A second sawmill had been constructed in Colfax along with others in Palouse and near Moscow. A horse-powered model was used by James Ewart on Union Flat, but the machinery was relocated to the Palouse River near Elberton where a larger sawmill was constructed in 1878. Other early sawmills were located at Moscow, Pine City, and Rockford. One of the smaller milling operations that survived the economic pressures of the era was Oakesdale's Barron Flour Mill. This five-story steam-powered facility was built with mortise and tenon construction in 1890. The facility was purchased by Pennsylvania native and second-generation miller Joseph C. Barron in 1907, who introduced the popular "Sweet Home" brand. Barron's son, Joseph, operated a smaller mill in an adjacent facility until the 1990s, and the original mill is now a National Historic Site.[14]

Among Latah County's earliest settlers, David Notman had heard about the legendary grasslands of the Inland Pacific Northwest while ranching on Big Thompson Creek north of Denver, Colorado. In 1873, he joined a group of friends and relatives who had come in a dozen wagons from his old home in Arkansas. They had decided prospects for the future were better risked in the uncertainties of this new land than in the grim realities of subsistence farming in the South. The Arkansas families included those of I. M. Woody and cousins John P. and John Freeze. Their trek began on April 4, 1873, in Benton County, Arkansas, and ended four months later with their arrival on August 3 in Walla Walla. Later that month Notman continued north across the Snake River to Deep Creek, northwest of present-day Potlatch. The Freeze families remained in the Waitsburg-Dayton area until 1876, when they joined the Notmans and others to form a rural community later known as the Freeze district. Others from the original Arkansas group, including Woody, were among the first settlers to establish themselves farther west from the Freezes, in what became the Farmington and Garfield areas.

Ranching in the Western Palouse

The earliest ranchers in the Rock Lake district included John Eaton—another veteran of the 1855–56 Indian Wars who arrived in 1870 after helping to operate the Kentuck Ferry for two years, Thomas May, and the William and Minnie Henderson family. The Henderson home, a two-story whitewashed Gothic structure built in 1872, survives as one of the oldest houses on the Palouse. A guest of the Hendersons in the 1870s described the interior of the one-room house that measured sixteen by twenty feet in no-frills terms. "Two corners were occupied by beds, a third by a cook-stove, and the fourth by a table. In addition, there were a cradle, several chairs and benches, cooking utensils, and a limited supply of dishes."[15]

In 1873 Henry Halsey settled farther east in the upper Pleasant Valley district beyond present-day St. John, where an ancient trail leading from the Palouse River to Steptoe Butte crossed the stream. Halsey established a livestock operation and built a log cabin that nine years later became home to cattleman George Howard, who disposed of the ranch's 2,600 sheep and acquired nearly a section of adjacent land. Later improvements were made to the ranch with the help of his wife, Emma, including the construction of a larger log home, complete with upper story gun ports, which has been kept in excellent condition to this day.

On the southwestern Palouse boundary, Mullan Road packer Thomas Benton Turner and his wife, Martha Jane, settled in 1871 at the confluence of Union Flat Creek and the Palouse River to raise livestock and sub-irrigated gardens and grain. In the same year, ten miles downstream, Albert and Ernest Hooper from Devonshire, England settled in the area where the small community named for them later emerged. The brothers brought with them a young Black man named Zanzibar (perhaps indicating his homeland), whom they later assisted in homesteading property on the Palouse near their property. Although an excellent swimmer, he drowned after getting entangled in a rope while leading a horse attached to the one he was riding across the Palouse River.[16]

The family of Andrew Jackson "A. J." and Melvina Smith established several ranches in the western Palouse region after the area was first scouted by one of their sons, Andrew, in June 1876. The Smiths had overlanded on the Oregon Trail in 1865 and settled initially in the Willamette Valley, but eventually sought more open spaces where they could both farm and raise livestock. Andrew returned with favorable news about settlement opportunities north of the Snake River and persuaded his parents and brothers John and Virgil to relocate in 1880. A. J. and Melvina settled on upper Downing Creek near present-day St. John, Virgil established a ranch on lower Downing Gulch, and John settled several miles to the east near Matlock Bridge (Kamiakin's Crossing) on the Palouse River. This scenic area was about two miles below DeLong's ranch, where the steep river bluffs were dotted with yellow

pine, and was the northernmost point on the Palouse River. The bridge was located on an important route—known to settlers as the Spokane Trail—that led through the Palouse Hills along an ancient Indian trail.

Matlock Bridge was named for the first settlers in the vicinity, Missouri natives Preston and Kerlista Matlock, who established a ranch on the river in 1872 and whose daughter, Sarah, later married John Smith. The brother who began the Smith family's exodus to the Palouse, Andrew, settled at Pine City in 1880 and operated the flour mill established there a year earlier by Anderson Edwards. At peak capacity in the 1880s, the mill could turn out 16 barrels of flour a day from about 100 bushels of grain. Other early Pine City area settlers included Peter and Annie Carlon and William and A. E. Davis, arriving in 1878, and Adam and Marinda Kile in 1881. Having surveyed much of the region prior to settling, former stagecoach driver James Gordon and his wife, Mary, claimed land in the Four Corners district north of present-day Malden in the late 1870s.[17]

By the mid-1870s, settlement of the region was still restricted to small bottomland farms while stockmen maintained increasingly large cattle herds and flocks of sheep on the hills and breaks of the Snake River and in the Channeled Scablands. In 1871 the *Walla Walla Union* reported that over 5,000 head of cattle had been taken across the Snake River since the previous fall into "the favorite region of the stock-raisers." The paper also covered the rise in immigrant traffic from the Willamette Valley to the Palouse Country.

The *Union* reported in the spring of 1872 that "most of those that are going there have more or less stock, and are attracted thither by the well merited reputation of the country for stock raising." The herds of several individuals grew to over a thousand head on the unfenced prairies of the Palouse, where, in Whitman County alone, 45,000 cattle shared the range with 58,000 sheep by the end of the decade. The stock typically wintered in the milder pastures in the western portion of the Palouse or in the sheltered Snake River Valley and was driven to the superior eastern ranges of Idaho in the summer.

By the end of the nineteenth century, Pendleton's famous Hamley Saddlery Company was creating saddles uniquely suited to the needs of Snake River ranchers and cowboys. Nicknamed the "Bear Trap," the Hamley Snake River model was considered a work of art and practicality by Palouse Country bronc-busters. Traditional styles with a low cantle in back and high horn for tying off a lariat made for a dangerous combination in some circumstances. Cowboys riding on uneven ground or slopes to rope wild horses for breaking and uncooperative cattle at branding time could sometimes be thrown up and nearly impaled or crushed if they landed on the protruding horn. A ranching family near Sprague suffered the double tragedy of Tom Lakin's death in 1905 in a horse accident followed by the fatal fall of his uncle, George Lakin, some years later. The Hamley Snake River featured the distinctive cantle and horn with high front swells made of wood blocks covered with leather. Mounted inside a "Bear Trap," with thighs pressed hard against such supports, a cowboy felt secure. Palouse Country native Dan Luft was among Hamley's foremost saddle-makers at the company shop in Pendleton, where exquisite leather inlay on company designs made Hamleys some of the most coveted saddles in the country—a tradition that continues among ranchers and collectors.[18]

Western Palouse cattle round-up, 1948.
Hutchison Studio Photographs of Washington State University and Pullman, WA., 1910-1973 (PC 70), Manuscripts, Archives, and Special Collections (MASC), Washington State University Libraries, Pullman, WA.

B. W. Davison homestead, 1885.
Hutchison Studio Photographs of Washington State University and Pullman, WA., 1910-1973 (PC 70), Manuscripts, Archives, and Special Collections (MASC), Washington State University Libraries, Pullman, WA.

Spotted Horses and Rodeo Champs

The few remaining Indian families who resided on the Snake River after the 1870s were determined to remain in their ancestral homeland and avoid removal to area reservations. Most of them had established friendly relations with White settlers in the river communities and sometimes worked the orchard harvest seasons while still fishing and tending their dwindling horse herds. Many of the animals abandoned by the Palouses who had participated in the Nez Perce War were caught by area horse traders like Walla Walla's "Cayuse" Brown to sell in Canada where they brought up to $8 a head. Many others were eventually destroyed by local farmers when they strayed across fenced areas and trampled crops.

Hatley horses and harvest near Colfax, c. 1895
Hutchison Studio Photographs of Washington State University and Pullman, WA., 1910-1973 (PC 70), Manuscripts, Archives, and Special Collections (MASC), Washington State University Libraries, Pullman, WA.

Smaller herds of the finer animals were safeguarded by the families of Yosyos Tulikecíin ("Someone Covered in Blue"), brother of Hahtalekin, who remained near Wawawai, Husis Poween ("Shot in the Head") at Almota, Poyakin at Penawawa, and the blonde-headed Chief Husis Moxmox, and Weeatkwal Tsiken ("Young Kamiakin") at Palus. One of the prime movers among the Palouses in the effort to legitimize their rights to ancestral lands was Husis Kute's nephew, Juklous, known to Whites as Sam Fisher, who encouraged the others to join together in a collective registration of claims. Fisher had grown up along the Snake River tending the horse herds of his father and relatives, and he developed a passion for both life in the valley and quality breeding stock.

In addition to a horse's intelligence, disposition, and sure-footedness, Sam Fisher found special appeal in the distinctive spotted pattern in the horse stock that came to be known as Appaloosa. Their name was derived from their Palouse homeland and was in widespread use throughout the region as early as the 1870s. Fisher gelded and used a "powerful medicine" to ensure the breed's distinctive spotted blanket markings, which were beautifully evident on such herd stallions as Calico Sam and Knobby. Other Appaloosa patterns include snowflake—white spots on gray—and leopard: dark spots against a lighter coat. To Fisher, one Appaloosa was worth more than a "truckload of other horses" and at times he ran well over a hundred head along the lower Palouse River Canyon.

Fisher's prized animals became well known to other Indians as well as among ranchers and cowhands throughout the region, who purchased them for work with cattle, pleasure riding, and as rodeo stock for such premier events as county fairs and the Pendleton Roundup. Fisher's knowledge came to be highly regarded by area horsemen who made the effort to find him and admired for his horse-raising expertise and his tenacious efforts to honor his people by maintaining a presence at Palus.[19]

Until his death in 1944, Sam Fisher and his wife, Helen, a survivor of the Nez Perce War, were also stewards of the tribe's ancient burial ground near their home. He freely traded his knowledge with local ranchers, most of whom raised draft horses for farm work, like Phillip Cox, whose Cherrydale Stock Farm near Hay was famous for producing the area's finest Percherons; Emery and Frank Gordon, who began raising horses in the Pampa-Rock Springs area in 1884, and Herb Camp of LaCrosse.[20]

Old friends from the river communities and Palouse Hills who knew the value of fine horse flesh also bought many of their favorite animals from Fisher. National rodeo star Faye Hubbard and his brother, Fern, grandsons of Wilcox pioneers Goalman and Nancy Hubbard, acquired some of their most beloved stock from Fisher including Faye's Ole Rex, a gray stallion with black spots. "We ran wild horses with him in Oregon, 'dogged' off him in Canada, roped off him all over the country," Hubbard later recalled. "He was just all-around useful and as tough as he was good-looking."

Hubbard went on to earn honors as World Champion Bulldogger at the 1939 New York World's Fair Rodeo, where he met Broadway composer Kay Swift. The unlikely friendship led to the couple's marriage and subsequent move to Cougar Rock Ranch near Bend, Oregon, where they raised Appaloosas and other horses used by fellow Palouse Country native Enos "Yakima" Canutt and film makers of popular Hollywood Westerns. Hubbard and Swift's quixotic relationship was chronicled in her autobiographical novel, *Who Could Ask For Anything More?* that appeared on screen in the 1949 RKO production *Never a Dull Moment.*

One of John and Nettie Canutt's sons from Penawawa, Yakima Canutt won international acclaim as four-time World Rodeo Champion beginning in 1917 and as the principal developer of Hollywood's "film fighting" and action stunt techniques. He acquired his nickname after winning the Pendleton Roundup competition while still in his teens. Some impressed

observers in the stands remarked that he rode "like a Yakima." Claiming "I can't remember a time when I wasn't on horseback," Canutt worked with such notable directors as John Ford and Stanley Kubrick on dozens of movie epics including *Stagecoach, How the West Was Won, Ben Hur,* and *A Man Called Horse.* Canutt was presented an Academy Award in 1966 for his unique contributions to the industry and was later inducted into the National Cowboy Hall of Fame. Canutt's Hollywood experiences influenced his younger cousin, Colfax native John Crawford, to become an actor; he also starred in several Western films as well as in the popular 1970s television series, *The Waltons.*[21]

Almota rancher Floyd Hickman purchased a mare from Sam Fisher that became the dam of Old Blue, named for the shade of this beautifully varnished roan. Servicing up to a hundred mares annually and living to his mid-thirties, Old Blue was considered to have had more influence than any other studhorse in the Palouse region for upgrading the quality of the region's Appaloosas, and gave Hickman his favorite horse, famed Toby I. Other prominent Appaloosa breeders in the area were George Adair of Potlatch and Moscow's George Hatley, who was a prime-mover in the formation of the international Appaloosa Horse Club. Others included Palmer Wagner, Les Sauer of Dusty, Chet Lamb and Lester Riley of Riley's River Ranch near Central Ferry, and Roy and Zaidee Parvin, whose Fourmile Appaloosa Ranch was located between Colfax and Pullman.

Due in large part to the tireless efforts of Palouse Country residents George and Iola Hatley, the National Appaloosa Museum and Heritage Center opened in Moscow, Idaho in 1974. The facility features exhibits on the breed's use by area tribes and as champion show and rodeo stock. Toby I, overall performance winner of the first National Appaloosa Horse Show in Lewiston a generation earlier, and Hatley's own Toby II were both descended from Sam Fisher's native Palouse herd.[22]

Wilcox Road Old-Timers   southeast of Dusty, Washington

Winter Barns   northeast of Colfax, Washington

CHAPTER V

Farming and Railroading

An immigrant to the Palouse region in 1874 observed many others "leaving the country because the people thought they could not grow crops and fruit." One early Idaho settler warned that while entry fees and commissions were nominal, the costs of improving new lands could be staggering and the labor burdensome. He wrote, "It is one of the severest struggles a poor man with a family can undertake in his lifetime to settle upon, pay for government land, and support his family all at the same time. He may try it and fail after much deprivation, toil and hardship. As a rule, in these territories, to conquer a piece of land and fence it, making it in any way valuable, and paying the necessary fees to land offices is worth all the land is worth."[1]

In spite of the challenges, regional settlement by stalwart immigrant farmers in the late 1870s was taking place at such a rapid pace on that by the end of the decade a government official observed that "the best pasturage of the territory… is rapidly passing into the possession of the farmers." By 1884 the number of cattle in Whitman County had been reduced to 20,000 head, less than half of what it had been. Palouse region farmers were gradually discovering the fertility of the hills and grain varieties suitable for production. The alluvial soils on the bottoms were actually inferior to the aeolian deposits of the hills, as the former were poorly drained and were much slower to warm in the spring. Soil temperature is an important factor in seed germination and damaging frosts often settled on the bottoms due to the downslope flow of cool air.

Transition from Stockraising to Farming

Locating a potential farm site in the Palouse region remained a formidable task throughout the 1870s. Travel expenses to the region were not inconsiderable, as prospective settlers had to make allowances for ferry service, meals, and other costs on the journey. Once in the Palouse, a hopeful immigrant could spend weeks or even months in search of a favorable location for a home. As a result, many men chose to leave their families while scouting the land and often remained alone on their

claims for an extended time to determine whether permanent residence would be economically feasible.

When his family joined the Palouse settler, all able members were needed to contribute to the success of the venture. This was particularly true with European immigrants, since the expense and distance of travel usually precluded hopes of a return to the homeland. Isolated in the rural Palouse, immigrant families began writing to their relatives back East or in

facing page

Storm Break Rolling Palouse

north of
Genesee, Idaho

Europe to interest them in moving to the region. Many joined their kinsmen in the area, and numerous rural communities emerged associated in name with an area of Eastern origin—Tennessee Flat, Texas Ridge, Missouri Flat, California Flat, New York Bar, and Minnesota Flat.

The Nez Perce Indian War of 1877 only temporarily interrupted the flow of immigrants to the Palouse Country. By 1878 the population of Whitman County had risen to 3,700, and in 1879 the Federal Land Office in Colfax transacted more business than any other district office in the entire nation. Clearly, a land rush of significant proportions was taking place. In the spring of 1879 Colfax's *Palouse Gazette* announced, "Immigration has commenced again, every boat up the Snake River is loaded with passengers for the Palouse Country, hotels are crowded, and people seeking land or business locations may be seen in every direction." That year, nearly 18,000 acres were under grain production, with almost half in wheat. Composite land claims for the 711 farms in Whitman County totaled 144,207 acres. Immigrants were flocking to the eastern Palouse region, as local advice deemed the best land lay within the twenty-mile strip west of the Idaho-Washington border.[2]

Some banks would not loan money on farmland located west of present-day Diamond because of the greater risks involved in farming the drier districts. The Potlatch River country was heralded in promotional literature as "the most fertile country in the world, ...well wooded, well watered." Palouse region farmers were raising an average of three hundred bushels of wheat and seventy bushels of rye by 1880, for which they typically received twenty-five to thirty cents per bushel at the Snake River landings. By the late 1880s, prices rose to forty and occasionally fifty cents a bushel. Most of the grain was shipped to commission merchants in Portland before local buyers began operating later in the decade. The population of Whitman County and Nez Perce County (which included present-day Latah County) swelled to 11,179 in 1880. At this time, the overwhelming majority were native-born European-Americans (82%). The largest foreign-born elements were the Germans (numbering 229), Irish (228), Canadians (209), and Scandinavians (156).[3]

Joseph DeLong's notation of "E. E. Huntley" in his account books likely referred to Elmer E. Huntley, whose mother, Phoebe, brought her three children on a two-month covered wagon trek to the Palouse region in the spring of 1880, following the death of her husband in Marion County, California. Originally from Maine, the Huntleys settled near present-day Thornton, Washington. Among their nearest neighbors were Marion and Louisa Baker, who had homesteaded two miles west of present-day Sunset in the summer of 1872. Mrs. Baker was also the wagon-master on their family's trip to the Palouse from Eugene, Oregon, while Marion followed with the cattle and horses. In 1886 the Bakers' daughter, Nettie, married Elmer Huntley. A distant cousin of the Huntley clan who had lived in Indiana and Missouri, William Huntley relocated to the Endicott area in 1884. Equally proficient with a ledger book and breaking plow, Huntley acquired 10,000 acres of farmland in the area through purchase and lease over the next fifteen years and established a chain of mercantile stores in Endicott, St. John, and Colfax in partnership with his brother, George Huntley.

Maine native Reuben Prince settled near the Bakers and Thornton Huntleys in 1878 and induced his brother Nathaniel, then living in California, to join him on unclaimed land adjacent to his farm. Nathaniel's wife had just recently died, leaving him to care for their three young children alone, so the offer of family assistance appealed to him. But three years after their arrival in the Palouse, Nathaniel also died and left his sixteen-year-old son, Henry, and two younger daughters in Reuben's care. The three determined children chose to remain at home and work to prove up on the homestead themselves, a goal they realized five years later.

Neighbors George and Margaret Comegys, also Palouse settlers of 1878, established themselves southeast of present-day Thornton where the Territorial Road crossed Thorn Creek. The grand scenery of the Comegys' new home inspired them to name it Belle Mead (Beautiful Meadow), where they remained for a decade. They then moved to Oakesdale, where Comegys joined financier E. H. Hanford in establishing the Oakesdale Commercial Bank. Comegys represented area citizens in the 1889 Washington Constitutional Convention, at which he played a leading role in drafting the new state's constitution.[4]

Among the earliest settlers in the vicinity of Steptoe Butte were Tennessee natives J. P. T. and Mary Minerva McCroskey who arrived with their ten children in 1879. The family first squeezed into a one-room cabin at the southern base of the butte until they constructed a 20-ft x 20-ft residence several weeks later. J. P. T. was a prodigious letter writer to relatives and friends back in Rockville and elsewhere in the Volunteer State, extolling the fertility and availability of land in the area. With ten children, peacocks and prairie chickens, cattle and horses, the McCroskey ranch, like many others in the Palouse,

was a beehive of activity outside, where labor was contributed by all in the fields and tending the livestock. Around the exterior of the house, the family carefully placed vast plantings of fruit and ornamental trees and raised a large garden. They passed evenings discussing the political issues of the day and lessons being taught at school.

In the 1890s, with the completion of a spacious and gracefully designed two-story home flanked by broad rows of dogwood trees and evergreens, the McCroskey ranch became a Palouse Country showplace. J. P. T.'s correspondence campaign succeeded in inducing dozens of other Tennesseans to emigrate to the Palouse region, where many settled on what became known as Tennessee Flat near Steptoe. Some immigrants credited McCroskey with leading more settlers to the region than any other one person. The McCroskeys' youngest son, Virgil T. McCroskey, later donated land to create Steptoe Butte State Park (1946) as well as Idaho's Mary Minerva McCroskey State Park (east of Farmington, Washington) in 1955. The Idaho tract's native landscape covers 4,400 acres and stretches nearly a mile from Mineral to Huckleberry peaks to offer incredible vistas of the eastern Palouse.[5]

Draw Bottoms to Hilltops

Rosalia-area settler A. J. Calhoun sowed both the flat and hills on his Spring Valley property in 1877, noting that, "If the hilltops wouldn't raise decent crops the country wouldn't amount to much." Congregational missionary George H. Atkinson rode from the Snake River through the Palouse Country to Spokane in May 1879 and noted the gradual change taking place in the region as farmers discovered the viability of growing crops on the hilltops. "Here and there the plow runs up the slopes and over the hills, opening the lighter or more reddish soils. The harvests of wheat from the uplands are proving to be the best." In a letter to the editor of the *Spokan Times*, Atkinson predicted that "the homestead which crosses the

small valleys and takes in a larger portion of the hills will be the most valuable."[6] Crops were gradually planted higher and higher on the slopes and—contrary to previous speculation—frost damage was generally minimal.

The farmers soon found it impractical to plow "up and over" the steeper hills, due to the strain on the animals and the resulting erosion problems. They devised a method of "backlanding" for tillage. In this process, the farmer began his field operation slightly above the base of the slope and followed the contour of a group of hills completely around to the point of beginning. Successive passes followed the same curved pattern and gradually worked the soil up to the top of the hills. Such experiments proved successful and in the spring of 1879, the *Palouse Gazette* reported on this most significant development:

> Our own observations have been confirmed by the experience of farmers that the hill lands prove to be best for all kinds of grain. While being about the country for the last ten days, it was noticed that grain is looking unusually well for this time of year, many hills so high that it would seem impossible to cultivate, being covered with a fine stand of wheat. The bottoms grow too heavy straw, are more subject to frosts, and being usually more effected by late spring rains, the crop cannot be sown so early as on the uplands, and consequently cannot be harvested before the fall rains set in. These ideas are mentioned for the benefit of new settlers, who, seeing that the bottom lands have been taken first, may think the hills or uplands have been rejected, while the latter are now generally preferred by those who wish to make grain growing their principal business.[7]

Greater acreages were steadily brought under cultivation, and the region's agrarian economy was further stimulated by the opening of the grain export business through Snake River navigation in 1876. One factor inhibiting development prior to this time was the relative isolation of the Palouse region from the larger marketing centers on the more populated Pacific Coast. The opening of shipping facilities at Almota by the Oregon Steam Navigation Company in 1876 enabled Palouse farmers to export nearly 10,000 bushels of wheat to Portland, while local reporters observed the unloading of "four threshers, three sulky plows, three reapers, three headers, fifteen wagons and 100 tons of produce."[8] In the following year, other shipping warehouses were constructed at Wawawai and Penawawa on the Snake River.

The volume of river traffic substantially increased in 1877; Henry Spalding, proprietor of shipping at Almota, recorded 1,000 tons of produce exported from the town. Deliveries to Almota that year included 500 tons of merchandise, 195 new wagons, 95 sulky plows, 100 Noble plows, 10 threshers, and a variety of other agricultural equipment. The Palouse, once synonymous with bunch grass and wild horses, was now becoming a haven for prospering farmers. In early 1880, only about 20,000 acres were under cultivation in Whitman County. By the end of the decade, that figure had risen to nearly 750,000 acres, as European-Americans had claimed virtually the entire farming district (though some areas in the western Palouse remained unplowed until 1920).

Many families in the countryside gathered to help build the enormous barns that were needed to store hay and protect livestock and farm equipment during the Palouse's snowy winters. As unique in design as the people who built them, many today lie in twisted hypotenuses of weathered wood, defeated by decades of wind and rain, others remain as vital and impressive as the year they were raised. The classic red walls of Thera's Adam Daubert barn have proudly stood for nearly a century and the unusual Max Steinke (DeChenne) round barn west of St. John and the T. A. Leonard round barn east of Pullman were constructed to simplify the task of feeding horses from the spacious hay lofts. The gleaming white horse stables trimmed in green on the McCroskey place near Steptoe Butte look as ready for use as when J. P. T.'s Tennessee relatives raced their animal nearby, and the enormous dairy barns adjacent to the University of Idaho on the western outskirts of Moscow remain among the largest in the Pacific Northwest.

The population of the Palouse region nearly tripled in the 1880s as the completion of the Northern Pacific Railroad facilitated immigration to all parts of the Pacific Northwest. By 1890, the population of Whitman and Latah Counties reached 28,282. Of that number approximately 2,000 were foreign-born; one-third of these were from England and Canada. Among the one million Canadians who came to America in the 1880s were two Scottish-Canadian brothers, Archie and Peter McGregor, who in 1883 claimed homesteads on Alkali Flat near present-day Dusty. To earn extra income, they herded sheep for ranchers along the Snake River, and in 1885 they acquired a small flock of their own. The McGregors invited other family members from Sydenham Township on Ontario's Lake Huron to come west, and in 1886 their brother, John, relocated to Whitman County. A fourth brother, Alexander, followed in 1900.

The industrious McGregors increased the size of their flock into one of the region's largest and pastured them on the winter ranges along the lower Palouse River until the annual summer drives to the eastern mountain districts. Pooling their profits and business acumen, the brothers entered into lucrative grazing leases and purchase agreements with the Northern Pacific Railroad, covering 25,000 acres in the southwest corner of Whitman County. In 1902, title was secured to the leaseholds, which gave the McGregors control of an agricultural empire extending 17 miles by 21 miles. The McGregors continued to run sheep for decades, brought large tracts of pastureland under irrigation, developed a substantial dryland grain farming operation, and later expanded their enterprises into wheat research and fertilizer production.[9]

Palouse Country steam threshing, c. 1895.
Hutchison Studio Photographs of Washington State University and Pullman, WA., 1910-1973 (PC 70), Manuscripts, Archives, and Special Collections (MASC), Washington State University Libraries, Pullman, WA.

The Rustler War and Rural Law Enforcement

Ranchers like the Huntleys, McCroskeys, Benjamin Manchester, Lucius and Lillis Smith, and others in the central and western Palouse regions were harassed by livestock rustlers in the 1880s and early 1890s, which led to the organization by some fifty men of the Stockmen's Protective Association in 1892. A February 1892 issue of the *Colfax Commoner* reported that fifteen head of horses belonging to Lafayette Wright of Sprague were found in Valley City, South Dakota! Another four hundred stolen from D. A. Fleweree of Colfax had still not been located.

Association members worked to break up a notorious horse-thieving operation headed by William "Big Bill" Masterson, who had established a ranch in Palouse Cove between present-day Ewan and Winona. The narrow box canyon sheltered natural springs and a small lake and was flanked by large basaltic columns to form an ideal hideaway for stolen livestock. The herds were moved eastward at night beyond Pine City and Farmington, to be sold in north Idaho and Montana. The Stockmen's Association joined with local marshals to eventually put an end to the depredations in the summer of 1892, when over two dozen rustlers were captured, including the Williams and Cooper gangs. Masterson's operation, however, continued to thwart the efforts of the ranchers. Standing six feet, four inches tall, Masterson was an imposing outlaw who wore a heavy mustache and, according to an acquaintance, was "uncouth, profane, insolent, and overbearing." He was also a crack shot and suspected of murdering Siowiarchy the Younger, son of a Palouse Indian chief, in a dispute over a horse.

Masterson's son-in-law and accomplice, Ed Harris, was arrested in Montana in July 1892 for selling stolen livestock and was brought by train to Spokane en route to Colfax to stand trial on the charges. In an attempt to free Harris, Masterson intercepted the party at the Pacific Hotel in Spokane. A gunfight erupted during the night, in which deputy Charley Miller killed Masterson after the outlaw wounded Pine City sheriff Luke Rawls. Harris was then taken to Colfax and sentenced to an eight-year term at the state penitentiary in Walla Walla. He escaped not long after his imprisonment, however, but was never seen in the area again. The Palouse Country Rustler War had come to an end.[10]

Most Palouse Country communities could not afford the services of a local constable, so from 1870 to 1900 law enforcement in most places was left to city marshals in Colfax and Moscow, who were periodically assisted by deputies. Their efforts to maintain domestic tranquility were often challenged by distance and the brutal circumstances of rural life. During the 1880s and 1890s, Colfax's *Palouse Gazette* regularly reported in lurid detail on cases involving gunfights and murder as well as occasional "crimes of infamy."

Three episodes of vigilante justice led to the overpowering of deputies on night shift at the Colfax jail and the lynching of the accused offenders. The first victim was a man convicted of an 1884 murder in Pullman, but some locals felt the wheels of justice did not grind fast enough for proper restitution. The grisly scene was repeated in June 1894, at a double lynching for two horse thieves who were unceremoniously tossed out an upper window of the Colfax courthouse. The same venue was used in January 1898 for a man held on a charge of murder and theft in Farmington. The area's only legal hanging, which drew a large crowd, took place near the Colfax courthouse on March 25, 1898.

I. A. "Brooks" Mackay and Joseph Canutt were Colfax's marshals for most years between 1888 and 1915, and they became legendary Palouse Country figures in their own time. Standing six feet tall and weighing two hundred pounds,

Old Place   south of Palouse, Washington

Palouse Solitude   north of Potlatch, Idaho

Sheriff Mackay exhibited a rare balance of terror and tolerance depending on the situation. An old acquaintance later elaborated on Mackay's approach: "On Saturday nights, instead of jailing the drunk farmers, Brooks, who knew them all, would take each one to his own team and wagon, slap the team on the rump and head them for home .... There were some tough customers reluctant to go, however, and Brooks could lead them off, two at a time, with a chain around the arm of each one. He used guns as a last resort. His main defenses were a strong right fist and a billy-club.... He was fearless."[11]

Henry Villard and General Tannatt

A native of Bavaria, Henry Villard came to the United States in 1853 and labored for several years at various occupations before studying law in Carlisle, Illinois. He then worked in the offices of several influential United States senators from the Midwest. Having a talent for journalism, he reported on various political campaigns for several newspapers, and these experiences led to personal acquaintanceships with Abraham Lincoln, Horace Greeley, and men in the highest circles of American and European business.

Villard became interested in the subject of railroad securities and finance and in 1873 joined a German protective committee which had heavily invested in Ben Holliday's troubled Oregon and California Railroad, as well as the Oregon Central and the Oregon Steamship Company. In 1874 Villard journeyed to Oregon as a representative of a committee to investigate the situation. He later noted that the trip changed the course of his life: "I felt that I had reached a chosen land, certain of great prosperity and seemingly holding out better promise to my constituents than I had hoped for."[13]

To bolster the region's developing transportation industry, he was supplied with the distinction of "Oregon Commissioner of Immigration" and by 1875 had established offices in Boston, Topeka, and Omaha that cooperated with the main Northwest Immigration Bureau in Portland in directing immigrants to the Pacific Northwest. The duty of railroad officials there was to provide these new arrivals with employment on construction crews or to sell them railroad land on which to settle. Special displays of Northwest grains, fruits, and vegetables were circulated; large advertisements regularly appeared in English, German, and Scandinavian newspapers throughout the country; and thousands of circulars extolled the Pacific Northwest as containing the "best wheat, farming and grazing lands in the world."

Villard observed that, geographically, the central artery of transportation throughout the entire Northwest was the Columbia River. He thus assumed that whoever navigated the great river and controlled the railways along its course would virtually monopolize transportation east of the Cascades. He journeyed into the region for the first time in May 1876 and stated later, "It was at that early date that a plan arose through the organization of the Oregon Railway and Navigation Company." Within a year, Villard's clever manipulation of several indebted concerns led him to the presidency of all three Northwest transportation lines that had been operated previously by Holliday. In 1878, Villard formed the Oregon Improvement Company to facilitate the construction of his network and to arrange for the orderly settlement and exploitation of his holdings in the region.[14]

The man Villard selected to be the general agent of the new company was Thomas R. Tannatt, who later arranged for colonization in the Palouse region by Volga Germans and other immigrants. Ultimately, Tannatt acquired a large estate in the Palouse region near Farmington for himself. A native of Manchester, Massachusetts, he was a prominent New Englander and retired brigadier general who had commanded Union forces south of the Potomac in 1862. During the defense of the U.S. capital, he became acquainted personally with President Lincoln. After the war, Tannatt became interested in developing railroad land grants in the Pacific Northwest. He wrote a letter to Villard in 1877, in which he offered several suggestions to aid in the westward settlement of immigrants. Impressed with the advice, Villard appointed Tannatt as the eastern agent for the Oregon Steamship Company. In 1878, Tannatt began directing the immigration program for Villard's other Northwest transportation companies. After the formation of the Oregon Improvement Company in 1878, Tannatt was elevated to the position of its general agent and his offices were transferred to Portland, Oregon.

Responding to the vast untapped agricultural potential of this region, Villard's Oregon Improvement Company purchased 150,000 acres (the odd sections in fourteen townships) from the Northern Pacific in the center of present-day Whitman County. These lands had been carefully selected and Villard intended to build his Palouse rail line directly through this district and populate it with dependable colonist farmers. The lands varied in price from $5 to $10 per acre and were sold on a six-year installment plan at seven percent interest. In March 1881, General Tannatt relocated his office to Walla Walla to be closer to the Oregon Improvement Company's operations in Eastern Washington. He made frequent trips to the company lands in the Palouse region and began arranging for their settlement. Villard took a personal interest in this program of colonization, which he outlined in the following 1881 stockholders report:

> A regular land and emigration department has been organized, the lands fully surveyed and appraised, 5,000 acres are now being broken up. The plan is to divide the lands into farms not exceeding 160 acres, to fence and improve no more than 40 acres upon each quarter

section, erecting thereon plain but substantial dwellings and the necessary outbuildings, so as to be able to offer farms ready for immediate occupancy at reasonable rates to incoming settlers. The Oregon Railway and Navigation Company is extending its system of roads right through these lands, and there is every assurance that our land operations will be successful and will result in a large profit to the company.[15]

In 1881, Tannatt began developing these properties with the assistance of A. A. Newberry, the Oregon Improvement Company's Colfax agent. Their crews methodically traveled from section to section in a special train of "six wagons heavily loaded with agricultural implements, tents, commissary stores, etc., forming the best outfit of the kind" that had ever entered the Palouse. Local farmers also found temporary employment by leasing their teams as well as a new market for their produce. The new work force turned to plowing and seeding 20,000 acres of company lands under Tannatt's capable management. For fencing and construction in the area, three million board feet of lumber were stored at the company flume at Dayton and delivered to the Palouse region in the spring.

Villard's massive investment in the region contributed to the economic transformation of the central Palouse area from grazing to farming. In addition, the marketing potential of the entire region was enhanced, as the railroad allowed Palouse farmers to capitalize on the growing European demands for Northwest grain exports. Palouse wheat export had begun as early as 1868, but had been limited to that which could be transported on the Oregon Steam Navigation Company down the Snake and Columbia Rivers. In 1879, only half the crop had shipped before navigation on the rivers closed for the winter in December. Railroad transportation would thus ensure a more dependable system of grain delivery throughout the year to both foreign and domestic markets. In November 1881, the *Palouse Gazette* observed, "A few not engaged in agriculture will dislike to see so large an area of grazing country broken up; but this is a narrow consideration, compared with the standing it will give our farming lands and the stimulus it will bring to our country." To begin populating the sparsely settled area with immigrants, the company also hired a number of writers "to go over every section of the country and give its true merits to the world, in newspapers, pamphlets, (and) magazines."[16]

In the early 1890s, an air of peculiar expectation seemed palpable throughout the Palouse Country. The early 1860s had witnessed the first penetration of the region by a scattered group of stockmen and subsistence farmers, mostly bachelors from the Walla Walla and Lewiston areas, who risked a beginning on the Palouse. The completion of federal land surveys in the region by 1873 provided legal means for the settlers to legitimize their claims, which gave significant impetus to the first real surge of immigration. Families began homesteading on the unbroken prairies north of the Snake River and clustered along the fertile bottomlands of its course from Wawawai to Riparia which previously had known only pithouse and mat lodge villages.

November Light

south of Palouse, Washington

The Columbia & Palouse Railroad

Surveys for the first railroad route through the Palouse region were undertaken as early as 1869 by such pathfinders as Levinius Swift, whose meanderings through the hills enabled him to find some of the most favorable sites to settle. After completing his work, Swift returned with his wife, Cornelia, to purchase land on Rebel Flat (near present-day Diamond) from the railroad, at a price of $2.50 per acre. Here they planted a small orchard and several black walnut trees along the stream, some of which still remain, and began turning the rich sod of the bottomlands. The prescient prose of Walt Whitman in the 1870s suggested in effusive terms the possibilities that awaited those who dared venture onto unclaimed landscapes like the Palouse. In the provocative essay "Democratic Vistas," Whitman wrote, "We presume to write upon things that exist not, and travel by maps yet unmade, and a blank. But the throes of birth are upon us.... It seems as if the Almighty has spread before this nation charts of imperial destinies, dazzling as the sun." When the sun appeared in the spring skies of the Inland Northwest in 1881, work began in earnest eastward from Palouse Junction (Connell) where the OR&N Co.'s Columbia & Palouse branch line advanced from the main Northern Pacific Railroad (NPRR) transcontinental route. The sounds of rock blasting, road grading, and spike driving were a prelude to a new period of immigration to the region. Providing its subsidiary with title to 150,000 acres of prime farmland in present-day Whitman County alone, the cash-strapped Northern Pacific was eager to promote the sale of its Palouse properties along the proposed route and plat a number of existing and future townsites.

Those members of the earlier vanguard who had attempted to settle in the area prior to 1880, only to "bust" from the inability to turn the stubborn sod, withstand the Indian scares, or contend with the sheer loneliness engendered by such isolation, decried the region in unmistakable terms. The Palouse region was "no place to take women and children," "unlivable wild country," and a "frosty land of such hills where no crops can grow."

As grading continued northeast to Kahlotus and Washtucna in 1881, the Northern Pacific's promotional department and affiliated Oregon Improvement Company aggressively campaigned in the regional and national press to change public perception of settlement prospects in the region by heralding its agricultural potential. Soon newspapers from Lewiston to Walla Walla to Oregon City were replacing their accounts of "foolish journeys to the rainbow's end" with testimonies of the Palouse Country's "inexhaustible soil up to eight feet deep" and recurrent high yields "without irrigation" of "never failing crops." These articles and railroad broadsides specified the liberal terms under which the Northern Pacific was prepared to part with its vast tracts, arranged in checkerboard formation on alternate 640-acre sections, where prices ranged from $5 to $10 per acre.

Villard's grandiose scheme for his railroad empire also reached fruition in late 1881. He had come to the realization that direct railway connections to the East were imperative if the Pacific Northwest was ever to be actively involved in the commerce of the nation and settlement of European immigrants. With this in mind, he had embarked secretly in December 1880 on collecting an unprecedented $8,000,000 "blind pool" from his financial supporters in order to purchase the controlling interest in Billings' stalemated Northern Pacific Railroad. In less than a year, he had raised more than he had asked for, and on September 15, 1881, he was elected president of the Northern Pacific. Work on both ends of the line again resumed, and Villard's dream of a northern transcontinental railroad under his personal control rapidly approached reality.

The editor of the *Palouse City Boomerang* extolled the virtues of the region's burgeoning economy while seeking to depict the area's unique topography in favorable terms: "The surface of this country looks as if it had been … ruffled, tucked, puckered and puffed, with several rows of trounces."[17] The unforgiving steep slopes were now being characterized in terms of comfortable bedding. The stolid farmers who remained did come to realize the Palouse's relatively mild winters coupled with wet springs and dry summers provided an ideal climate for growing soft white wheat. By the fall of 1882, the railroad passed through LaCrosse and Winona to Endicott, and in 1883 it extended along Rebel Flat to Colfax.

Levinius Swift's original area survey had bypassed a Palouse River canyon route into Colfax in favor of the more advantageous path from Mockonema Flat to Guy (today's town of Albion). For decades, the rumor persisted that Colfax city fathers raised $20,000 to bribe the Columbia & Palouse's chief engineer into redirecting the rail line down the three-degree slope into Colfax, the steepest grade along the entire system. Northern Pacific president Henry Villard had become the sower, casting forth seeds of settlement with his Columbia & Palouse line, moving farther inland week after week. As in the parable, some seed took root on fertile ground, where communities large and small were platted that remain vital throughout the next century; some fell among stones to sprout for a few years and perish by the wayside; and others, like Plainville, seemed to vanish before the maps bearing their location were even printed.[18]

Changes in company management and financial difficulties periodically stalled further progress in the early 1880s, but Pullman and Moscow were both reached by 1885, sparking great celebrations. The first train, clad in red, white, and blue bunting, arrived in Pullman to the music of the community brass band. At the newly completed depot, speeches were given proclaiming a new era for town and region, while unimpressed grizzled

workers prepared to lay the next stretch of ties and rails to Moscow. The completion of the line in September met with more music and a volley of Grand Army of the Republic (GAR) cannon fire. Another memorable celebration was held several months later in Pomeroy, south of the Snake River, which soon became Garfield County's largest city. The town was located about midway on the well-traveled route between Dayton and Lewiston, where J. M. Pomeroy had first settled in late 1864. Villard's OR&N Co. line finally arrived in the fledgling community in January 1886, after fevered construction the previous year from Grange City at the mouth of the Tucannon.

The rail line also breathed life into the hamlets of Marengo, Pataha City, and Starbuck, and facilitated transport of northern Garfield County farmers' grain to coastal markets. Although colorful Marengo-area frontiersman Louis Raboin had died in 1856, others, including his son-in-law, Massachusetts native Henry Chase, made homes in the area and the location was platted as a townsite by Sewell Truax in 1876. Marengo soon boasted a flour mill, hotel, stores, and school. Located just three miles east of Pomeroy, the community of Pataha City was first settled in 1861 by James Bowers and surveyed as a townsite in 1878. That same year, John Houser established a substantial stone flour-milling operation, upgraded in 1889 with steel rollers, that remained in operation until 1943. Starbuck, platted along the OR&N line in 1894, was named for Villard associate and Oregon Improvement Company president William H. Starbuck of New York. By 1900, the bustling community had two hotels, freight warehouses, stores, a blacksmith shop, and a livery stable.

North of the Snake River, a Columbia & Palouse branch line extended eastward from Moscow toward Juliaetta in the late 1880s. The main route turned north from Pullman, with grading proceeding at an aggressive pace, to connect Garfield, Farmington, and Tekoa in 1886. Two years later the line completed the master circle route by building from Farmington to

Oakesdale and southwesterly to St. John down to the junction at Winona. General Tannatt found the area around Farmington to be among the most pleasant in the region, and retired to a large farm there in 1888. He often employed newly arrived immigrants from Europe as fieldhands, like Jacob Adler, who remembered the general as being "a stern but fair" taskmaster. He would also serve as a member of the State College of Washington's first board of regents.[19]

Work began in the next century on the Union Pacific's (UP) plan to tap the Palouse grain district. By then, reorganization of the railroads led to the UP's control over the Oregon Railroad and Navigation Company, which built a line connecting its parent company's railhead opposite Riparia on the Snake River with the Columbia & Palouse line at LaCrosse.

The river was spanned at Riparia by the OR&N Co's massive Joso Railway Bridge, which was completed in 1914 after four years of construction. Named for local sheepman Leon Jaussaud, the bridge still stands, nearly 4,000 feet long and at its completion 260 feet high, making it the tallest bridge in the entire Union Pacific system at the time. The first highway bridge across the lower Snake was built at Central Ferry in 1924. Ferry service had begun at this strategic point in the 1870s and was operated by twin brothers Alvin and Alfred Hastings, natives of Pataha Flat, in 1895. The ferry operation was taken over by Robert Young in 1917 and continued until the bridge was built. This route became a principal thoroughfare for travel from the Palouse region to Dayton and Walla Walla.[20]

Grain Milling, Storage, and Marketing

Completion of the Northern Pacific transcontinental and subsidiary lines in the 1880s and 1890s coincided with a surge in regional grain production. More lands had come into production with wheat varieties like Pacific Bluestem, Little Club, and Red Chaff, which farmer experimenters had found more suitable to Inland Northwest growing conditions. Spring barley strains derived from Manchurian (Manchury, originally from Russia), German Oderbrucher, and English Chevalier were also successfully raised. Moreover, the revolution in agricultural mechanization enabled more extensive farming across the country as the 150 man-hours needed to plant, cultivate, and harvest an acre of cropland in 1840 had been reduced to about 40 hours by 1890.

Harvests in Washington and Oregon yielded a 300% increase between 1880 and 1900, with wheat production reaching as astounding 25,000,000 bushels in 1900. Whitman County alone was contributing annual wheat yields of some 10,000,000 bushels and nearly an equal amount of barley and

oats combined to become the nation's leading grain-producing county by the turn of the twentieth century. The bustling central Palouse community of Endicott boasted the area's largest storage facilities by 1905, with six warehouses and a capacity of 500,000 bushels of sacked grain.[22]

The surge in production between 1880 and 1900 depressed wheat prices from about 85 cents to 65 cents per bushel. Both factors contributed to the success of a network of entrepreneurs who provided storage facilities to area farmers, expanded milling operations, and sought international markets for high-quality Palouse soft white wheat flour. Among the first to perceive opportunities afforded by the economic situation, completion of railroad networks, and the opening of foreign markets was a group of Jewish businessmen whose work ethic and insights further contributed to regional development. Led by Colfax's Aaron Kuhn, a German immigrant of 1873, the tight-knit circle of Palouse Country grain traders also included Julius Lippitt and Simon Dreifus. All three operated general mercantile businesses in Colfax, became active in city politics, and regularly met for fellowship with other prominent residents in the city's Masonic Lodge. In addition to shared marketing interests, Kuhn, Lippitt, and Dreifus also established local banks in order to extend operating capital to Palouse area farmers of proven character and ability.[23]

Aaron Kuhn had arrived in America at the age of sixteen and operated stationery and cigar stores in Nevada, California, and Idaho before coming to Colfax in 1883. His businesses prospered with the region's development, and Kuhn invested a share of his profits in local real estate. Julius Lippitt had settled in Colfax in 1878 and was soon shipping Palouse grain through his brother, Phillip, who lived in San Francisco at the time when the West Coast grain trade was headquartered in that city. By the 1890s, however, a shift in production northward moved West Coast market decision-making to Portland, Tacoma, and Seattle. By that time, Kuhn and Lippitt had become important figures in the Northwest grain trade, with Kuhn shipping as much as 1,500,000 million bushels annually through his Interior Warehouse Company network at sixteen locations in Whitman and Latah counties.

In 1901, Kuhn built the half-mile-long Wawawai Tramway to transport grain from the Palouse plateau down to the Snake River steamer fleet for export to Portland, while railroads moved much of the region's wheat to Puget Sound ports. Northern Pacific Railroad officials had decided in the 1870s to designate Tacoma as the line's western terminus, to take advantage of Commencement Bay's deep-water port. By 1900, NPRR grain warehouses stretched for 2,300 feet along Tacoma's boisterous mile-long eastern waterfront grain storage district, justifiably touted as the "World's Longest Wheat Warehouse." Tacoma had become the state's leading grain exporter and the nation's fourth largest, exceeded only by shipments from Minneapolis, Kansas City, and Portland. But in 1900, seventy percent of West Coast wheat exports went to China and Japan, the result of

an ambitious marketing campaign involving the Palouse region with some of the world's most influential leaders in the secretive global grain trade.

As early as 1865, Inland Northwest wheat had been shipped to Portland from Walla Walla on Dorsey Baker's famed "Rawhide Railroad" to Wallula for transfer to Columbia River steamers, and in the 1870s Portland traders were shipping flour directly to the Liverpool trading exchange by sea. This period witnessed the transition of grain trading from the ancient continental traditions of bartering cartloads of produce to flour mills within a few miles of the harvest to some of the earliest marketing schemes on a truly international scale. The rapid spur in European demand for foodstuffs during the early nineteenth century had taken place as a result of the Industrial Revolution and concurrent dramatic population increase.

In the United Kingdom, Parliament's repeal of the protectionist Corn (Grain) Laws in 1846 represented a major opportunity for foreign traders to enter the lucrative British market and among the first to seize upon the opportunity were a small group of European entrepreneurs whose separate efforts would lay the foundation for the great grain family trading empires of the modern era. Two of the most prominent— Simon Fribourg of French Lorraine and Léopold Louis-Dreyfus of French Alsace—were Jewish traders whose inclination and location led to their grasp of the opportunity to supply the demands of Great Britain's markets with the abundant grain resources from Russia's Black Sea region.

Circumstances of the era also led the Bunges of Antwerp and Andrés of Switzerland to establish similar connections, since Russia at mid-century could not consume all the grain the Black Sea and Volga regions were capable of producing. Entering into such agreements, however, required the combined skills of international diplomacy and banking with the steel nerves of a ship captain. The swarthy Black Sea polyglot port of Odessa became the center of Russian grain exports, as Greeks, French,

English, Germans, Italians, and Spaniards freely mixed with native Slavic peoples to bargain for the region's ample produce. In doing so, they also introduced—both intentionally and by accident—a number of the region's most popular wheat varieties as seed for farmers and breeders in Europe and the Western hemisphere. The 1870s "Communication Revolution" made possible by the completion of transoceanic cables greatly facilitated international trading, which also contributed to the rise of several American grain marketers.[24]

Brothers Will, Samuel, and James Cargill began building and buying elevators from Minnesota to Chicago, "Elevator King" Frank Peavey launched his chain that would stretch from St. Paul to Portland by century's end, and Charles Alfred Pillsbury began construction of his first flour mills in Minneapolis. By 1875, the United States had replaced Russia as Great Britain's principal grain supplier, and, six years later, the U.S. vessel *Dakota* inaugurated the first wheat shipment directly from Tacoma to England. Most of the grain exported to Europe had come from the seeds of varieties that had been raised for generations in South Russia and England.

Attention to trans-Pacific Asia in the 1880s, however, led to economic relationships that would transform the marketing of Palouse and other Northwest soft white wheats preferred by consumers in China and Japan to make noodles and other products. During the same period that businessmen like Kuhn, Lippitt, and Dreifus were becoming established in Whitman County, entrepreneur Theodore B. Wilcox had matured from a young Salem, Oregon, bank clerk to general manager of Portland Flouring Mills. The Massachusetts native grasped early the incredible economic potential represented by East Asia's half-billion inhabitants and began a series of acquisitions with backing from Oregon financiers to build additional flour mills in Tacoma, Spokane, Harrington, and Odessa—a wheatland community named for the Russian homeland of many of the region's Russian-German immigrants.[25]

In 1886, Wilcox formed Pacific Elevator Company to handle bulk storage and delivery to his mills just when Northwest exporters began testing Asian markets. Two years later, he established Puget Sound Warehouse Company to grow his network of grain-handling facilities to 350 locations in order to ship bulk wheat to England and flour to China. Wilcox established the Puget Sound Flouring Mill in 1889 adjacent to the NPRR wharf in Tacoma, where massive grindstones hummed rhythmically around the clock. Wilcox's foresight and methods—sometimes characterized by his competitors as ruthless—led to a pivotal move in 1890, when he arranged for Canadian diplomat Albert Rennie to represent his interests in Hong Kong. British brokers had established a monopoly on China's foreign trading arrangements, but Rennie was a Commonwealth official who could facilitate the bargaining sought by Wilcox. The resulting sales accords with Chinese and Japanese grain brokers proved so successful that Rennie began working fulltime for Wilcox in 1895, as Palouse Country and regional grain production continued to feed the capacity of his far-flung operations.[26]

The period also witnessed the opening of NPRR steamer shipping service from Tacoma to the Orient in 1890 through the company's alliance with a British firm, forming the Northern Pacific Steamship Company, Union Pacific Steamer Company operations from Portland in 1889, and Great Northern traffic on vessels from Seattle to Hong Kong in 1896. Elevator magnate Frank Peavey constructed a million-bushel-capacity grain warehouse in Portland in 1895 and could ship to Liverpool via the Isthmus of Panama in a mere four weeks.

Peavey's experiments and other economic factors raised concerns in his mind about the challenges of storing and shipping sacked grain. He had grown highly interested in the concrete bulk storage facilities he saw in Romania and elsewhere, which led to his decision in 1898 to sell his entire West Coast operation to Wilcox in the famed "Million Dollar Deal" through which 256 of Peavey's warehouses were transferred to Wilcox's Western Warehouse control.

In contrast to generally lower harvests worldwide in 1900, the Palouse Country contributed to Washington's record-breaking 25,000,000 bushel crop, representing a three-fold increase from the 1895 yield. Puget Sound longshoremen labored to ship a remarkable 1,400,000 barrels of Northwest flour that year to Hong Kong on exotically named ships anchored along the mile-long wooden docks. Vessels regularly in port at Tacoma included the *Persian Empire, Pass of Melfort, Loo Sok, Emin Pasha, Phra Nang, Victoria,* and *City of Delhi,* with many bearing four masts that spread several acres of canvas and capable of holding 5,000 tons of cargo. Return trips brought loads of Japanese tea and Chinese silks, rice, and burlap grain sacks to the chaotic docks of Tacoma, Seattle, and Portland, where dockworkers in 1900 earned 35 cents an hour for ten-hour shifts. Reflecting the cycle of harvest, processing, and delivery, the export season was busiest from October to March, with many vessels making several round-trip Pacific voyages each year.

By 1900, Wilcox was the Northwest's unrivaled "Flour Magnate," whose brands were known from the Malabar Coast and across China to Vladivostok. Cheney, Washington, benefited from its strategic location on the main Northern Pacific transcontinental line and became a major grain warehousing and milling center. Colfax businessman John C. Davenport built the first flour mill there in 1880. Farm implement dealer F. M. Martin established the Martin Grain and Milling Company flour mill at Cheney in 1908, that ran twenty-four hours a day, six days a week, and became one of the largest mills in the Pacific Northwest. F. M. Martin's son, Clarence Daniel Martin, inherited the Cheney enterprise in 1925 and kept the company going for the next 30 years, selling the mill business to the National Biscuit Company (Nabisco) in 1943. In 1902, he acquired Aaron Kuhn's Palouse grain operation, enabling Kuhn to purchase controlling

interest in Traders National Bank of Spokane, the forerunner of Spokane & Eastern Trust Company and Seattle First National Bank. Following Wilcox's death in 1918, his warehouse and milling empire was acquired by Sperry and later absorbed by General Mills in 1929.[27]

Loading grain ships on the Tacoma elevator wharf, 1920.
Courtesy Washington State Historical Society

Cradle, Threshers, and Combines

The period from 1880 to 1920 also witnessed a revolution in agricultural mechanization in the Palouse. A determined farmer with a single shear "footburner" plow could break out only about forty acres of land each year, usually after the thick native grasses had been burned off. A seemingly Sisyphean struggle still loomed ahead, however, as the thickly fibrous root system penetrated the ground for two to three feet. To prepare a seedbed, farmers devised crude harrows by pounding long nails or wooden pegs into wide beams.

The first seeding was done by hand broadcast by a farmer, who moved at a measured pace with a sack slung over the shoulder, to cover a swath about fifteen feet wide. The field was then harrowed again to cover the seed and the farmer prayed for rain and for an early sprout that would root the grain and create a ground cover before winter. The introduction of the shoe drill in the middle 1880s greatly improved plant emergence, as the seed was placed at a calibrated depth beneath the soil, and the implement could be connected to a harrow to smooth out the ground. Threats included weeds—especially cheatgrass—as well as rodents and uncooperative weather, which could do considerable damage to a promising crop.

The arduous task of summer harvest was first done using a primitive cradle, or scythe, connected to long wooden ribs that would hold several hand swathings to then be dropped

Gildersleeve Falls

Palouse River near Hooper, Washington

in the stubble and tied into larger shocks. The calloused hands that knew this labor then either flailed the cuttings or, more often, winnowed them first by tamping down a circular area to form a hard surface and spreading the stalks across the area. Teams of horses would then trample the stalks for at least two hours before the straw was removed with pitchforks. The seed was carefully shoveled with as little dirt and roughage as possible into burlap gunny sacks, to be eventually dumped and winnowed to separate grain from chaff and dirt. An entire family might harvest only two acres in a day and hope for favorable winds from which might be gleaned seventy bushels of grain.

A few farmers could afford to purchase small mechanical fanning mills, but these were expensive and required considerable strength to turn the internal blades and generate sufficient wind to clean the grain. In the early 1880s, small, horse-drawn reaper-binders appeared in the Palouse region that would deposit grain bundles on the ground, which were then hauled in wagons to large stationary separators, or threshers. These reapers increased harvest output tenfold over the hand scythe method. Threshers were first introduced in the 1840s: they were powered by several teams of horses tied to rotating sweep bars on the ground that turned a tumbler rod attached to the machine. The system experienced numerous breakdowns and the horses used for this work were soon replaced by coal- or wood-fired steam engines.[29]

Larger headers with twelve-foot sickle bars and reels were introduced in the middle 1880s. These three-wheeled contraptions were pushed by horses or mules behind the header and driven by a "header puncher" who steered by means of a rudder wheel connected to a board between his knees. His hands guided the lines to the horses and operated a lever to adjust the height of the sickle that cut the grain, which fell onto a wide and rapidly moving canvas draper, reinforced with hardwood slats. On the downhill side of the header was a sloped elevator, on which the draper carried the cuttings upward and dropped them into a header box wagon, built with one side lower than the other to fit under the elevator.

In addition to the wagon driver, a loader worked inside the wagon to equally distribute the grain with a pitchfork in a laborious routine considered one of the most strenuous of the entire operation. Another header box would move into place when the first was full, and the loader would jump into to it to continue working while the full header box was driven to the thresher, a beehive of harvest activity. At a centrally located area in the field, usually near a country road, a small army of workers moved continuously amidst the cacophony of roars and whistles from the steam engine, thresher, and horse-drawn wagons. Successful farmers treated their livestock with the attention demanded by resources so vital to work and sustenance.

Family members of all ages often made pets of bummer lambs, runt piglets, abandoned calves, and other offspring without mothers to tend them. But few farmstead relationships between owner and creature were more special than those between a farmer and his beloved draft horses, usually Belgians, Percherons, or Clydesdales. Weighing as much as one ton each, these gentle giants bore affectionate names like Fanny and Hank. Each one evidenced dispositions and capabilities that had to be taken into consideration as the farmers arranged their teams for pulling heavily loaded wagons and weighty field implements. One of the most delightfully told and illustrated stories about these memorable creatures is Spangle artist-author Nona Hengen's *Plodding Princes of the Palouse* (1984).

As many as two dozen experienced workers were needed for stationary thresher operations, and it was not uncommon to see women from the family driving teams. The overall harvest operation was supervised by the "straw boss," often the owner of the thresher and engine who rented their use out to area farmers. He handled the hiring of the core crew from reliable acquaintances, relatives, and other helpers from the several

Palouse Hills horse-drawn threshers, c. 1900.
Hutchison Studio Photographs of Washington State University and Pullman, WA., 1910-1973 (PC 70), Manuscripts, Archives, and Special Collections (MASC), Washington State University Libraries, Pullman, WA.

thousand "bindle stiffs" who converged on the Palouse region from Spokane and other cities each summer looking for harvest employment. The boss also worked with the farmer to determine the sequence of areas and fields to be cut, and oversaw all aspects of the workers' myriad responsibilities. Teamsters were needed to drive the two or three headers that usually comprised an outfit's contingent and others for handling the two-horse teams that took the three or four header boxes back and forth to the threshing area from the headers.

The wagons were unloaded into large piles by the driver and a "spike pitcher," another demanding role, and a "stacker" who properly arranged the grain into two or three high piles. A "forker" then set to work on a large platform mounted on a wagon called a "derrick table," named for a high four-beam derrick that rose some fifteen feet above it. At the top of the poles a pulley was suspended, through which a rope ran, connecting to a derrick team of six to eight horses to a six-pronged steel Jackson fork. The forker positioned the

following spread

Macintosh Road Winter

north of
Pullman, Washington

Jackson onto one of the piles and yelled to the derrick team driver to move the horses ahead so the fork's load could be hauled to the table and dropped with a trip rope. In later years, the main pulley rope was connected to a net in the bottom of the header box wagon that could be lifted to deposit the load directly onto the derrick table, which eliminated the need for the Jackson fork.

Two "hoedowns" then used hoe-shaped forks to carefully guide the grain at a measured pace onto a long canvas feeder that led to the thresher's gnashing mouth, out of which long metal fingers moved back and forth to pull in the grain. This grueling work usually went in shifts, with two hoedowns replacing the other pair in half-hour shifts. These workers determined the maximum rate of intake by listening to the growl of the metal monster. They had to be careful not to choke the creature by plugging it up with too much grain, which risked breaking a drive chain or shaft, or the laborious task of extracting the partially digested stalks by hand from inside the tightly jammed innards, using every possible contortion of limb and colorful language. This chore, usually attended to by several of the younger workers, was especially unpleasant if the straw was infested with countless miniscule spines of scabrous tarweed, perhaps a Palouse native, that stung like fire if touched.

A rapidly rotating cylinder with rows of short steel tines was narrowly mounted above a set of stationary iron "concaves" with large teeth to shatter the kernels out of the heads. The particles then fell through a series of rocking sieves to an auger at the base of the machine and into a storage bin. The sieve action combined with the effects of a wide-bladed fan created a virtual wind tunnel through which straw and chaff were blown out the back of the thresher. These tailings were stacked by "straw pitchers" until a long and powerful "wind stacker" pipe was introduced after the turn of the century that blasted the straw twenty feet away to form a pile. Other important needs of the thresher were tended to by an "oiler,"

who kept the moving parts well lubricated and assisted the mechanic, or "separator man," in maintenance work.

The inner workings of the thresher were turned by an enormous rubberized drive-belt, some sixty feet long and crossed in the middle, which ran from the steam engine's power wheel to deliver up to forty horsepower on the 1890s Case, Rumely, and other models to the machine's main pulley. The huge engines were ponderous steamers, some up to twenty feet long, and were tended by an experienced engineer. The long distance from the thresher was a fire prevention measure.

The fireman's job was considered one of the most exhausting of all, and it was certainly the hottest. These workers earned the crew's highest wages. The fireman rose at 4 a.m. to clean out the ash pit and boiler flue soot and light the firebox with straw. When sufficient pressure was reached, he blew the whistle to wake the rest of the crew, who usually slept outside in their bedrolls with their feet toward the strawpile. During the day, the fireman had to constantly fuel the flames, usually with straw delivered by a "straw buck," who used a pitchfork to provide a steady supply to the engine from the main pile behind the thresher. A "water buck" was in charge of the cigar-shaped wooden water wagon, which carried up to 500 gallons, and a hand pump that kept the steam engine and horses supplied.

The water wagon remained close in case a fire broke out—a farmer's worst nightmare—which could occur if a spark escaped from the engine or from a malfunctioning thresher bearing. Exploding boilers were rare but always a risk, and accidents were not uncommon among forkers and hoedowns, who were sometimes hit by moving equipment. Navigating a header box on steep slopes could also be very difficult as well as hazardous, since the horses tended to drift downhill while the wagon remained on course. America's longest serving Supreme Court Justice and Eastern Washington native William O. Douglas remembered driving a header box when it struck a rock and started to tip over. He jumped free just as the wagon tumbled down into a ravine.[30]

Twirling sprockets run by flat chains turned the cylinder, fan, augers, and other components that howled throughout the day. A mechanic was needed to keep the thresher properly operating, a "roustabout" to run errands, gather the enormous amount of foodstuffs necessary for the crew's consumption, and facilitate communication among the workers. A "sack jig" filled gunny sacks with the grain while two nimble-fingered sack sewers sitting on two grain sacks raced to close the bags using long steel sack needles flared at the end. They formed a corner "ear" on the left side of the sack, rapidly tied it off with two half-hitch loops, and then moved across the top with nine lightning stitches before closing it off with an identical ear on the right side.

Weighing about 140 pounds each, the sacks were then stacked nearby to await loading by a teamster onto flatbed wagons with short side-racks. The wagons were often hitched together in a group of two or three to be pulled by eight-horse teams to local warehouses and outside storage platforms. Here men carefully arranged the sacks into formations that could reach several stories high. During a good fourteen-hour day with eighteen workers, an experienced threshing crew running two headers could harvest sixty acres and fill 1,200 sacks with 2,700 bushels of grain.[31] Such intense labor and long work hours generated enormous appetites. One of the surest ways to keep a good crew was to ensure they were well fed with plenty of fresh meat and potatoes, vegetables, and applesauce. Sometimes workers were also treated to fresh fruit desserts. Women working in a portable cookshack toiled from the predawn hours to feed the workers up to five times each day—breakfast by 6 a.m., midmorning lunch break, dinner at noon, afternoon lunch break, and supper after 8 p.m. The men ate in shifts behind screened windows, on long narrow benches and tables.

The abundance and quality of harvest food was legendary among most crewmembers, who considered the cook's job even more demanding than their own, and a matter of great concern to farmers' wives and other women who often assumed this responsibility. Pulitzer prize-winning author H. L. Davis, raised at The Dalles, Oregon, portrayed a threshing crew's harvest season his 1953 novel, *Team Bells Woke Me and Other Stories*. Nard Jones's *Wheat Women* (1933) presents another perspective from his trilogy of novels about the hopes and cynicisms of early settler life east of the Cascades.

By the early 1890s, implement manufacturers like Holt Manufacturing, John Deere, and McCormick were combining reapers and threshers to make "combines" which in the hilly Palouse region could require as many as thirty-two head of horses to be pulled and were powered by massive drive chains from large metal-cleated side wheels. The first one to make an appearance in the Palouse Country drew crowds of gawkers to the farm of "Wheat King" Lillis Smith near Endicott in the summer of 1893. A reporter from the *Palouse Republic* proclaimed Smith's Holt "the seventh wonder of the world" that seemed to require "all the horses in the neighborhood…to drag the great machine over the hills and through broad fields of ripe grain."[32]

Such complicated contraptions of chains, sprockets, and cogs still required sizeable crews. A driver was needed to direct teams of up to thirty-five horses or mules from a seat perched precariously out in front of the machine, while trying to minimize the animals' trampling down standing grain. Just harnessing the herd could take several hands a full hour in the early morning and again in the late evening to take the animals out of harness. A "header tender" stood behind on a wooden deck to raise and lower the cutting platform according to the slope and height of the grain. This area was shared with a machinist, who served as the overall boss of the operation and controlled the combine's rack and pinion leveling mechanism with a lever in front of the bulk tank, where up to fifty bushels of clean grain could be stored. A single sack sewer sat on a bench beneath the bulk tank where the kernels fell through a downspout into burlap sacks that were sewn shut and stacked nearby until six to eight could be dropped onto the ground. This process still required wagons for collecting the sacks and transporting them to local warehouses.

Palouse Country Innovators

A number of inventive minds devised improvements for the machines, usually built in the Midwest or California, so they could function more efficiently on the steep slopes of the Palouse Hills. Given the amount of capital needed to launch such enterprises, the equipment's relatively high cost, and the limited market, only a few of these enterprises prospered, including Moscow's Rhodes Harvester and Idaho National Harvester companies, the Colfax Harvester Company, and the Dunning-Erich Harvester Company of Harrington. Farmers and manufacturers modified their combines to be pulled by tractors and powered by a separate engine after these technologies became available at the turn of the twentieth century. Such improvements increased the harvest to forty-five acres a day.

By 1920, the economic benefits of mechanization in the Palouse region were becoming more pronounced, given the costs of hired help and maintaining livestock throughout the year. The new machines substantially reduced farmers' reliance on draft animals, and thousands of horses and mules were sold in order to purchase combines, trucks, tractors, and the larger field implements that accompanied them. These changes also reduced the need for additional workers during the harvest season, which angered laborers from area cities who had come to depend on the seasonal employment. Protests also came from leaders of the Industrial Workers of the World (Wobblies), who tried unsuccessfully to organize their labor. These conditions across the Inland Northwest provided the backdrop for Zane Grey's popular 1919 novel, *The Desert of Wheat*.

For William O. Douglas, whose labor in the fields funded his studies at Whitman College, the conditions for seasonal workers in the Palouse region during this period would deeply influence his distinguished career in jurisprudence. While harvesting on the Ralph Snyder ranch near Washtucna, Douglas fell into the company of a transient crew that included an IWW member whom he only knew as "Blacky" and who befriended the rookie wagon driver. What Blacky lacked in ambition, he made up for in kindness and compassion, but he also evidenced "a desperate loneliness." Douglas had always based his judgments on the Puritan work ethic, which held that prosperity in life was the result of proper moral choices, and society's malcontents were victims of their own unrighteousness. As a scrawny lad suffering from the lingering effects of polio, Douglas had read the journals of Lewis and Clark and become acquainted with Indians on the Yakama Reservation near his birthplace. He knew from these experiences that valid exceptions existed to the principles so widely affirmed in the wider culture.

Douglas's experiences with the itinerant bindle stiffs in the Palouse region formed fuller understandings in his inquisitive mind. "Many of these wanderers had real grievances," he observed, "and responded by protesting, sometimes crudely, sometimes eloquently, that their plight was serious, the injustices heaped upon them real. They sang, they swore, they did outrageous things at times. But they were seeking a place of some security in a free society." By his own account, these formative years in the sweltering harvest fields of the Palouse Country forged ideas that shaped William O. Douglas's liberal ideas and years of service on the nation's highest bench, the longest Supreme Court tenure in American history.[33]

The next generation of Palouse farmland innovators led to significant improvements in tillage and harvesting equipment as well as fertilizing methods. In the late 1940s, John Deere

Palouse pull-type combines, 1956.
Hutchison Studio Photographs of Washington State University and Pullman, WA., 1910-1973 (PC 70), Manuscripts, Archives, and Special Collections (MASC), Washington State University Libraries, Pullman, WA.

Spokane regional manager Clyde Moody teamed with Everett Kroll and Elwood Widman of Moscow, Idaho's Everett Will Tractor Company, Dave Neal of Garfield, and Endicott's Conrad Hergert, owner of one of the region's first John Deere dealerships, to prepare specifications for a prototype self-propelled and self-leveling ("hillside") grain combine. Holt Manufacturing Company of Stockton, California, had manufactured several hundred self-propelled threshing machines from 1917 to 1921, but it did not continue production, as farmers preferred the reliability and maneuverability of combines pulled by draft animals and tractors. Baldwin brothers Curtis, George, and Ernest of Nickerson, Kansas introduced their first trademark silver and red Gleaner combine in 1912, which was built for level land operation and mounted on a Fordson tractor, so it was not a fully self-propelled machine. Production ended in 1928 when Henry Ford discontinued production of the Fordson Model F. The first commercially successful self-propelled combines were the level-land models Massey Harris 21 (1940), International Harvester 123 (1942), John Deere 55 (1947), and J. I. Case 9 (1948).

The area team assembled by Clyde Moody had remarkable talent for visualizing complicated solutions to structural and mechanical challenges, ranging from steel bracing for heavy equipment to establishing standards for combustion engines. In the early 1950s, Moody arranged for John Deere to bring some of the group to company headquarters in Moline, Illinois, headquarters to help design a hydraulic self-leveling mechanism using an activated lever and valve device. During the same period, Frank Farber of Moscow's Idaho Machine Company and local Helbling Brothers International Harvester (IH) dealership (successor to McCormick International) to fabricate a similar system for IH combines that could level in four directions. Such cooperative efforts inaugurated a new era of harvest machinery for the Palouse region, with 1953 field testing and the 1954–55 release of John Deere's 55H and International's McCormick 141H. In 1957, Kroll joined John Deere's Arrow Machinery in Colfax and received a patent for an improved leveling device

that used a water-antifreeze mixture to push against a diaphragm-activated microswitch. Dealerships debuted John Deere's larger 95H combine in 1958, alongside International's popular IH-151, followed by the IH-403 in 1962, with all these models widely used throughout the decade.

John Deere's completely redesigned 6602 hillside combine in 1971 featured a wider header, hydrostatic drive, and a significantly wider stance for safer operation on steep slopes and slick straw. But on sloping terrain, the accumulation of unthreshed stalks on the downhill side of a combine's interior could still limit the complex machinery's ability to function optimally. This tendency also contributed to aggravating internal slugging that could damage equipment and consume precious operating time. One of the most notable late-twentieth-century innovations in harvesting technology was the advent of the "axial-flow" rotary system, which replaced the threshing cylinder and concave base with a substantially longer rotor situated parallel to the main frame. This

Bill Walter, "Harvest on the Edwin Curtis Farm near Colfax, Washington," 1954.
Photograph shows prototype John Deere 55H followed by Case self-propelled and John Deere pull-combines.
Dennis Solbrack Collection

substantial change allowed for a wider distribution of kernels onto augers below the rotor and greater expulsion of straw and chaff out the back. In the 1970s and 1980s, Spangle, Washington, native Edward Hengen served as a senior project engineer at John Deere's sprawling harvester works in Davenport, Iowa, to devise an axial-flow threshing drum and higher-capacity header-auger feeding system. Similar equipment was patented by New Holland and International Harvester in the 1970s and introduced in the popular high-capacity NH TR70 in 1975 and the IH 1440 and 1460 in 1977. International's larger 1470 hillside model equipped with Hanson mercury switches came one year later. Gleaner introduced its first rotary combine in 1979: the N6, powered by an Allis Chalmers engine. The appearance of these massive machines throughout the Palouse region significantly improved operator safety on steep slopes and grain cleaning efficiency while also reducing the length of the harvest season.[34]

Divine Protection

north of Potlatch, Idaho

CHAPTER VI

Crossroads and Communities

Many of the Palouse's first communities had already emerged as small rural trading and postal centers before rails approached their outskirts in the 1880s and 1890s. These places became the nexus of country life, where both economic and social exchanges were made in a forum of hospitality. Many town names honored their founders including (Albert J.) Hooper, (Edward T.) St. John, and (William) Spangle. Others were named for the eastern hometowns of their first inhabitants or surveyors such as Fairfield and Farmington (Minnesota), LaCrosse (Wisconsin), Genesee (New York), Winona (Michigan), Waverly (Iowa), Malden (Massachusetts), and Moscow (Pennsylvania).

Samuel Neff, who named Moscow, was also said to have favored the word because Russia's capital sounded like a scenic and holy place—fitting for a new community in "Paradise Valley." Many towns platted along the rail route were given names of such railroad company officials as vice-presidents Thomas F. Oakes(dale) and Daniel Lamont, directors Benjamin Cheney, John Sprague, and William Endicott, and sleeping car magnate George Pullman. The namesakes of other communities were of Native American origin—Latah, Washtucna, Kahlotus, and Palouse. Tekoa was named by its postmaster's wife, Mrs. Daniel Truax, for the imagery presented by the Biblical reference in II Samuel to the "city of tents."[1]

The surveyors who platted Palouse Country townsites laid out standard grid patterns of streets and lots in accordance with the lines of the federal land surveys. In many cases, the locations of rivers and streams, steep hillsides, and additions by landowning developers conflicted with rigid conformity to the cardinal directions. Streets occasionally turned at odd angles or twisted along peculiarities of the terrain. In addition to the colorless alpha-numeric rules for naming streets (e.g., First Street and Avenue A), Palouse area communities commonly featured the two categories of names used across the country: trees and presidents. Perhaps life along Elm, Chestnut, Walnut, and Ash brought hope to local residents that deciduous stands of such non-native species would soon shade their grassy homesites.

Over half of the region's communities also contain streets named for Washington, Adams, Jefferson, and Lincoln. Only the name Whitman—in tribute to martyred missionaries Marcus and Narcissa—is accorded such honor on as many street signs in the area. Tekoa also honored Jackson and Taft, Colton favored McKinley and Harrison, and Garfield platted Monroe and Cleveland. Prominent residents also received such recognition, including McConnell and Lieuallen (Moscow), McKenzie and Neill in Pullman (Kamiaken Street runs through the center of town), Greif (Colton), McCoy (Oakesdale), Loomis (St. John), Shindler (Malden), and Manring (Garfield).

facing page

Manning Bridge

west of
Colfax, Washington

Between 1899 and 1910, seven hamlets and sidings along the Washington, Idaho & Montana (WI&M) Railroad line east of the company town of Potlatch paid tribute to the Ivy League. Tiny Princeton, located closest to Potlatch, probably inspired the designations, though it had been named in 1896 by founder Orville Clough in honor of his original home, Princeton, Minnesota. The hamlet served as a stopping point for the Palouse-Hoodoo (Woodfell) stagecoach. Harvard, platted in 1906, was named by founder Homer W. Canfield, who owned considerable property along the WI&M route.

Vassar, Idaho, appeared in 1907, but its name may also have been in tribute to James R. Vassar, a Civil War veteran who had settled nearby on Vassar Meadows. Yale, Purdue, and Wellesley soon appeared along the railway, although, among schools in the West, only Stanford was accorded similar status in the eastern Palouse region, even though Inman A. Stanford had settled earlier in the vicinity. Like Mount Hope and Staley, most of these settlements have more letters in their names than residents. Still, other Palouse community names owe their origins to an obvious local quantity, quality, or geography, as with Hay, Dusty, and Rockford.

The first commercial enterprises in the region were the Palouse River sawmills and gristmills that were built at Colfax and Palouse City in the 1870s. By the end of that decade, local businessmen had established general mercantile stores at these and other sites where settlers clustered. These businesses brought relief to families that had previously relied on long annual treks by wagon to Walla Walla to purchase household necessities. Samuel Neff established a general store in Paradise Valley in 1873, but sold his business about two years later to Almon Lieuallen, who moved it to a new location at the corner of First and Main streets. William Ragsdale's general store opened in Palouse City also in the 1870s, and in the next decade more than a dozen others were established in the region including Lippett Brothers of Colfax, Moscow's

Pullman, Washington, 1889.
Courtesy Whitman County Library, Colfax, Washington

McConnell and Maguire, Stewart, and Lee in Pullman, and Huntley Brothers, which operated stores in Endicott, St. John, and Colfax.

The aroma of spices and coffee mixed with the scent of fresh leather in the stores' cavernous interiors, where farmers, ranchers, and timber workers could procure everything from flour, corn meal, and sugar (the latter selling for as much as 25¢ a pound) to kerosene, window panes, and squirrel poison. Horehound hard candy and licorice found their places near bolts of gingham, calico, and linen. Reflecting the needs of a nascent business class, some stores even advertised suits by Chicago-based Hart Schaffner Marx, although such sartorial needs for Palouse area farmers were generally restricted to church functions and occasional civic duties. Other businesses soon followed the mills and mercantile stores, with most early Palouse communities having blacksmith and livery services, a meat shop, saloons, lumber sales, dentist and real estate offices, a train depot, local bank, and grain warehouses.

Among the first structures erected in each town were a church and a school, and in several communities the pastor also served as the first schoolteacher. Rev. Cushing Eells, son of Spokane Indian missionaries Myron and Myra Eells, worked with Rev. George Atkinson of Portland as a circuit-rider to organize the earliest churches and several schools in the Palouse. Indefatigable "Father Eells" joked that he covered a district from the Snake River to the North Pole and toiled to be a good steward of divine blessing. He subsisted on 37 cents a week and traveled everywhere on his beloved sorrel horse, Le Blond. The region's first organized church was Colfax's Plymouth Congregational (1874) followed by others in Cheney and Sprague.

Moscow's Zion Baptist Church (1876) was among the first of its denomination in the area, and other early congregations in many communities included Catholics, Methodists, Methodist-Episcopalians, Christian, Presbyterians, and Lutherans. Eells' Colfax legacy had international influence through the ministry of one of his successors at Plymouth a generation later. British cleric James Bainton assumed responsibilities at the church in 1901 and remained many years in the community. His son, Roland, graduated from high school in Colfax and went on to earn distinction as one of the world's foremost scholars of the Reformation era. The best-selling author served for forty-two years as a professor of ecclesiastical history at Yale Divinity School, but never lost touch with his Palouse Country roots.[2]

Oakesdale, Palouse, Moscow, and Sprague boasted opera houses in the 1890s, featuring plays by such traveling professionals as the Graham Company Players and the Curtis Comedy Company. National figures like the hatchet-bearing crusader Carrie Nation came to rail against "evil of all kinds including tobacco and alcohol use" while other stage guests included hypnotists, professional wrestlers, and musicians. At the turn of the century, these structures also served as the region's first silent film theatres. Virtually every town had fine lodging and meals available at hostelries like Moscow's Barton House, Juliaetta's Grand Hotel, the Hotel McMichael at Spangle, the Palace in Pullman, Almota House, Duff's Hotel

in Colton, and Colfax's Ewart House. Many featured second-story ballrooms beneath stately mansard roofs. Perhaps the Palouse's most elegant lodging was at Waverly's extravagant Harbottle Hotel, a palace on the prairie built in French Empire style. The ornate three-story brick edifice came with the local sugar beet factory, but seemed to harken back to New Orleans cane country.

Moscow, Idaho, 1889.
Courtesy Whitman County Library, Colfax, Washington

In these places, large gatherings of couples danced the Virginia reel and other quadrilles as well as more formal minuets and waltzes to the accompaniment of popular Palouse Country musicians like the Cy and Andy Privett String Band. Among the most famous inns far and wide was James A. "Cashup" Davis's grand Steptoe Butte Hotel. Visible for miles around, the substantial two-story structure, perched at the very top of the butte, opened in 1888. Guests first entered a substantial exhibition hall, displaying dozens of grain sheaves creatively displayed across the walls and in floor vases. The hotel offered stunning vistas of the Palouse landscape, enhanced by views through a brass telescope in a glass-enclosed turret crowning the building. Rumor held that a careful observer could use the instrument to view the streets of faraway Walla Walla.

Rock Lake City boat builder and hosteller Willis "Dad" Evans had a similar vision for a lakeside destination resort. Evans and his wife, Emma, opened the Cliff House in 1903 on a rocky tongue overlooking the southwest shore of Rock Lake. They offered tourists Sunday afternoon excursions to the head of the lake in a coal-fired steam vessel thirty feet long for $1.50, twice the daily room rate. Sprague area settlers organized the Merrie Crew Boat Club in the 1880s for sail boating on Colville (Sprague) Lake. John and Francis Kebla acquired lakefront property about 1910 and built Sprague Lake Resort: a sprawling complex of cabins, a dance hall built on stilts over the lakeshore, store, and park. Laborers hauled in tons of sand and lumber to create a scenic beach and dock for their tour boat, the *Silver Star*. For years, the resort served as the site of one of the Palouse Country's most spectacular Fourth of July celebrations. Accommodations were available even in the smallest Palouse Country settlements, where travelers could find respite at the Hotel Lamont, Hooper's Hotel Glenmore, and Texas City's Hotel Stewart, where late-night poker games occasionally ended in gun-play.

Two nefarious businessmen used Endicott's Commercial ("Hill") Hotel to plot the murder of a local country doctor who had threatened to close a house of ill-fame operated by the pair. Many such "parlor houses" were located in the Palouse region in the late 1800s, especially in the larger railroad and logging communities, where some had as many as a half-dozen. The doctor in Endicott also acquired the area's first Model T Ford franchise and expected to unload a shipment of vehicles when they arrived by rail in the summer of 1914. The conspirators placed gunpowder in a cylinder of one of the cars, but unfortunately Henry Schierman, a recent German immigrant from Russia in need of employment, had been hired to drive the vehicles down from the flatcar. When he turned the ignition switch on the tampered car, an enormous explosion ripped through the engine, sending debris flying in all direc-

Endicott, Washington, 1911.
Hutchison Studio Photographs of Washington State University and Pullman, WA., 1910-1973 (PC 70), Manuscripts, Archives, and Special Collections (MASC), Washington State University Libraries, Pullman, WA.

tions. The hapless driver was killed instantly when a piece of glass struck his temple, leaving a destitute family in a strange new land. The case went unsolved for nearly a century.[3]

The economic vitality of several communities was based to a great extent on a single enterprise. In Cheney, Pullman, and Moscow, state institutions of higher learning ensured an abiding employment base, as did the location of county seats in Colfax for Whitman County and Moscow for Latah. For years, residents of Moscow had lobbied for a separate county in the northern part of Nez Perce County, which was headquartered in distant Lewiston. Through the extraordinary lobbying efforts of Congressional representative Willis Sweet, and businessmen Charles Moore and William McConnell, along with other Moscow political activists, the new county was authorized through Congressional mandate—the only such case in American history. McConnell derived the name "Latah" from the Nez Perce words *La-tah* (pine) and *Tah-ol* (pestle) to mean "Place of Pines and Pestles."[4]

The bitter struggle between Cheney and Spokane for county seat status and the contested 1880 election outcome resulted in the notorious night theft of county records from Spokane to assure Cheney residents that their city would attain the honor and reap the subsequent benefits of employment. The victory, however, was short-lived. The 1886 county election proved definitively that the balance of population power had swung east, and the books and jobs returned to Spokane. Sprague was designated Lincoln County's seat of government when the area was detached from Whitman and Spokane counties in 1883, but only after the Harrington and Davenport communities accused the town of submitting votes from children, train passengers, and the cemetery. Several years later, the honor was won by more centrally located Davenport.

In 1899, Fairfield businessman E. H. Morrison established the Washington State Sugar Company and arranged for a $500,000 investment to construct a three-story processing factory in Waverly after determining that the sugar beet crop could be grown profitably in the area. The facility employed 400 seasonal workers and 150 others to operate the factory in two shifts, which processed up to 6,000 tons of sugar beets annually. Complications plagued the operation of the complex extraction machinery, however, and some farmers found grain production to be less labor intensive and more commercially viable than raising sugar beets. Within ten years, the company was forced to curtail operations. A regrettable consequence of the factory's effluent was the extirpation of anadromous fish runs along Latah Creek, where salmon had flourished for ages.[5]

In some area communities, the railroad continued to provide relatively high-paying jobs long after the rails had been laid through the region. Roundhouses for servicing and repairing the massive steam engines and railway cars were established on the main Northern Pacific transcontinental line at Sprague in 1882 and at Farmington in 1886 by its subsidiary, the OR&N Co. The tiny town of Malden was designated a division point by the Chicago, Milwaukee & St. Paul Railroad (CM&SP or "Milwaukee Road") in 1906 for its Idaho-Cascade route, which swelled its population from a few dozen at the turn of the twentieth century to 800 at the end of the decade. At these points, the railroad employed dozens of mechanics and repairmen and housed its crews of engineers, stokers, brakemen, conductors, and other personnel. The abandoned CM&SP line is now the Milwaukee Road Trail Corridor. The former Spokane, Portland & Seattle Railroad (SP&S) has been converted to the Columbia Plateau Trail for hikers and cyclists and runs 132 miles from Fish Lake in Cheney to Pasco via Lamont, Hooper, and Washtucna.

Boom and Depression

Designated headquarters for the NPRR's Sandpoint-Pasco Division in 1881, Sprague was rapidly transformed from William Newman's original stagecoach stop and scattered flat of a few dozen houses at the head of Sprague Lake into a small city of 1,700 residents by the end of the decade. In the Palouse Country, this population was second only to Moscow's 2,000 residents, where the "Merchant Prince of Idaho," William McConnell and his wife, Louisa, served as two of the area's greatest boosters. McConnell used his considerable political influence in the Idaho state legislature to locate the state university in Moscow. He went on to serve as Idaho's third governor from 1893–95 and in the U.S. Senate.

The story of life in Moscow during the 1890s is evocatively portrayed in Carol Ryrie Brink's juvenile novel Caddie Woodlawn, winner of the 1936 Newberry Award for the nation's outstanding contribution to children's literature. Born in Moscow in 1895, Brink went on to write a trilogy of critically acclaimed adult novels about the area including *Buffalo Coat* (1944), *Strangers in the Forest* (1959), and *Snow in the*

River (1964). A previously unpublished manuscript, *"A Chain of Hands,"* was released by Washington State University Press in 1993 as the inaugural volume in a reissued collection of her work, edited by historian Mary Reed.

Colfax's population swelled to 1,650 by 1890 while Pullman and Cheney, still awaiting college faculty and enrollments, numbered 868 and 647, respectively. Palouse Country businessmen like James Perkins and William McConnell built magnificent homes from the flourishing enterprises they established by supplying area residents with household necessities, lending farmers money to acquire larger acreages, and marketing grain and livestock. Evidence of their success is displayed in nineteenth-century Victorian repositories of communal memory that serve as portals to the past and expressions of civic pride.

These timeless works by patient craftsmen include such masterpieces as Garfield's R. C. McCroskey House, Tekoa's A. B. Willard Home, and the residence of R. J. Howard in Rosalia, with its distinctive rooftop cupola. James A. and Minnie Perkins' home in Colfax (restored by the Whitman County Historical Society in the 1970s) is a rare example of western Italianate architecture, while the E. H. "Hanford Castle" overlooking Oakesdale displays a blend of nineteenth-century styles crafted in brick and stone. The William and Flossie Sanborn home in Sprague is the mirror image of a brick Victorian structure originally used for offices across the street. Both were erected by a local railroad official in 1880.

A cornucopia of nineteenth-century architectural style and composition is strikingly evident along Moscow's Fort Russell Historic District of over one hundred structures northeast of the city's downtown area. The McConnell Mansion itself is a lesson in structural eclectics generally conforming to Eastlake style but incorporating elements of Victorian and Queen Anne architecture. The McConnells' daughter, Mary, was raised in the home during the years it served as the city's social center, and she later married Senator William Borah. After Mary McCo-

The Perkins House in Colfax, Washington, 1889.
Courtesy Whitman County Library, Colfax, Washington

nnell Borah's death in 1976 at the age of 106, the home was substantially restored to its original condition, with many interior furnishings from the family, to serve as headquarters and museum for the Latah County Historical Society.

The neighboring "House of Seven Gables" is a two and one-half story fairy tale chalet built for flour mill owner Mark Miller. The manor features stained glass windows and upper story notched purlins thrusting through wide carved bargeboards. The Jerome Day Mansion was built for the son of silver magnate Henry Day, with both men providing the principal financing for Moscow's Idaho Harvester Company. Henry Day had made a fortune with F. M. Rothrock and others in the 1890s as principal shareholder in the Silver Valley's Hercules Mine near Mullan, Idaho, that produced $85,000,000 worth of ore during its first twenty-five years of operation.

Jerome Day spent lavishly on the residence, which was built in Queen Anne style with colonial influences evident in the metal crenellations and white columns along the lengthy curved veranda. Nearby Butterfield House is one of the Palouse Country's few examples of Georgian Revival architecture;

another can be seen in the elegant lines of Colfax's brick Post Office with distinctive cream-colored window trim and arches. Moscow also has one of the Pacific Northwest's original Carnegie Libraries, which was built in Spanish Mission style with funds endowed by the famed industrialist Andrew Carnegie to improve public education throughout the country and especially in rural areas that could not afford to build such an edifice.

Many Palouse Country historic structures did not survive the region's "great fire era" that devastated large portions of many towns including Colfax (1881, 1882, 1891), Pullman (1886, 1888, 1890), Palouse (1888), and Moscow (1890). Oakesdale (1892) and Kendrick (1893) did not escape the scourges and other conflagrations also struck Troy (1893), Sprague (1895), Farmington (1897), Endicott (1905), and Lamont (1910, 1913). Communities located in lowland areas like Rock Lake City and Sprague or on the banks of the Palouse River as with Colfax and Palouse also periodically experienced destructive floods.

From Moscow's magnificent mansions to the simple John Kelly log cabin built near Oakesdale in 1872, the grounds of Palouse area homesites hosted capacious coves of colorful plantings. Most were brought by Palouse settlers from the East or purchased from nurseries in Walla Walla. Blossoming General Jacquimonts and Paul Neyrons appeared in rose gardens and rows of colossal scarlet-blossomed hollyhocks and trumpet-flowered hibiscus guarded homes and outbuildings. Virginia creeper vines embraced walls with southern exposure while white catalpa flowers, one of the few ornamentals bearing its Native American name, appeared in front yards in springtime. Successful country flower gardeners all had their secrets for raising blooms in such abundance and variety. My Grandma Johns watered houseplants only from containers filled with crushed eggshells, her enormous begonias were always started in pots lined with potato peelings, and coffee

grounds were worked into the compost along the border of the yard for the brightest yellow and orange nasturtiums.

As in boomtown Lewiston during the 1860s, walking the boardwalks of Sprague in the 1890s provided lessons in cultural diversity, as one could hear conversations in a babel of foreign tongues. While most early residents like Iowa natives Matthew and Mary Brislawn and Nathaniel and Harriet Davis of Illinois were American born, other settlers represented virtually every European nation. The Davises came to Sprague in the 1890s, where Nathaniel's milling skills readily led to his employment at one of the town's gristmills. About the same time, the Olaf Petersen family arrived from Denmark to homestead in the vicinity, as did Swedes like Nils and Vendia Anderson and Robert and Adrina Franseen, along with Robert and Emily Potts and John and Anna Costello from Ireland. Christian and Louisa Kintschi emigrated from Switzerland while Jacob and Anna Stromberger were German-speaking immigrants from Russia's lower Volga region. Many other families in the area came from Germany, Norway, and England.

Sprague also became home to the Palouse's only colony of emigrants from Portugal's Atlantic Azores, consisting of the Anthony and George Pereia, Frank and Manuel Silva, and Joseph and Manuel Simas families. Many of the men worked as herdsmen for area ranchers like F. M. Rothrock and the Harders before saving sufficient capital to acquire their own land. In the early years of the twentieth century, brothers John and Marcus Escure, Basque natives from the Pyrenees Mountains of northern Spain, settled southeast of Sprague, where they eventually established sprawling Rock Creek Ranch for raising cattle, sheep, and other livestock. Combining Old World values of frugality and hard work with progressive ideas on rangeland capacity and animal nutrition enabled the Escures to expand their holdings to cover 15,600 contiguous acres. The entire ranch was acquired in the 1990s by the U.S.

Bureau of Land Management and is now the Rock Creek Recreation Site, providing valuable native habitat for threatened species including black- and white-tailed jackrabbits and the rapid-chattering burrowing owl.

F. M. Rothrock and Harry L. Day used their Hercules Mine earnings to launch a number of regional commercial enterprises. Rothrock was a rancher at heart and his preferred endeavor became operating the Hercules Ranch which he and Day established in 1914 on the shores of Sprague Lake. Within several years, they expanded their holdings to 20,000 acres, where vast herds of Shorthorn cattle and sheep pastured for marketing throughout the region. Rothrock made the sprawling fourteen-room Hercules Ranchhouse his headquarters, where prominent Northwest cattlemen and prospective buyers were entertained on the white-pillared veranda during exhibitions in the adjacent show pavilion.

Rothrock also acquired nearby Golden's Racetrack, which became one of the area's most popular venues for competitive horseracing. Emblazoned in bronze upon a massive basalt slab at the Hercules Ranch's main entrance was Rothrock's personal creed: "Agriculture is the foundation of all prosperity; livestock is its cornerstone." The ranch continued under Rothrock's management for twenty years before he sold his interest and went on to operate Spokane's Union Stockyards. In 1937, he organized the first Spokane Junior Livestock Show, which became an enduring tradition. Neither Day nor Rothrock were immune from the effects of the Panic of 1893 and subsequent five years of economic depression that engulfed the entire nation. In the words of Enoch Bryan, who had been appointed president of Washington's new land-grant college at Pullman just two years earlier, "The Northwest had come up to the very moment when the storm broke, in the full tide of prosperity." Exhibits showcasing Idaho and Washington's fisheries, forests, orchards, and wheat farms "had astonished and delighted" crowds visiting the 1892 World Columbian Exposition.[6]

Almost overnight in the early spring of 1893, however, Northwest wheat prices that had hovered for some years around 40 cents a bushel dropped to 30 cents, and within nine months had sunk to 18 cents a bushel—far below the cost of production. The situation unfairly came to be associated with the 1892 election of Democratic candidate Grover Cleveland. Seeds of the disaster had actually been planted several years before that fateful year, as tens of thousands of acres of newly claimed farmland were coming into full production in the Palouse region and other rural districts throughout the West.

Overproduction of grain in the early 1890s depressed commodity prices and farm income while mortgage rates and payment schedules remained constant. For these reasons, the problems of the decade especially affected farmers who had financed land purchases from the original landowners or the railroad through local banks. Unsound banking practices and reckless railroad spending had already leveraged the nation's economy, and when mortgage payments could not be met on homes and farms across America, foreclosures brought family evictions. Widespread loan defaults resulted in bank failures at the same time that thousands of railroad miles went into receivership.

In late 1893, the lines of the Northern Pacific, Union Pacific, and the OR&N Co. all came under new ownership. Complicating the situation in the 1890s was a significant increase in silver production from new mines in the mountain states, like those in northern Idaho. The production of silver in the United States had increased by 65 percent between 1880 and 1890 while the amount of gold produced over the same time fell by almost exactly the same proportion. The Silver Purchase Act of 1890 authorized the U.S. Treasury Department to acquire excess silver as its price fell against the value of gold bullion.

The final blow to the precarious situation for many Palouse farmers came in the summer of 1893, when incessant rains ruined the grain harvest. August days that had not experienced more than a trace of moisture in local memory saw heavy storms that wrought devastation upon what was expected to be a bumper crop. To many residents in the region, the unprecedented failure of crops dashed their last hopes of making a living, but with unemployment increasing everywhere, few other options were open for relocation. An air of despair swept upon the land like a biblical plague, persisting until federal intervention began boosting grain prices and farmland values in 1898. Despite the 1896 state elections in Idaho and Washington favoring Democrat William Jennings Bryan, GOP nominee William McKinley narrowly won the popular vote and electoral margin.

Many Palouse farmers came to attribute the welcomed changes to Republican policies after McKinley took office in 1897. Active reduction of federal revenue over expenditures had taken place, however, during the administration of fellow Republican William Henry Harrison from 1889 to 1893. Such practices had helped fuel the crisis in the first place. The new prosperity and reorganization of the northern railroads under the efficient management of J. P. Morgan and James Hill led to the region's "Great Decade of Progress" from 1897 to 1907. Gold discoveries in Alaska sent forth a steady stream of placer miners in 1897 and brought new reserves to the precious metal into treasury coffers in the same year that Australia and New Zealand sent over 15 million dollars' worth of bullion to purchase wheat from the Inland Northwest. Wheat prices in the Palouse region shot up to 75 cents a bushel, leading to a rise in immigration and land values. Farmers who had survived the depression of the 1890s were delighted with the new prospects but sought every possibility to secure and further improve their situation. New attention was paid to scientific improvements in agriculture advocated by personnel serving under presidents Bryan and Franklin Gault at the land grant colleges' experiment stations in Pullman and Moscow.[7]

The Palouse Press, Folk Art, and Sporting Events

As the Northern Pacific's "immigrant trains" brought recurrent streams of newcomers to the Inland Northwest in the 1880s and 1890s, the new transportation networks facilitated the export of grain and other produce from the Palouse. Communities throughout the region gradually prospered and newspapers appeared in many of them to inform a growing readership of local events and boost the virtues of settlement in the vicinity. Area political contests, social affairs, school events, and economic issues affecting life from Spangle to Uniontown and from Genesee to Washtucna were regularly featured in the Palouse press. Performances of the Lamont Mandolin Orchestra and the Uniontown Brass Band were announced and reviewed next to news from Seattle on grain exports to China, Japan, and Korea, markets important to Palouse farmers, and national headlines on the controversial agrarian policies advocated in the Cleveland and Harrison administrations.

Palouse Country businessmen L. E. Kellogg and C. B. Hopkins published the first newspaper north of the Snake River with the inaugural issue of the weekly *Palouse (Colfax) Gazette* on September 29, 1877. The *Spokan Times* appeared two years later. Several other local papers were established before the end of the nineteenth century, including the *Moscow Mirror* (1882), *Pullman Herald* (1888), *Sprague Advocate* (1888), *Palouse Republic* (1892), and *Fairfield Standard* (1895). The early Palouse press generally issued weeklies in which editors made clear their political affiliations. Moscow's readership was large enough in the 1890s to allow three competing weeklies—the *Mirror*, *Times-Democrat*, and *North Idaho Star*.

Over one hundred distinct newspapers were published in thirty-six towns in the Palouse region between 1877 and 1920. Several communities had more than six weeklies during this period, but rarely with more than two were in publication at any one time. The widest variety of news—though often short-lived—was in Juliaetta (*Advance, Enterprise, Gem, Potlatch, Register*), Oakesdale (*Advocate, Breeze, News, Observer, Sun, Tidings, Tribune*), and Tekoa (*Advertiser, Blade, Globe, Manitou, Sentinel, Topic*). Others that appeared for smaller circulations included the *Elberton Wheatbelt, Ewan Telephone, Malden Register, Valleyford Enterprise,* and *Thornton Tidings*. Some papers did not hide their small-town informality; for example, the ephemeral *Winona News* announced publication beneath its banner "whenever something happens." An extensive collection of these newspapers is filed at the Palouse Boomerang Print Museum in Palouse.

Something newsworthy did happen every June in the Palouse region, to inaugurate the arrival of summer. Hundreds of residents from far and wide gathered along the Palouse River at Elberton on June 21, for a special event that combined settler family picnicking with Chautauqua presentations and evening revival camp meetings. During the day, couples waited in line and gazed upward in awe at hot air balloon ascensions while children scurried up and down the wildflower meadows playing Run Sheep, Run and Fox and Geese. The grand affair invariably included a game of baseball, with teams drawn from communities throughout the region.

The origins of the Palouse Empire Fair date to April 1887, when James Perkins and others organized a fair association in Whitman County, in order to raise capital stock of $20,000 to build a park, horseracing track, stables, and exhibition buildings. The Latah County Agricultural Fair was organized in 1888 and was held annually near Moscow's Mountain View Park. The Whitman County site was along the Palouse River, a mile north of Colfax, and the first fair was held there in October 1887. Residents throughout the region flocked to the event, which featured a variety of commercial and agricultural exhibits. The *Palouse Gazette* reported, "Horseshoes, honey, a new sack sewing

needle, a rare collection of birds' eggs, the new Domestic sewing machine and the latest hats were among the exhibits of the first county fair, which opened on October 4 and lasted five days. So many livestock were brought in that carpenters worked all night to erect additional sheds." Show cattle included Durhams, Holsteins, Herefords, and Jerseys, and numerous draft horses with their colts were represented. One noisome pavilion displayed caged turkeys, geese, chickens, and ducks along with a cornucopia of fall vegetables, including a newsworthy 25-pound beet. An array of "lovely things that only the mind of woman can conceive and her deft fingers fashion," wax and paper flowers, and an enormous brightly colored pyramid of rare flowers, crochet, and needlework were all on display.[8]

The traditional designs favored by some quilters hinted at places of origin for many Palouse area families, both foreign and domestic—Irish Puzzle and Dresden Plate, Ohio Star and Kansas Sunflower. The only patterns known to be indigenous to the Pacific Northwest are Oregon Trail and Lewis and Clark. Certainly among the most unique quilts ever fashioned in the Palouse region was one of cream-colored calico bearing signatures in red floss of 276 pioneer residents of Moscow. Included among the names are Lieuallen, McConnell, and Adair with stitched identification showing it was "Made by the Ladies Industrial Society of the Baptist Church of Moscow, Idaho, May 8, 1897." The remarkable creation is displayed at the Latah County Historical Museum in Moscow.

Carnivals were added to the fair in 1903 and Grange exhibits were shown in 1907, with first prize awarded the remarkable sum of $125. Due to problems with recurrent flooding on the Colfax site and the public's demand for other locations to showcase the region's bounty, the fair was held in Garfield for several years during the 1920s and in other communities the following decade. In 1948, Charles McSweeney, Hugh Huntley, and Byron "Bo" Henry acquired thirty-one acres of property on the Palouse Highway, along Rebel Flat near Mockonema, to establish the more permanent Palouse Empire Fairgrounds and the half-mile Mockonema Downs racetrack for pari-mutuel betting.[9]

Area newspapers also reported on sporting events that took place at the area's two land grant colleges, and Palouse area residents came to look upon one game with growing interest year after year following the inception of the "Battle of the Palouse" in 1893. The annual game pitted the football squads of Washington Agricultural College and the University of Idaho playing against each other in an era devoid of padding and goal posts. Featuring the "old style" offense of mass formation and a center rush of players clad in baseball pants, the teams faced each other for four brutal quarters on a muddy field in Moscow. Although the Cougars managed the most wins in the grudge match's first decade of play, the teams' first meeting ended in a decisive 10–0 Idaho victory.

The year 1892 also marked the appearance of a small booklet, published in Massachusetts and written by Springfield College physical education instructor James Naismith, titled *The Official Guide to Basketball*. Naismith had devised the game to overcome the boredom associated with calisthenics and specified in the guide the size of the ball, backboard position, height of the basket, and rules of play. Within ten years, the game had caught on in Pullman, where Cougar coach Fred Thiel added it to the physical education program. The first official game was played on December 7, 1901, against a YMCA team in Spokane, because the college had no gymnasium at the time. The hosts won the game, but the next year the Cougars posted their first win in an 18–13 contest against the Spokane team on December 13, 1902. Legendary J. Fred "Doc" Bohler took over as coach and athletic director in 1908 at what was then the State College of Washington and led the team to a national championship in the 1916–17 season.[10]

The first Palouse Country high school squads were organized in Colfax, where a girls' team began playing in 1902, followed by a boys' squad two years later. The more experienced females bested their male counterparts in their first game played against each other in 1904. In the winter of 1905–06, Endicott and Garfield played the first game between area schools in an Endicott grain warehouse, after the local team had moved 2,500 wheat sacks into another facility across the street over Christmas vacation. The hosts won the game, 9–3, in a "gymnasium" featuring two long shelves to hold six coal lamps protected by hogwire, and a wood floor that inflicted frequent slivers whenever someone fell.

Teams were soon organized in Palouse (1906) and St. John (1910) to create the first county league comprised of both boys' and girls' teams. Since dribbling was prohibited in Naismith's original rules and no ten-second line violations existed, scores were extremely low in the early years of the game. Out-of-bounds fights over possession were also frequent, as referees usually awarded the ball to the player who bested others in the struggle for control. Spectators found these skirmishes to be some of the more entertaining aspects of the game, especially when most of the players ran after loose balls down stairways or in a darkened corner for which many early area gyms were notorious.

During the second decade of the century basketball spread to virtually every school in both Whitman and Latah counties with new high school teams organized in Pullman, Moscow, Colfax, and in smaller communities like Johnson, Hay, Pine City, and Thornton. Even at dozens of the one-room country schools that dotted the rural Palouse, young boys and girls tossed up balls of tied rags into an iron hoop nailed to the side of the building. The transition from traditionally outdoor sports to the more controlled atmosphere of indoor basketball continued to be difficult, however.

As one newspaper noted in 1915, "Sunset's idea of a basketball game and ours differ pretty materially. If we are going to play football we want to get out doors and call it by its right name. But perhaps we don't know what basketball is anyway." The first Whitman County high school basketball tournament was held at WSC in 1922. No distinctions were made among teams on the basis of school enrollment and the tourney was

Red Rays

base of Steptoe Butte, Washington

Golden Twilight   Little Kamiak Butte north of Pullman, Washington

won by the local Pullman club. The critically acclaimed film *The Basket* (1999), substantially filmed in the western Palouse region near Lamont, features the story of rural basketball and one-room country school education against the backdrop of World War I.

Private academies were established by Colfax Baptists in 1876, later Colfax College, under the tutelage of Leoti West, whose enrollment of seventeen students for the fall term swelled to a hundred by the following June. The United Brethren in Albion founded short-lived Edwards College in 1885. However, only Uniontown's St. Andrew's Parochial School, also established in 1885, and St. Joseph's Academy in Sprague (1886) survived as alternatives to public education in the Palouse region into the twentieth century. Both Catholic schools established outstanding reputations for their academic programs and attracted students from as far away as Alaska and California.

Upper Columbia Academy near Spangle was established by the Seventh-day Adventist Church in 1945, but traces its origins to an academy founded by the denomination at Viola, Idaho, in 1917. During the first two decades of the twentieth century, over one hundred country schools operated in the Palouse, a legacy of Jefferson's plan to establish a school in every township in addition to the larger community schools.

Lancaster, Washington native Glen Miller enrolled at Cheney Normal School in 1919 to obtain a degree in education and served as a teacher and administrator in schools at Sunset, Ewan, and St. John. Miller's hometown had the distinction of being perhaps the only Palouse community with two names— Lancaster to most locals, and Willada to the railroad and mapmakers. Over the years he and his wife, Beulah (whom he met at the Sunset school), provided local residents with services ranging from hair-cutting to dance lessons. Glen subsequently leased farmland near Ewan, which he worked at night. The Millers were eventually able to purchase their first farm, which led to the establishment of the Miller Land & Livestock Company.

During the couple's lifetime, their holdings came to include 27,000 acres of Palouse Country grainfields and rangeland, making the Millers the largest private landowners in the Inland Northwest. My first encounter with Glen was at the Palouse Empire Fair in the 1970s, where I happened upon him and Uncle Ray Reich discussing the finer points of fence-building. Glen was making a point with such gestured enthusiasm that I did not find it incongruous that someone who had spent a substantial portion of his life driving a Caterpillar tractor and riding on horseback still gave his grandchildren tap-dancing lessons.[11]

Years later, when the Endicott community voted to construct a new school, we sought to incorporate a number of pieces from the original structure. Someone mentioned that Glen had salvaged the school's original cast iron bell, which had been used for decades to announce the beginning and end of classes. Due to the deterioration of the belfry portico, the bell had been removed and sold at auction to a local resident and later acquired by Glen. I volunteered to seek the return of the relic for remounting in the new structure, and with that objective I visited the Millers at their home on the old Hugh Huntley place. (Regardless of current residents, farms in the Palouse region are often known by the name of some distant owner from the early settler period.)

After driving a couple miles down a dusty gravel road, I approached the unmistakable entrance to the Miller residence. As a Texas longhorn steer warily eyed my approach, it became obvious that Glen was interested in collecting more than just land. The Miller house was surrounded by enormous cast bells securely mounted to iron cradles and other frames built to hold these weighty objects. The largest bell of all, from a mission church in Oregon, rested on a flatbed trailer parked along the yard. After explaining our interest to the Millers, they generously offered to donate the community treasure back to the school, where it remains in the courtyard to this day.

Lodges and Secret Societies

In addition to annual gatherings at special events like the Elberton summer celebration and county fairs, Palouse area residents also found social and practical benefits from membership in a variety of fraternal and benevolent lodges and auxiliaries. Most were organized in the region after members of these groups migrated from the Midwest and East to reside in Palouse area communities. These societies provided opportunities for fellowship among townspeople and their rural neighbors, and membership—by invitation only—usually entailed elaborate initiation rites, secret ceremonies for degree advancement, and service for civic improvement.

Among the organizations most active in the Palouse region in the late nineteenth century were the two largest in the nation. The Free and Accepted Order of Masons was heir to the medieval guilds of stone masons and cathedral builders, and their women's auxiliary was known as the Order of the Eastern Star. The Shrine Club and The Daughters of the Nile were philanthropic Masonic affiliates. The Independent Order of Odd Fellows also had its origin in Europe, as did its affiliated Daughters of Rebekah Lodge, founded in 1851 by Colfax's namesake, U.S. vice president Schuyler Colfax.

The town of Colfax also hosted the Kamiak Tribe of Order of Redmen and Women's Order of Pocahontas. Other societies with widespread membership in the Palouse region included the Woodmen of the World and Women of Woodcraft, originally established as a life and health insurance company; and the Grand Army of the Republic, formed for fellowship among veterans of the Civil War. Also active in the region were the Maccabees, the Benevolent and Protective Order of Elks, Improved Order of Red Men (with the offices of great sachem, great senior sagamore, great prophet, and great keeper of wampum); and the Knights of Pythias, led by a chancellor commander; masters of arms, works, and exchequer; and inner and outer guards. A Memorial Day visitor to virtually any cemetery in the Palouse region will find freshly cut flowers beneath gravestones on which are engraved epitaphs containing such inscriptions as GAR, K of P, and IOOF.

As a boy growing up in the Palouse, I was aware that, in the past, local chapters of the Knights of Pythias and Pythian Sisters had met on the top floor of the Wakefield Building, a large brick structure in the center of town. There was an air of mystery about the place, as the high windows above the locked outer door revealed an immense cobweb-laced stairway that seemed to stretch far into the darkness of some inner sanctum. A cousin, Jim Lust, had access to the door key and attempted to frighten us for some time with tales of skeletons hidden away in the Knights' chambers.

Old enough to defend a measure of bravery, I joined several friends in slowly climbing the stairs late one afternoon. We made our way past any vestiges of defending commanders and inner guards to a room with large wooden plaques bearing long gray spikes. Our docent informed us that these had been used to test prospective candidates of the order. He pushed against one set made of immovable iron and told us to strike the other plaque with full strength. For good reason we refused. He proceeded to hit the other spikes, which bent backwards as they were fashioned from some kind of rubber.

We then continued into the main hall, shrouded in gloom from parchment-colored window shades, and spotted an ebony casket on a dais at the front of the room. A chill swept up my spine and we saw that the box had no lid. We moved as a group to view the contents, reason telling me to expect a practical joke. But as we stepped onto the landing, our eyes first spied the skull. One more pace revealed an entire human skeleton—just as Jim had promised—but we instantly decided against a more thorough investigation of what we thought were the remains of Damon or Pythias himself. We never did learn whose bones made that building their home.

following page

Barn and Wheat

south of
Moscow, Idaho

Spring Willows and Wheat   looking south from Steptoe Butte

Scholz Road Canola 2   west of Dusty, Washington

The Grange Movement and Soil Conservation

The roots of another organization popular among early Palouse Country residents ran deep into America's rural history. The Patrons of Husbandry, or Grange, was an agricultural fraternal society organized in 1867 as a result of President Andrew Johnson's and journalist-farmer Oliver Hudson Kelly's efforts to develop means for reconciling the animosities that persisted between the North and South after the Civil War. The term Grange was derived from a word used in the Middle Ages for a country manor with barns, stables, granaries, and other structures necessary for animal husbandry or agriculture.

Grange organizers in America were familiar with the Masonic Order and used the lodge as a pattern for much of their structure and ritual. The role of each local Grange officer was associated with an occupation on a typical English estate including a master, overseer, steward, chaplain, gatekeeper, and other offices. The Grange movement was envisioned to be progressive with women equally represented in the leadership with designated titles drawn from Greek mythology—Ceres, goddess of grains; Pomona, goddess of fruits; and Flora of the blooms. The Grange was organized with officers at the local, county, state, and national levels with seven farm implements used as symbols in the formalities of each degree.

The plow, for example, "should teach us to drive the plowshare of thought diligently through the heavy soil of ignorance," the hoe "is emblematic of that cultivation of the mind … thus promoting the growth of knowledge and wisdom," while the "ancient and honorable" sickle "speaks of peace and prosperity, and is the harbinger of joy. It is used not merely to reap the golden grain for the sheaf, but, in the field of mind and heart and soul, to gather every precious stalk, every opening flower, every desirable fruit." The Horn of Plenty and Bible were all-encompassing symbols representing the values of harvest blessing and godly wisdom.

A panoply of problems faced Northwest farmers when the first Granges were formed in Washington (1873) and Idaho (1874). The region's Grangers deplored the excessive profits made by several farm implement manufacturers and the artificially high freight rates charged by the Northern Pacific Railroad. Putting into practice their preachings about citizenship activism, the organization sought every legal means to improve their economic plight by lobbying state legislatures and Congressional regulatory commissions. Their efforts brought concessions from manufacturers and the transportation industry, which enhanced the role of the Grange in both states.

Local farmers assembled in James Ewart's log cabin to organize the first Grange in the Palouse region in 1897. Two years later, others were established at Whelan, near Pullman, and at Spangle (Pine Grove). In 1903, the State Grange Session was held in the Palouse region for the first time, with Pullman hosting the event. The warm reception given participants by WSC President Enoch Bryan was calculated to foster stronger bonds between the region's farmers and the land grant universities.

Nearly twenty Granges came to be organized in the Palouse region, with most located in smaller communities like Ewartsville, Whelan, Dusty, Winona, and Pine City as well as near Moscow and Pullman. Grange halls were built in these and other areas in response to state campaigns to ensure the viability of the movement. In 1918, the state organization formed the Grange Wholesale Warehouse Company, later known as Grange Co-op Wholesale, which combined the purchasing power of smaller Grange cooperatives to market equipment and petroleum products to farmers more economically. The prime mover behind this important effort was Pullman-area Granger William Smith. A dozen years later, the state Grange cooperative merged with the Midwest's Farmers Union Central Exchange (CENEX) to create one of the nation's largest agricultural supply enterprises, which integrated ownership of oil wells and refineries with bulk handling and services at the regional and local levels.

Grangers were also well-known for campaigns aimed at educating youth and the general public about the importance of agriculture to all segments of society. No visit to Palouse Country county fairs was complete without viewing Grange displays fashioned in intricate designs of rural scenes using multicolored mosaics of grains and legumes. Exhibition themes focused public attention on the significance of agriculture in daily life and evidenced Grangers' spirit of fellowship and hard work. The *Pacific Grange Bulletin* (later the *Agricultural Grange News*) began publication in 1908 to better coordinate activities within the organization and to feature prose and poetry by rural authors that merited publication. Sara Archer penned the following lines to commemorate one of the earliest agricultural fairs in Spokane:

Another year of garnered hopes. Of bending boughs on orchard slopes;

Of stubble-fields where Ceres reigns of bursting barns and stag'ring wains;

The tardy sun seeks southern sides; and Hesperus is quick to rise.

The Washington and Idaho Granges also used their growing influence to fight for rural electrification and conservation practices. Efforts to bring electrical power to farms were greeted with widespread support and eventual success, following the organization of public utility districts and Columbia River hydroelectric dams a generation later. The Grange campaign to promote an ethic of land stewardship was rooted in moral principle and enunciated by Grange enthusiast Theodore Roosevelt. President Roosevelt visited the Palouse region in April 1911 and addressed an enormous audience at Moscow, speaking from a platform made of Palouse wheat sacks.

Using the White House "bully pulpit," the president had earlier proclaimed, "The conservation of our natural resources and their proper use constitutes the fundamental problem which underlies almost every other problem of our national life. Unless we maintain an adequate material basis for our civilization, we cannot maintain the institutions in which we take so great and so just a pride; and to waste and destroy our natural resources means to undermine this material basis...."[12]

Roosevelt went on to define stewardship of the land in terms that balanced principle with practicality: "Conservation means development as much as it does protection. I recognize the right and duty of this generation to develop and use the natural resources of our land; but I do not recognize the right to waste them, or to rob, by wasteful use, the generations that come after us." The Country Life Commission, appointed when Roosevelt was in office to investigate the major problems confronting rural America, concluded that the tillage practices followed by many of the nation's farmers could better be described as "mining." Soil fertility was at risk throughout the country and especially in highly erodible regions like the Palouse Hills. The commission's report concluded that the situation "has now become an acute national danger..."[13]

Roosevelt's reasoned ethic of land stewardship for sustainable agriculture was promulgated by Granger leadership that sought to alter farming practices nationwide that threatened the country's most precious resource-fertile topsoil. The Palouse Hills had acquired one of the most unenviable reputations as an area where an average of twenty-five tons of topsoil per acre eroded away annually, resulting in the loss of nearly 20,000,000 tons of soil each year. Erosion rates were critical throughout the cropland area, but the most serious damage occurred on the steeper slopes of the south-central Palouse.

Unprotected summer-fallow or newly planted fields were extremely vulnerable to water erosion in the fall, as rills formed to drain the water after even moderate rains. The frozen sur-

Hutchison Family Picnic, c. 1933.
Hutchison Studio Photographs of Washington State University and Pullman, WA., 1910-1973 (PC 70), Manuscripts, Archives, and Special Collections (MASC), Washington State University Libraries, Pullman, WA.

face soil in early spring was equally at risk from rainfall that could not be absorbed, but instead washed down in muddy masses of dislocated loam. The epochal forces of nature that required a millennium to form one inch of fertile humus could be washed away in a single day's heavy rainfall on an unprotected Palouse side-hill. In just two generations, such neglect transformed the dark chestnut earth on many slopes into the exposed pale clods of clay nubbins.

The Palouse Country's legendary "inexhaustible soil," once heralded by railroad promoters and land speculators, was, in fact, a fragile but priceless patina overlaid upon significantly less organic subsoil. Over half of the entire Palouse region's soil erosion was taking place on the steepest 25 percent of the basin's cropland. The magnitude of the problem not only decreased the fertility of the land but also contributed significantly to the degradation of fish and wildlife habitat and the formation of massive silt deposits in the Palouse, Snake, and Columbia rivers. Grangers worked together with soil scientists at the region's colleges to identify and advocate measures to moderate the crisis. Grange publications, extension service bulletins, and farmer workshops recommended

several practices that could be expected to reduce Palouse erosion rates by more than half without significantly reducing income-divided slope farming, greenbelts along streams, and planting trees on the steepest hillsides.[14]

Perhaps the Grange's erudite founder O. H. Kelly had perceived deeper significance in what the goddesses Ceres and Pomona represented than their common association with nature's bounty. The ancient Greeks were among the first civilizations to note with grave concern the effects of unbridled farming on once fertile landscapes above their Corinthian shores. Kelly read Plato, who regarded the environmental changes of Hellenic Greece with alarm, as noted in the famed philosopher's dialogue with Critias. "What now remains of the formerly rich land is like the skeleton of a sick man," he observed, "with all the fat and soft earth having wasted away and only the bare framework remaining .... The soil was deep, it absorbed and kept the water in the loam, and the water that soaked into the hills fed springs and running streams everywhere. Now the abandoned shrines at spots where formerly there were springs attest that our description of the land is true."

But most of Plato's countrymen would not hear of exchanging their ingenuity and diligence for understanding and conservation. Soil erosion continued at an alarming pace in ancient Greece and degraded the waters of the northeast Mediterranean, weakened the region's economy, and forced the Greeks to plant their grains and vines on the increasingly marginal soils of Attica's highest slopes. The great British historian Alfred Toynbee wrote that this lamentable situation significantly contributed to the fall of Classical Greek civilization. Some Palouse area farmers began to speak of agriculture in terms of living on sustainable topsoil interest rather than spending hillside capital. Yields may have been slightly lower than that of their neighbors, but the benefits over time far outweighed and more than paid for any inconvenience or limitations.

The federal government was slow to respond with financial incentives for conservation practices, which hampered efforts by Grangers and other interest groups to preserve the basis of the Palouse Country's vitality. However, landmark congressional acts created the U.S. Department of Agriculture (USDA) Agricultural Adjustment Administration (AAA, 1933) and the Soil Conservation Service (SCS, 1935). The AAA introduced subsidy payments to farmers who voluntarily reduced their production acreage by 15 to 20 percent. They would be guaranteed a parity price for their crop, as the plan intended to reduce commodity surpluses that had depressed grain prices for years. Counties were assigned wheat allotment inspectors to assist interested farmers in complying with the terms of the act. The SCS was heir to the soil conservation initiatives undertaken in the Republican administration of Democrat Franklin Delano Roosevelt's uncle, Theodore Roosevelt.

In 1923, Peter and Maude McGregor's son, Maurice, returned to the family's sprawling Hooper ranch following graduate studies in finance at New York University, and was appointed to the AAA's first Washington State board of supervisors in 1933. McGregor had long expressed concern about the problems of farm surpluses and soil erosion. In the early 1930s, he noted that the family cropland was "approaching a critical stage" and required soil rebuilding if the enterprise was to be viable for future generations. Under Maurice's leadership, the McGregors implemented a series of innovative conservation practices, including the planting of crested wheatgrass on depleted areas, streambank protection, and the elimination of stubble burning. He expressed deep concern over what WSC scientists termed area farmers' "lack of appreciation of the seriousness of the situation" and "attitudes of indifference" regarding soil loss.

The decade of the 1930s came to represent one of the most significant shifts in agricultural practices—for those willing to change traditional approaches—since the introduction of mechanized farming in the previous century. Farmers like the McGregors turned to stubble mulch summer-fallowing to build cropland humus and to provide more land cover to protect topsoil. Three generations of "clean fallowing," in which the stubble of the early tall wheats was completely plowed over and recurrently weeded, left vast tracts at the mercy of the elements.

In September 1930, Pullman was designated one of the USDA's first ten Soil Erosion Experiment Stations, in cooperation with the two land grant colleges in the vicinity, under the leadership of William Rockie and Paul McGrew. Following the organization of the SCS in 1935, soil conservation enabling acts were passed in Washington and Idaho to fund state committees that would work in cooperation with the new federal agency. The Pacific Northwest's first conservation district, North Palouse in west-central Whitman County, was organized in January 1940 as one of a dozen districts in the Washington and Idaho Palouse. Five-member district farmer supervisor committees and staff conservationists worked together to promote the new minimum tillage "trashy fallow" techniques, reduce stubble burning, and encourage tree and native grass plantings on highly erodible slopes and marginal farmland.

In the spring of 1942, a group of state SCS staff members—including State Conservationist Harry Carroll (Pullman), Regional Conservationist G.B. Swier (Spokane), agronomist Verle Kaiser (Moscow), and W.R. Spencer (Fairfield)—arranged a tour of soil and water conservation practices for interested farmers and state officials on the McGregor Land and Livestock Company ranch near Hooper. Following this inspection, the Washington Association of Soil and Water Conservation Districts was formed in May 1942 at a meeting in Ritzville. Key Palouse Country leaders at the state and national levels in these strategic efforts to improve farm management practices included Ervin King, Lars Nelson, Verle Kaiser, and Russ Zinner.[15]

Hutchison root cellar near Endicott, c. 1939.
*Hutchison Studio Photographs of Washington State University
and Pullman, WA., 1910-1973 (PC 70), Manuscripts, Archives, and
Special Collections (MASC), Washington State University Libraries,
Pullman, WA.*

facing page

*Leonard's Barn
Summer*

east of
Pullman, Washington

CHAPTER VII

Education and Transformation

Institutions of higher learning established in the Palouse region in the 1890s have contributed significantly to the region's agricultural development as well as to the general education and culture of residents throughout the Pacific Northwest and beyond. Both Pullman's Washington State University, originally Washington Agricultural College (1891), and the University of Idaho at Moscow (1892) were established under the provisions of the 1862 Morrill Land Grant College Act and the Hatch Agricultural Experiment Station Act of 1887, which obligated them to serve the interests of area rural populations through liberal arts education, vocational training, and agricultural research.

Eastern Washington University's roots were in the creation of Cheney Normal School, a teacher training college established in 1890, which equipped hundreds of young educators for the rigors of service in the one-room country schools and stately community brick structures throughout the Palouse region and greater Northwest. Established in 2000, the Cheney Normal School Heritage Center is the renovated one-room Jore School located in the center of the EWU campus. The historic building showcases the heritage of rural education inside the traditional wainscoted country school walls where young people once studied with chalk slates and copybooks on pine floors.

Bryan Hall and its clock tower, Washington State College, Pullman, 1928.
Hutchison Studio Photographs of Washington State University and Pullman, WA., 1910-1973 (PC 70), Manuscripts, Archives, and Special Collections (MASC), Washington State University Libraries, Pullman, WA

facing page

Old Timer's Summer Morning

east of
Colfax, Washington

Washington State University began in a rectangular building known as "The Crib," built of brick from clay dug at the summit of College Hill, where the structure stood for many years. Located between present-day Holland Library and Compton Union Building, a portion of the original wall was incorporated into the library's south face. Castellated Thompson Hall, built as the college's original administrative building in 1894, is now a National Historic Site. The University of Idaho's flagship structure was the imposing Administrative Building. Although destroyed by fire in 1906, the classic design of its 1909 replacement in Tudor Gothic style set the architectural standard for further construction on the university's scenic 450-acre campus. In 1908, the prestigious Massachusetts-based landscape design firm Olmstead Brothers was hired to give a New England nuance to the school's sweeping grounds.[1]

The populations of the "college towns" soared as these three schools successfully expanded their programs and enrollments. Pullman more than tripled its numbers between 1890 and 1910, increasing from 868 to 2,602 residents, and the most significant growth elsewhere in the region over the same period took place in Moscow (2,000 to 3,670) and Cheney (647 to 1,207). Cheney also benefited from its strategic location on the main line of the Northern Pacific Railroad and became a major grain warehousing and milling center.[2]

Administration Building, University of Idaho, Moscow, 1933.
Hutchison Studio Photographs of Washington State University and Pullman, WA., 1910-1973 (PC 70), Manuscripts, Archives, and Special Collections (MASC), Washington State University Libraries, Pullman, WA

facing page

Palouse Country Barn Fall

south of
Moscow, Idaho

College Experiment Stations

The agricultural experiment stations established in Moscow in 1892 and in Pullman the following year were first met with a measure of skepticism by area farmers and ranchers who were suspicious of outside experts. Yet several progressive residents of the area joined together to purchase acreage large enough for test plots near both schools. Within several years, the research teams won over considerable numbers of their constituents by respecting them for overcoming the challenges of life on the Palouse and by demonstrating the practical results of scientific methods for improving crop and livestock production. In 1893, Louis F. Henderson, whose mentor had been prominent naturalist David Starr Jordan, arrived in Moscow to head up plant sciences at the experiment station and teach at the university, where his classroom readings from Shakespeare were almost as well-known as his research in plant pathology.

Agronomist William J. Spillman arrived in Pullman to serve on the college's faculty in 1894. Popular Inland Northwest barleys at the time included Coast, a Spanish Mediterranean descendant from California, Russian Manshury, and English Chevalier. The most commonly grown wheats in the Palouse region at that time were the soft yellow-white spring varieties Little Club, named for the shape of its head, and Pacific Bluestem. Spillman found most farmers planting these and other tall, low-protein variet-

1890s US Hybrid Wheats (Jones Fife)
Courtesy USDA National Library, Beltsville, Maryland

ies in the spring rather than risking winterkill, to which early plantings of these two popular grains were susceptible. This practice resulted in severe wind and water erosion on fallow lands and the growth of unwanted thistle, cheatgrass, Jim Hill mustard, and other invasive weeds. Spring planting generally failed to develop the secondary root system needed to absorb available moisture and good stands often lodged, or were knocked flat, after moderate rains while the heads shattered in brisk winds. Spillman initiated an ambitious wheat breeding program in 1899 and found that offspring from crosses of various parent stocks created a variety of characteristics in the second generation.

Spillman's pioneering research paralleled the groundbreaking work nineteenth-century Austrian biologist Gregor Mendel was conducting with peas—a single chromosome species. Mendelian laws first explained the basic principles of heredity and gave rise to the field of genetics. Spillman worked with the more complicated triple chromosome sets in wheat, crossing over 300 pairs to select plants in each generation with the desired characteristics. The decade of Spillman's tenure in Pullman also witnessed the introduction of several wheat varieties by the U.S. Department of Agriculture and private Eastern breeders. Each variety, however, experienced problems in the region. Red Chaff was often damaged by Palouse winters, Early Baart did not yield

facing page

Red Barn and Spring Wheat

north of
Colfax, Washington

well, Fortyfold and Jones Fife shattered easily, and Russian Red, actually of English origin, was of such poor milling quality that it brought considerably lower prices.[3]

Following Spillman's departure in 1902 for a position with the Department of Agriculture, the wheat breeding program was capably continued by Claude Lawrence. Finally, in 1907, a series of promising hybrids that Lawrence and Spillman had developed in 1899 were released to area farmers for commercial production. Hybrid 128, a variety resulting from a cross between Little Club and Jones Fife, proved to be the most winter hardy and productive strain. Results of the program's research in the Palouse region and other experiment station recommendations were more fully disseminated among area farmers following the enactment of the Smith-Lever Act of 1914, which established an agricultural extension service cooperative among the federal, state, and county levels. The work of the county extension agents facilitated rural education in farm management practices, home economics demonstrations, and 4-H programs.[4]

Lawrence and others worked patiently for years with their experimental varieties in Pullman and Moscow and released the soft red winter variety Triplet in 1918. However, like other varieties of the time, its kernels became infested with the black fungus "smutting bunt," which drastically reduced yields and the quality demanded by shippers and millers. Plant geneticist Edward F. Gaines had begun breeding for resistance to bunt in 1915 at the Main Experiment Station in Pullman. After nine years, Gaines' research led to the release of the hard red variety Ridit, followed by the soft white club wheat Albit in 1926, a popular variety originally developed in 1920 by crossing Hybrid 128 with White Odessa. The scientists also took into account farmer concerns about marketability, since the hard classes were used domestically for breads and breakfast cereals, while most of the whites were for pastry flours and export to China and other Asian markets for making noodles.

Continued problems with smutting, the appearance of the fungal disease rust on wheat leaves and stems, and a proliferation of varieties for marketers to grade led to the organization of the Cooperative Western Regional Wheat Improvement Program in 1930. Funded by Congress through the Department of Agriculture, eleven states participated in the program, which was administered in the Palouse region by Edward Gaines, Orville Vogel, and plant pathologist O. E. Barbee in Pullman and by V. H. Florell and C. A. Michels at Moscow. The two teams worked closely together to develop more and larger nurseries by acquiring additional lands adjacent to the experiment stations and in areas of various microclimates and soil classes across the region. These efforts under Vogel's direction led to the development of more specialized soft white wheats like Orfed (1943), Marfed (1947), Brevor and Elmar (1949), and Omar (1955) for areas of high rainfall, semi-hards for intermediate lands, and hard reds for low rainfall areas.

Using Brevor crosses with dwarf Japanese Norin 10 obtained during the post-war Allied occupation, Vogel introduced the semi-dwarfs Gaines and Nugaines in the 1960s for resistance to lodging, and yields often exceeded 100 bushels per acre. For his distinguished contributions to plant genetics that also gave rise to the Green Revolution of vastly improved wheat production in Central America, India, and Sudan, Vogel was awarded the National Medal of Science in 1975 by President Gerald Ford. Due to the enduring efforts of the college experiment station staffs, their allied cooperative extension service agents, and local farmers, the Palouse Country became and remains the highest yielding dryland grain district in the world.[5]

A department of forestry was established at the University of Idaho in 1909 under Charles H. Shattuck, who created the first college arboretum west of the Mississippi river, planting some 300 different varieties of trees near the campus. Known today as the Shattuck Arboretum and Botanical Garden, many of the original plantings of oak, beech, chestnut, fir, and pine from around the world survive amidst lilacs and peonies on sixty acres along the south rim of the campus. The trees are evidence of Shattuck's efforts to find species that could adapt well to conditions in the Palouse region and be used for research on conifer disease resistance. The department was elevated to college status in 1917 under Dean Francis G. Miller, who was induced to migrate across the state border from WSC, where he had served as head of the forestry department. The practice of the two schools enticing professors from one to the other was not uncommon and generally represented a rivalry far less damaging than the Vandals' periodic theft of Butch, WSC's Cougar mascot, from his cage on the Pullman campus.

Under Miller, one of the nation's largest college forests was acquired one parcel at a time through tenacious effort and considerable political maneuvering to obtain the necessary funds for purchase and as gifts from the state. The tract eventually grew to cover 7,000 acres in the Moscow Mountains, just north of the city, where extensive research was conducted on productivity, insect infestation, diseases, and other aspects of forest management. Edward Iddings and Cuthbert Hickman were also hired at the university to strengthen the college of agriculture, where the two pioneered important work on Palouse area cattle raising, horse breeding, and legume production. Dry peas were first introduced to the eastern Palouse region about 1910 and slowly became an important alternative crop, while dry beans were introduced with less success about the same time in the Genesee district. The Palouse would eventually supply 90 percent of the dry peas and lentils consumed in the United States, with the nation's largest genetic stocks of these legume varieties located at the USDA Plant Introduction Station in Pullman.[6]

Immigrant Profiles

Native-born European Americans continued to be the most populous group in the Palouse region in 1900, when the combined population of Whitman and Latah Counties reached 38,811. Although the rate of growth never reached the phenomenal pace of the 1880s, the healthy 29 percent increase of the 1890s was strongly reinforced by another 26 percent rise by 1910. That year, the two-county area's population peaked at 52,098—the highest of any decennial year. Ninety percent of the people were native-born Americans, but significant numbers of European immigrants continued to settle in the Palouse during the first two decades of the twentieth century. Relative to the total population, immigrant numbers declined after 1910, when they constituted 10.4 percent of the region's populace. European emigration was interrupted in 1914 with the outbreak of the First World War.

The unsettled international situation was concurrent with final settlement on open but marginally productive public lands on the western periphery of the Palouse. Few immigrant farmers came to the region after 1915, as its economic base remained overwhelmingly agricultural. Farm labor needs were generally met by self-sufficient families, and few opportunities for new employment existed in the small agrarian communities. The area experienced a five percent decline in numbers between 1910 and 1920, as the population of Whitman and Latah Counties fell to 49,415. The trend would continue for several decades, as farm mechanization and economic conditions allowed fewer farmers to acquire larger holdings.

By 1900, the Palouse's American Indian population had been largely displaced, great measured squares marked in fences had been imposed on its rolling terrain, and the land had been thoroughly peopled with families from virtually all states in the Union and every European nation. Bolstered by geographical and cultural advantage, native-born Americans predominated by the end of the century. Children of the foreign-born often grew up bilingual, speaking their family's language at home and English in the public schools.

Most churches associated with a European homeland offered an additional service in English during the First World War as the region's growing second-generation of European-Americans contended with both internal and external pressures to "not be different." New identities emerged in the region as dozens of vigorous rural communities in Whitman, Spokane, and Latah counties boasted a two-story brick school, state bank, churches, and mercantiles while local newspaper editors bore frequent witness to the "fulfilling of pioneer dreams" in the early years of the new century.

European immigrants to the region were typically members of the lower and middle agricultural classes with little chance of inheriting land. They often chose to emigrate during times of economic adversity on the continent. In many cases they were young and healthy, determined to build a more prosperous life in the "Promised Land" of opportunity. Another aspect of their selection began after their initial migration, since many first settled in Midwestern states where they engaged in farm work, until various conditions compelled some to reconsider their situation. Crop failures as well as climactic and social adjustments left the beleaguered Midwestern immigrants with three alternatives: they could return to the homeland, resign themselves to the local circumstances, or risk a new quest for security in a land rumored to be as fertile and pleasant as any on earth—the Pacific Northwest. The latter course was chosen by the first European immigrants who settled in the Palouse.

Many came expecting to find land in Oregon or Washington and soon learned of the great potential for newcomers in the Palouse. After their arrival, another stage in the selection process continued to sift out the immigrants dedicated to building a permanent and productive life. Unlike American-born settlers, the Europeans were more keenly aware of their isolation and were less likely to relinquish their homestead rights. They had endured the struggles of a journey

stretching halfway around the globe and which had often consumed many years of their lives. In the Palouse region they were determined to finally demonstrate to themselves and to others that they were capable of achieving the success that they had so long sought. The environmental conditions of the Palouse region were conducive to supporting an industrious, law-abiding agrarian populace. Crop failures were virtually unknown and the transportation problems that had inhibited widespread settlement during the earliest years of settlement had been overcome by the railroads in the next decade.

In the earliest stage of resettlement, the immigrants often journeyed alone or in small groups to explore the new setting. If prospects were good, the newcomers may have corresponded with family and friends back home and persuaded them to follow. In this way in the 1870s Michael Schultheis acquainted the German Catholic colony in Minnesota with opportunities in the Colton-Uniontown area, just as Archie and Peter McGregor contacted their kinsmen in Ontario a decade later about life in southwestern Whitman County. At

Henry & Mary Repp and Henry & Anna Litzenberger families, c. 1885.
Richard D. Scheuerman Collection,
Manuscripts, Archives, and Special Collections,
Washington State University Libraries, Pullman, WA.

that time, the Volga German farmers Phillip Green, Peter Ochs, Henry Litzenberger, and Conrad Schierman, who settled near Endicott in the fall of 1882, were describing the area to relatives in the Midwest and in Russia. Sounding Green out on the possibilities of a move from Kansas, his brother-in-law replied that, "…if life yielded as little as the last years it would be better we moved to you."[7]

The second stage of migration began as a small stream of migrants followed to the new place. Similar circumstances were repeated with the Swiss Mennonite Joseph Stevick, who landed at Almota in 1885, the Norwegian Lutheran Peder Wigen and his kinsmen who pioneered settlement southeast of LaCrosse in 1901, and dozens of others like them. So enticing were the prospects for prosperity in the Palouse region that the population leaped to over 52,000 by 1910 when the rural Palouse became the most densely settled rural area of the Inland Northwest.

Reflecting the final phase of resettlement patterns seen elsewhere in the American West, large numbers of villagers from specific areas in the East and Europe joined in the movement as the extended family network grew substantially with each passing year. The nucleus of the Colton-Uniontown German Catholic colony became other families from the 1867 wagon train that followed Schultheis. Walla Walla press accounts from the 1870s and 1880s contain frequent reference to these arrivals. A typical entry from 1878 reads, "Another wagon train of immigrants passed through the city today destined for the Palouse Country." Most groups at this time were native-born Americans and the articles often mentioned areas of origin and specific destination: Iowans to Oakesdale, Ohioans east of Colfax; families from Tennessee to Steptoe and from Illinois to Spangle. Waves of newcomers were entering from the north and south onto the rolling unclaimed Palouse prairies, called "the Mecca of immigrants" by the *Walla Walla Union*.[8]

That significant numbers from entire European villages joined in the pilgrimage is evident in the experiences of Palouse's Russian German, Swiss Mennonite, and Norwegian Lutheran communities. The schoolmaster in the Volga German colony of Yagodnaya Polyana, Russia, for example, estimated in 1910 that nearly one-fourth of the village's 2,500 inhabitants had left for the United States or Canada during the previous two decades. The number of Whitman County Russian-born residents that year was 589, and the overwhelming majority were from that very village. In the southwestern Palouse region, the McGregor sheep operation recruited experienced French herders from the eastern province of Haute-Alps early in the nineteenth century. Many of these men, like brothers Emile and Maurice Morod, Ernest Biques, and Maurice Vasher, remained with the company to make their homes in the Palouse.

Selbu Lutheran Church near Hay, Washington, 1929.
Hutchison Studio Photographs of Washington State University and Pullman, WA., 1910-1973 (PC 70), Manuscripts, Archives, and Special Collections (MASC), Washington State University Libraries, Pullman, WA.

The formation of the Potlatch Lumber Company in 1903 ushered in a new phase of employment opportunity in the Palouse region for immigrants from southern Europe who were recruited by the Spokane offices of the All Nations Employment Agency and Northwestern Employment Agency. Though company officials preferred northern European workers, Italians and Greeks were directed to Potlatch as early as 1908 to meet the demands of a burgeoning business that employed hundreds of men to cut down and process the massive white pine forests of the eastern Palouse. Ethnic enclaves soon emerged in Potlatch as the company instituted a policy requiring employees to live in the town.

Greek, Italian, Japanese, and Scandinavian neighborhoods developed on the north side of town where the sounds of weekend bocce-ball matches and aromas of barbecued lamb and other Mediterranean delicacies revealed Potlatch's cultural diversity. The community also hosted an inter-faith "Union Church," a Catholic Church, and evening English classes offered to those intent upon naturalization. Some Italians later relocated to the neighboring communities of Onaway and Princeton after the company relaxed its residence policy, while other Italians and Yugoslavs were employed at the company's Elk River sawmill.[9]

Among workers recruited in 1902 for construction of the Camas Prairie Railroad along the north bank of the Snake River was a young Greek immigrant, Gust Delegianes, from the small farming village Kandila in the mountainous Peloponnesian Peninsula. The railroad to Lewiston was opened in late 1909 and upon completion of his work along the line near Penawawa, Delegianes decided to seek employment in the bustling port community because the climate and small farms on the bottomland and adjacent slopes reminded him of his native land. His brother Christ had immigrated in 1904 and eventually found work first as a bootblack and then as a railroad shop mechanic in Seattle. Gust encouraged

his brother to join him in Penawawa where local orchardists eagerly sought dependable laborers for summer work and fall harvest. Gust found work on the Silas Smith ranch where he learned how to prune, irrigate, and tend the countless other chores requisite for successful orcharding. Christ joined his brother in Penawawa about 1912 and the two formed a partnership to lease the Smith ranch. About the same time two of their cousins, brothers Mike and George Delegianes, also arrived in the area.

The Delegianes family partnership prospered on the land leased from Smith and after a couple years the three men decided to buy about three hundred acres of their own four miles upriver from Penawawa. In 1914 they planted seventy acres to Moorpark apricots, Alberta and Hale peaches, Mount Morincy cherries, and other fruit and also raised vegetables and melons, all of which at first were arduously watered from barrels carried on wagons. Within several years the orchards and gardens were in full production while the men also maintained over two hundred adjacent acres in pasture. A small Greek colony emerged in the vicinity as other Greeks including John, Louie, and Nick Deleganes worked in area orchards for extended times. Several members of the Deleganes (Delegans) family were married and raised their children in the community, teaching them to observe traditional Greek Orthodox festivals and name days as well as maintaining other distinctive cultural traditions.[10]

The African American experience in the Palouse region during the settlement period involves a similar history of intolerance and frequent discriminatory treatment by the Euro-American majority. African Americans were attracted to the Pacific Northwest in the late 1800s, seeking a place with less prejudice and more opportunity than was available to them in the South. Although African Americans in Washington Territory could not vote until Congress enacted the Fourteenth Amendment to the Constitution in 1866, they were permitted to legally purchase and own property in the territory, unlike Oregon. Relatively few risked breaking away from their scattered enclaves of settlement west of the Cascades to move eastward. Only nine Blacks were registered in the 1880 census for Whitman and Nez Perce Counties, and they were employed as manual laborers. Among the earliest African Americans in the Palouse region were the Wells brothers—Joseph, Louis, Grant, and Crom. The four North Carolina natives settled in Latah County in 1889, where they worked at logging and blacksmithing.

Among the first African Americans to homestead in the region was William King, a native of Wake County, North Carolina, who immigrated to Spokane in 1902 before bringing his family west a year later. After working as stonemason in the city for many years, he joined others in a 1910 homestead lottery for 36 quarter sections adjacent to the southern boundary of the Coeur d' Alene Indian Reservation. King's number was drawn, and he relocated to his claim, later known as King Valley, near present-day Tensed. At the time of his death in 1927, the family had purchased nearly 500 additional acres in the vicinity, and they eventually acquired some 1,500 acres covering nearly the entire valley. The experience of most African Americans during the early twentieth century, however, was characterized by manual labor for area farmers during the work year with winters spent in Spokane or Lewiston.[11]

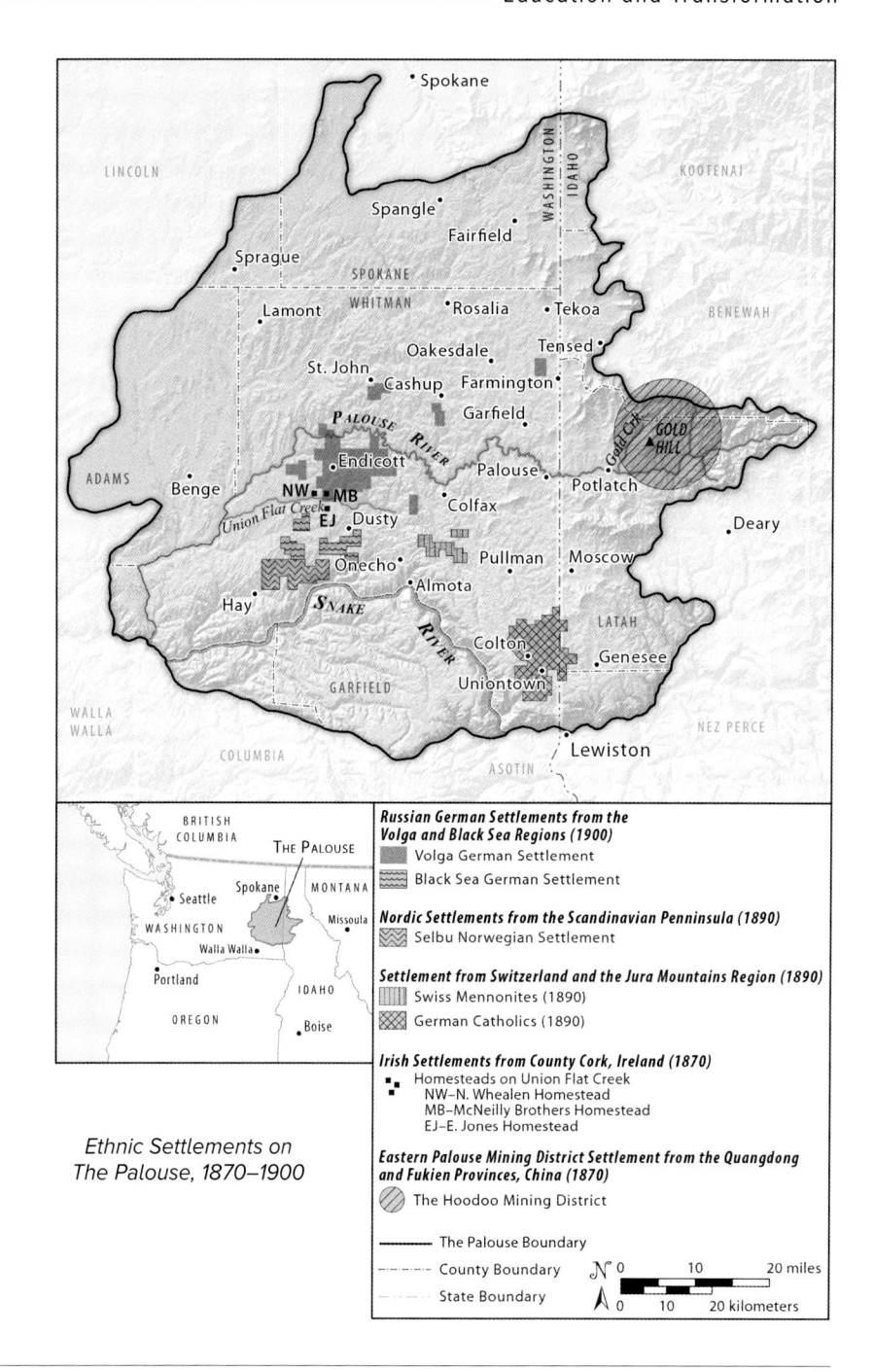

Ethnic Settlements on
The Palouse, 1870–1900

A New Social Order

The period of large-scale immigration to the Palouse region came to a close by 1920. After World War I interrupted European emigration, the first of three increasingly restrictive United States immigrant quota laws was enacted in 1921. The effects of these events, coupled with the fact that Palouse lands were virtually all claimed and settled by 1915, effectively curbed further immigration to the region. Since the late 1870s, the majority of Palouse area residents have been American-born, though by 1920 the total number of foreign-born in Whitman and Latah Counties (2,862) represented 8.6 percent of the total population (31,323). However, due to the large birth rates among the foreign-born, their first, second, and third generations constituted approximately one-third of the total population in the Palouse. The four largest European groups each constituted over 10 percent of the total foreign-born in 1920, these being the Russian Germans (17.0 percent), Swedes (16.6 percent), Germans (14.8 percent) and Norwegians (10.6 percent). Smaller European elements were the Irish, Swiss, English, Scots, Greeks, and Italians.[12]

The new social order in the Palouse, as elsewhere in the American West, also contributed to assimilation. No longer was one confined to a level of society on the basis of birth, as had been the case in many nineteenth-century European nations. The Homestead Act rendered all eligible citizens potential economic equals on the unclaimed frontier. Learning English and engaging in American politics were not seen as threatening the individual and national identity of the immigrant. Rather, free public education and the democratic process were viewed as blessings generously offered, which enabled the newcomers to capitalize on the opportunities of life in a free land.

Still, the immigrant could maintain elements of personal identity through the institution of the church. It was more than sanctuary of religious faith, although this was of preeminent value to devout immigrant settlers. The church also protected the native language and the many cultural traditions associated with the Old World. Catholic, Lutheran, Methodist, and Mennonite immigrants in the Palouse region often reached accommodation in their areas of settlement with American-born members of their respective denominations through cooperative services or shared premises.

Likewise, the diverse rural populace generally came together to establish local farm cooperatives for marketing crops, and although several parochial schools were established in the Palouse, in most areas public schools received broad local support. Many newcomers to the Palouse found more than just opportunities for employment: they found a new homeland. Though typically characterized by a rolling terrain of fertile land, the Palouse landscape varied from a vast expanse of rangeland in the west to the undulating hills of the central Palouse region and eastern forested mountains of Idaho. The snow-capped peaks of the Bitterroots gave Norwegian farmers in the eastern Palouse region the impression of a "New Norway," just as the timbered slopes of the same area seemed familiar to the immigrants from Sweden's southern highlands.

In the same manner, the Volga Germans, whose people had labored for over a century on the steep slopes of the Volga *Bergseite*, eagerly sought the unbroken hills of the central Palouse region, as did many of their fellow Teutons from Prussia, Saxony, Hesse, and Baden. The settlers' plows also changed the landscape, as cultivation exposed the fertile but fragile Palouse slopes to the destructive forces of wind and rain. The same toil that replaced the native grasses with

facing page

Cumulonimbus

from
Steptoe Butte

the world's highest yielding dryland grains and legumes has caused serious environmental problems through erosion and sedimentation of the soft, mellow earth. Crop and livestock production also brought biotic change through the inadvertent introduction of foreign plant species, transported here with seed grain and in transcontinental boxcars.

The cultural backgrounds of families in the Inland Pacific Northwest remain as varied as the region's landscapes, to which many immigrants formed mystical attachments because of geographic similarities to their homelands. Motives for coming to the region have been as complex as the individuals who harbored them, with hopes for prosperity and eagerness to flee adversity with both playing important roles. In other instances, adventurous souls responded to wanderlust that had worked for generations to weave the

colorful fabric of American, European, and Asian culture. This spirit, combined with idealistic visions of life in the Far West, lured many foreigners and Easterners to find new homes in the Palouse region during the period 1860 to 1920.

In 2000, nearly one-third of the area's residents still claimed a single dominant ethnic ancestry, indicating the peculiar resilience of rural Palouse ethnic cultures. To be sure, historical and geographical factors in the region have led to cultural change; yet ethnic groups in the Palouse region remain characterized by distinctive social, religious, and occupational patterns of Eastern American and foreign origin. From the Swiss Mennonites and Russian Germans of Whitman County to the Swedes and Norwegians of Latah and Spokane counties, cultural identities forged in the region's colorful era of settlement are retained and celebrated.

Palouse River outing, c. 1910.
Hutchison Studio Photographs of Washington State University and Pullman, WA., 1910-1973 (PC 70), Manuscripts, Archives, and Special Collections (MASC), Washington State University Libraries, Pullman, WA.

Dahmen Barn Canola

Uniontown, Washington

following page

Freeze Church, Summer Wheat

north of Potlatch, Idaho

Feed My Sheep

Freeze Church Spring

north of Potlatch, Idaho

CHAPTER VIII

Appreciation and Renewal

In recent decades, Palouse Country residents have spearheaded numerous domestic and global food security efforts. In the wake of the collapse of the Soviet Union, for example, a group formed WestWind Ministries in 1991 in response to appeals from newly independent Russian leaders to provide food and medical assistance to schools and orphanages in the Russian Far East. A coordinated "Operation Karelift" effort, involving the National Association of Wheat Growers, Washington-Idaho Pea & Lentil Association, and The McGregor Company of Washington, Idaho, and Oregon, led to delivery of over a thousand tons of aid to areas in greatest need. Farmers hauled truckloads of wheat for processing into flour while Northwest barley, lentils, and beans were combined into nutritious soup mixes.

In September 1994, when Russian president Boris Yeltsin made an unprecedented visit to Seattle to report on newly normalized relations between the United States and Russia, he cited "this help in our hour of need" in the context of the food campaign as a key factor in his historic visit. Yeltsin's gala reception was hosted by Washington Governor Mike Lowry, himself a native of the Palouse Country hamlet of Endicott, Washington, where his father, Robert, had managed the local grain grower cooperative in the 1950s. Lowry's dedication to humanitarian causes and migrant farm worker causes was the subject of many tributes following his passing in 2017. Officiant Kacey Hahn of St. Matthew's Lutheran Church in Renton opened the late governor's memorial with explicit reference to moral responsibility from Leviticus 23:22: "And when you reap the harvest of your land, you shall not reap your field right up to its edge, nor shall you gather the gleanings after your harvest. You shall leave them for the poor and for the sojourner."

With the outbreak of war of Ukraine in February 2022, many of the original KareLift partners joined with other groups through "Operation Harvest Hope" to raise funds and send Northwest commodities to help feed the several million refugees who fled the conflict to safe havens throughout Europe. The war between Russia and Ukraine—nations that provide some 30 percent of world wheat and barley exports—destabilized global grain markets and put at significant risk the wellbeing of millions in the Middle East and North Africa, whose lives depend on imports and subsidized bread.[1]

facing page

Harvest Bounty

west of
Dusty, Washington

Jim Gerlitz, *Palouse Colony Harvest*, 2017
Oil on canvas, 18 x 24 inches
Author's collection

Tradition and Innovation

Palouse Country grainfields that have long provisioned world markets are favored landscapes for artists and increasing numbers of tourists, many of whom travel great distances to marvel at the undulating hills. W. Craig Whitcomb of Lewiston, Idaho, has painted rural scenes for a half-century in watercolor and acrylic, with subject matter ranging from isolated Northwest grain elevators to English thatched cottages and Japanese landscapes. His work *Amber Waves* (2008), a finalist in the first annual "H'Art of the Palouse" banner competition, shows an immense abandoned grain elevator in vivid rusty reds and blues rising from a field of ripe grain. Vibrant watercolors of Northwest grain and legume fields scenes by Andy Sewell of Viola, Idaho, have appeared on posters for the Pullman-based National Lentil Festival. His dramatic piece *Doubletime Before the Storm* (2021) shows the skillful choreography of two John Deere combines moving in tandem with tractor-pulled grain carts in the face of threatening clouds and lightning. Sewell, a graduate in fine arts from the University of Idaho in Moscow, spied the late afternoon scene near his eastern Palouse home. The golden browns and dark shadows of land and sky express Sewell's appreciation for the primal forces of nature that make harvests possible. Other richly colored agrarian landscapes by Sewell include *Palouse Summer Glory* and *Palouse Country Summer*.

Tradition and innovation have presented cultural tensions since the dawn of civilization, and responsible influence from each has contributed to humanity's wellbeing. Like van Gogh paintings of gleaners and reapers with factory smokestacks on the horizon, agrarian fine art and literature foster better understandings of tensions that involve emotion and reason, and local and universal values. Among other recent developments in grain production, the advent of minimal tillage operations using specialized power equipment has greatly reduced soil erosion on American farms while increasing

yields. The emerging New Agrarianism of the twenty-first century moves beyond nostalgic romanticism to moderate use of industrial energy within the context of natural systems for soil fertility. Wise approaches to innovation respect stewardship of the land and the long-term wellbeing of others. Duke Divinity School environmental theologian Norman Wirzba writes of a New Agrarian ethic that honors modern science as well as ancient religious appreciation for the transformative mystery of soil, water, and grain for human sustenance. Implicit acknowledgement is also made of fair compensation for farmers and other workers. "How we make bread, how we share and distribute it, are of profound moral and spiritual significance," he writes in *Food and Faith: A Theology of Eating*: "[E]very loaf presuppposes decisions that have been made about how to configure the social and ecological relationships that make bread possible."[2]

Although based in Baltimore, landscapist Katherine Nelson has traveled cross-country regularly since 2001 to the Palouse's undulating grainlands. Her fluid charcoals and dye sublimates capture the summertime chiaroscuro of swirling slopes, saddles, and swales laden with grains and legumes. Nelson has also contributed to Oregon State University's Art About Agriculture program and to Glen Echo, Maryland's Yellow Barn Gallery exhibitions. She traces threads of her fascination with the region to her diplomat father's interest in Turkish rugs: "I remember their luxuriant textures and shapes, which influenced my affection for rolling landscapes. The Palouse is a tapestry of woven connections among seasons, fields, and people. The effect is thoroughly spiritual and provides a place of reflection, solace, and beauty that overcomes the noise of the outside world." To emphasize the rhythmic effects of light for line and shadow, Nelson works entirely in black-and-white, which evokes heightened awareness of layering, texture, and movement. "My 'Portraits of the Palouse,'" she explains, "are metaphors for the human prospect. 'Harvests' to me are exhibitions that depict the land as hallowed space through views of heritage farm architecture and landscape vistas. Implicit rural values relate to the natural environment, hard work, and community, and are relevant anywhere."[3]

Public awareness of land stewardship takes on special significance in a day of unprecedented industrial and technological change as world population and pressure for land use continue to grow. As a boy, I experienced our family's 1962 cross-state trip from the Palouse Hills to Seattle's optimistically titled "Century 21" World's Fair. Visitors were dazzled by exhibits on space travel and consumer abundance. A half-century later, Milan, Italy, hosted the 2015 "Feeding the World" Fair, with themes related to the problems of food security, sufficiency, and safety. A UN-sponsored session discussed the disturbing flatline of world grain yields since 2000, and how one billion inhabitants of the developing world were at risk of chronic malnourishment after decades of decline. The world's population in the medieval era peaked at approximately 300 million inhabitants, but rose to a billion by about 1800, doubled to two billion in 1927, and reached three billion in 1960. Demographers at Milan predicted this exponential growth rate would result in ten billion world inhabitants by 2050, bringing attendant challenges for food resources, species diversity, and stewardship of soil.

Recent Palouse Country fine art exhibitions have explored these themes, sponsored by the Pullman Arts Council, Moscow Arts Commission, and Colfax Arts Council. They have featured works by lifelong Palouse Country resident Vicki Broeckel, Anna Blomfield, and photographer George Bedi-

Katherine Nelson, *Ideas About Infinity*. Detail: Grainfields from Steptoe Butte, 2018.
Charcoal and dye sublimate on opaque and sheer fabric, 3 ft x 9 ft.
Courtesy of the artist

Vicki Broeckel, Fields of Gold, 2022
Oil on canvas, 18 x 24 inches
Collection of the artist

rian. Jacqueline Daisley lives on a farm near, Pullman where the surrounding countryside inspired her curvaceous masterpiece, *Palouse Hills—End of Harvest* (2018). Blomfield embarked on an artistic farrago in the fall of 2006 to explore and depict Palouse grain production throughout the seasons. Originally from Great Britain, she studied painting and printmaking at St. Martin's School of Art in London and in Liverpool before moving to California in 1987 to work as an animator and muralist, then to Moscow, ID, in 2006. Her popular online "frogblog cartoon-diary" commenced on November 7, 2006, when she observed, "If I wanted to buy a combine harvester there are 3 dealers in town to choose from."

Relocation to the Northwest brought unexpected agrarian vistas and serendipitous friendships with area farmers, combine dealers, shop mechanics, and others engaged in agricultural pursuits. "I was entranced with the landscape, the people, and the various crops" she remembered; "each one had a story to tell and show." Over the course of her five-year residence in the region, these encounters yielded dozens of such colorfully illustrated posts as "Out Amongst the Wheatfields (8.28.07)," "Threshing Bee (9.3.08)," and "A Combine Chorus Line (4.25.2010)" with commentary provided by the artist's alter ego Froggie, who traveled year-round in Studio Subaru. Characterizing her captivating genre as "visual storytelling," Blomfield combined illustration and information to transport and amuse readers through expeditions to such locations as harvest fields, grain elevators, inspection stations, and rural railroad sidings. Public "gallery" showings of her popular work were appropriately held in repurposed silos and barns and at the farm equipment dealerships she had first noted in her earliest online posts.[4]

Pullman, Washington, artist Henry Stinson has painted beautiful representational canvases of harvesting combines and other modern farm equipment in action but is especially known for whimsical views that reflect his lifelong fascination with gadgets and electricity that attest to modern American society's ubiquitous connections to technology. An enormous untitled exterior wall mural painted by Stinson in 2019 evokes the classic *American Gothic* pose as it might have appeared in a 1960s episode of *Lost in Space*. The painting reflects the artist's interest in a world where people and livestock increasingly share rural landscapes with drones and satellite-controlled, computer-monitored field equipment.

Jacqueline Daisley, *Palouse Hills—End of Harvest*, 2018.
Oil on canvas, 42.5 x 32 inches
Author's collection

Sustainability for the Long Term

Stories and paintings that relate a range of interpretations regarding contemporary and future existence add voice and visibility to diverse perspectives on land use. Consolidation of family farms in recent decades into larger corporate enterprises and the commodification of grain—William Cronon's "transmutation of one of humanity's oldest foods," warrant high regard for stewardship of the land. Reinvigoration of Americans' deep-seated social memory and cultural capacity can guide landowners and public officials who contend with environmental challenges and finite production acreage. When Conrad Blumenschein told me about leaving Russia for America just before the outbreak of World War I, ten families lived on a dozen farms of about 320 acres each, scattered along the road between my hometown of Endicott and the Palouse River some seven miles to the north. (Two landowners lived in town.) Numbering some fifty people, most attended one of two Lutheran churches in the area—the Missouri Synod in the country, and the Ohio in town—and two country schools enrolled the area's children through the eighth grade. Many of these families were related to each other and regularly gathered for summer harvest labors, fall butchering bees, and various ceremonies and celebrations.

A half-century later, when I began interviewing first-generation Palouse Country immigrant elders in the 1960s, the number of farms had fallen to nine, with some consolidation of property holdings among the remaining seven families consisting of thirty-two individuals. The size of area farms had increased to an average of 550 acres, and both country schools had consolidated with the larger town district that offered instruction through grade twelve. My father was able to complete our month-long harvest on about that much acreage by keeping in good repair the old tractor and pull-combine that had teamed up for at least a quarter-century to make the annual run. The price of a bushel of wheat rarely rose to $2 from 1960 to 1973, at which point a controversial U.S. trade deal to supply the Soviet Union with grain boosted prices to as much as $6.25 per bushel. The long-sought optimism felt by growers ushered in a year of equipment upgrades and land purchases, followed by years of economic challenge, with fewer young people returning to the farm.

The broader demographic impacts on Palouse Country rural life and labor are consistent with trends over the past two centuries that have changed the nature and necessity of worker communities. In 1840s pre-industrial America, for example, a farmer could produce an acre of hand-broadcasted wheat, yielding about twenty bushels, from approximately fifty hours of annual work, using simple implements like a single-shear plow and scythe. (Soil exhaustion and other factors in early nineteenth-century France and Germany contributed to average yields of less than half that amount, or about ten bushels per acre. Yields on unmanured fields in England were in the range of fifteen. Continental Europeans commonly faced substantial crop failure and famine at least once every ten years.) A single day's harvest by an able-bodied scythe-wielding reaper could cover up to one acre. By 1900, an American farmer equipped with horse-pulled gang plow, harrow, and mechanical drill still produced about twenty bushels, but in about ten hours of annual per-acre labor. An experienced crew operating a reaper-binder and steam-powered thresher at that time could cut about forty-five acres a day, for some 1,200 bushels (31 tons) of grain. A farmer in 1940 using a gas-powered tractor, three-bottom plow, and combine with twelve-foot header further reduced annual per-acre labor to 3.5 hours.

Dryland grain yields increased three-fold nationally during the twentieth century, and Palouse yields of eighty bushels per acre are common today, along with diesel-powered, satellite-guided equipment that makes crop rows of linear perfection. High-capacity combines now cost as much as $1 million each and feature sidehill leveling, cruise control, and electronic monitoring of threshing functions that automatically adjust to crop load. Modern farmers invest about

fifty minutes in total annual per-acre labor and, using a combine header forty feet wide, can harvest 250 acres in a ten-hour day to yield up to 30,000 bushels (900 tons) of wheat, or 72,000 bushels of corn. Sickle-section cutter-bars endure: modern versions feature four-inch-wide chromed, serrated triangular sections arranged toothlike in a row that run the length of the header and move back and forth at lightning speed. Such mechanical marvels represent the output of a

Henry Stinson, Untitled Wall Mural, 2019.
Fonk's Store, Main Street, Colfax, Washington
Columbia Heritage Collection Photograph

thousand reapers and twice as many binders who labored in harvest fields before the Industrial Revolution. (Substantial numbers of others were tasked with carting unthreshed stalks to barns, flailing grain, tending livestock, and other related tasks.) A phalanx of these modern behemoths cruising through a field of golden grain evokes appreciation for techno-mechanical ingenuity and still stirs ancient feelings of gratitude for agrarian bounty.[5]

Harvests Yesterday and Today—Different Times, Identical Location.
Lautenschlager & Poffenroth (1911) and Klaveano Brothers Threshing Outfits (2019)
Four miles north of Endicott, Washington
Author's collection

"God is in the Details"

Contemporary agrarian art and literature offer insightful if variable perspectives on the transformation of rural landscapes and ways of country life. Stories and paintings can be elegiac and abstract as well as hopeful, with expressions of agrarian renewal evident in newfound appreciation for regional heritage and stewardship of the land. These considerations juxtapose values related to the natural world with those of private development and global capitalism. There is little to regret about archaic rural prejudices, grinding aspects of exhaustive dawn-to-dusk farm labor, and highly erosive tillage practices that once characterized areas like the Palouse. Small town redevelopment efforts are examining how local stories, specialty crops, and other resources might be shared to better contend with shifting labor patterns and demographic change. Harvest bees and church benefits still aid neighbors in times of special need. At the same time, the annual harvest experience requires seasonal urgency, and the instinct for necessary provision unites humanity worldwide through the rituals of planting and harvesting and thanksgiving.

Reflecting on contemporary agrarian experience, novelist Bruce Holbert observes that in places like the Palouse, "God is in the details—turning a wrench, discing the summer fallow, spraying and rod-weeding, planting and cutting." He considers these to be prayers "of the ancient sort, the ones you offer not for an answer as much as to be heard. Their reward is the opportunity to perform similar acts tomorrow and the next day. Their faith is not invested in an end; it is the opposite, a prayer to continue and in it is a kind of patience with the fates that few outside this place share." The inhabitants of Holbert's stories are not portrayed to explore the classic American theme of personal freedom amidst the conformist mainstream. Instead, they seem to take for granted a life of mystery and misery amidst economic hardship and the vagaries of nature, and speak perceptively from deep within as they move about in clouds of uncertainty. Holbert explores the abiding toil and periodic terrors of country life in *The Hour of Lead*, winner of the 2015 Washington State Book Award for Fiction, and in other novels and writings. His short story "Ordinary Days," in which the Mason Hills are cast for the Palouse, features an exploration of rural change and meaning-making as a farmer takes his fourteen-year-old daughter on a drive through the countryside:

> The wind through the wheat stalks alternated like the back and forth of the sea, green or brown or golden or tawny swells depending on which direction you looked and which time of year. My father had always claimed its authority, like God's, was omnipresent. Omnipresent not omnipotent. The difference mattered to him. We resided in Nighthawk. Grain siloes paralleled the railroad lines like castle keeps. An enormous American flag flapped upon the tallest. The town is only a few cross hatched roads lined with well-kept but unassuming houses and lawns, a school tucked against a hill.

> The Mason Hills were once peppered with such communities but farming requires fewer people and more equipment and land so kids who twenty years ago inherited ranches now attend college and opt for city jobs. Shrinking towns bled children to those a little less tenuous through yellow school buses until they were only wide spots along the highway and even freight trains no longer blasted their whistles when they passed.

> In Nighthawk, the grocery closed at 5:00 but the owner distributed keys to the locals. After hours customers hung post-its on the cash register to update their bill. Each

year, the Red Cross circulated a large donation envelope from house to house that held hundreds of dollars in cash. Neighbors and acquaintances claim to know you but so do those with whom you just exchange a nod in town. When a person gets sick it plucks a string in a spider's web and all the other strings vibrate.[6]

Nostalgia for some halcyon past contributes to the popularity of rural art but tempered with consideration of what has been lost and what has been gained. These contrasting themes are explored in contemporary photographic art and are the special interest of Richland native John Clement and Southwesterner Don Kirby. The stark, mysterious black-and-white photography of Kirby's *Wheatcountry* shows unpeopled agrarian vistas from Texas to Washington. Essayist Richard Manning writes of the contrast between the imaginative West of the national consciousness—reshaped since settlement and largely uninhabited—and landscapes tended by farmers who contend with the vagaries of weather and maneuver through an array of government programs to provision the masses. Kirby's monochromatic views bear the titles of nearby locations scarcely known or seen by outsiders, but that conjure memory and meaning to locals. His Palouse series includes Diamond and Lancaster (places where farmers came from miles around to procure seed wheat), Harrington and Pomeroy (home to area flour mills), and the Snake River port of Central Ferry, which remains one of the Northwest's largest grain exporting terminals.

Having grown up in the vicinity, I immediately recognized Kirby's image *Wheatfield III, Repp Road, Endicott, Washington*, which shows a prodigious stand of ripening wheat cloaking an enormous swirl of sloping summer-fallow beneath a stack of cumulus clouds. The Repp family had the only pool for miles around before the town built one in the 1960s, so they kindly taught a generation of us how to swim. The matriarch of the clan only recently passed away at age 104 and her nephew Mike

Lowry—our state's twentieth governor, who contributed to normalized US-Russia relations in the 1990s—may well have helped harvest that very hill. Trends in the depopulation of the countryside are found throughout the nation, even as affordability of houses in small towns has helped keep some populated with newcomers to sustain local schools, churches, and clubs. Shrinking numbers of farmers remain as vital carriers of intimate knowledge about the land and growing conditions, and of practical skills that keep bringing forth the crops.

Color images of "Northwest Drylands" photographer John Clement, like *Wheat Moon*, *Freeze Church Summer*, and *Bringing in the Sheaves*, show the influence of two prominent American watercolor artists, whose works Clement has closely studied since starting his career in the 1970s—Winslow Homer and Andrew Wyeth. Although the substantial portion of Homer's paintings depict realistic Eastern landscapes and ocean scenes, Impressionistic views like Schooner at Sunset captured Clement's imagination just as they inspired a generation of modern American artists like Wyeth and his father, Nathaniel. Clement studied the watercolors of the younger Wyeth and learned that the drier Pennsylvania prairie and underlying abstractions in paintings like *Christina's World* held lessons in originality for photography of the arid Columbia Plateau grainlands. Clement's picturesque landscapes, which earned him induction into the Professional Photographers of America International Hall of Fame, typically feature evidence of humanity's waning presence—dilapidated barns and fences, retired farm machinery, and fields of maturing grain. His ideas about the "saturating luminosity" of dawn and dusk suggest affinity with the nineteenth-century American Luminists and pioneers of color photography, whose detailed agrarian views beneath soft, hazy skies engender feelings of melancholy and meditation.

Cultural tensions rise with proliferating perils of climate change, concern about impacts on soil biomes and wildlife, and global food security needs. Establishing balance involves mediation of the ancient urges for veneration and exploitation, and consideration of technocratic limits and trade-offs in agricultural improvement. Soil scientists estimate that no-till farming has reduced erosion on American farms by 40 percent since it gained widespread use in the 1980s, as well as having lowered American diesel consumption by two-thirds, for some 280 million gallons of annual savings. For Promethian bioentrepreneurs, CRISPR (the acronym for "clustered regularly interspaced short palindromic repeats") gene modification and related technologies offer the prospect of crop improvement, although prominent biologists acknowledge that cellular arrangements can be altered in ways that are not fully understood.[7]

Whether on a Palouse Country farm or in a Chicago high-rise, one may live with fidelity to place by learning and practicing domestic arts and community building. Family care and homemaking need not require moving "back to the land," although new paradigms for remote working are facilitating rural residency. In any setting, folks can summon moral courage to eat together, shop locally to support practitioners of local crafts, connect young people to worthwhile endeavors, and affirm the values of environmental care. Policies and practice of self-reliance and promotion of the common good that characterized republicanism in the ancient world are relevant more than ever in an era of threatened landscapes, endangered species, and marginalized labor. Meaning-making in classical thought came through an honorable paideia of civic engagement and reflection. Intellect detached from action risks loss, and empathy apart from action is purposeless. Apparent in

literature and art ranging from Virgil and Horace to British Georgics, French Rustics, and Russian Itinerants, a holistic life of labor—such as harvesting, craft, and community—promotes personal as well as cooperative wellbeing. A related education grounded in distinctly local connectedness through stories and art, mealtime fellowship, and field study, offers prospect of cultural renewal.

Leo Tolstoy's 1897 exposition on aesthetics, *What is Art?*, embraces a wide range of creative expression from painting and sculpture to literature, folklore, and liturgy. He characterizes their highest forms as conveyance of the makers' regard for human dignity and the natural world in ways that astonish, mystify, and benefit the common good. That Tolstoy points to artists like Jean-Francois Millet and Léon Lhermitte and authors Nikolai Gogol and Anton Chekhov as aesthetic exemplars is significant for their use of agrarian themes to present such universal values. The characters who inhabit Tolstoy's stories have heroic capacity, even when leading solitary lives. They walk familiar paths to work together in the fields and better understand the people and world around them. Among the most stirring moments in Tolstoy's *Anna Karenina* is when landlord Konstantin Levin, who sought the full life of mind, love, and labor, joins a scythe-wielding brigade in an afternoon of great satisfaction: "He… wished for nothing, but not to be left behind the peasants, and to do his work as well as possible." In a day of tension over progressive approaches to a more sustainable future, an ancestral regard and consideration of Biblical figures Ruth and Boaz, muzhik harvesters, and Palouse Country farmers offer restorative interpretations of land use and the human prospect.

Windy Wheat

"The Way It Used to Be"

On an overcast morning in April 2024, a dozen descendants of legendary Columbia Plateau tribal leader Chief Kamiakin gathered at The McGregor Company farm supply headquarters near Colfax, Washington. They embarked on a daylong excursion commemorating Palouse Country homeland campsites. I smiled at a colorful entryway farm supply poster that proclaimed, "Big Roots Run Deep." Company chairman Alex McGregor welcomed the delegation of elders and youths who had driven from the Yakama and Colville Indian Reservations to visit areas once frequented by their famed ancestor and other Snake River-Palouse bands. In the 1920s, Alex's great uncle, Peter McGregor and his son, Maurice, had provided legal representation to several Indian families residing at the ancient village of *Palus* near Lyons Ferry. They included the Kamiakins and famed Appaloosa horse breeder Sam Fisher and wife, Helen, who was among the last survivors of the 1877 Nez Perce War. The title to properties they had acquired through the Indian Homestead Act was threatened by others who sought the land. The McGregors' partnership with members of the band led to enduring friendships and subsequent ruling by the General Land Office in Spokane in favor of the tribal litigants.

Although the last member of the Snake River-Palouse at Palus died in 1954, relatives of these families who gathered in the spring of 2024 near Colfax had never forgotten their Palouse Country identity. One of the elders spoke of this regard in terms of moral obligations to water, air, land, and the creatures upon it. His words were reminiscent of those spoken by Chief Kamiakin and other tribal leaders to Governor Isaac Stevens at the 1855 Walla Walla Treaty Council. During those tense meetings, the two sides struggled mightily to reconcile Indigenous spiritual values and Euro-American economic interests. In a spirit of goodwill at the recent Colfax gathering, Snake River-Palouse historian Clifford Trafzer, Rupert Costo Chair of American Indian Studies at the University of California-Riverside, presented fieldtrip participants with Costo medallions to commemorate their important contributions to regional heritage and cultural appreciation. Kamiakin family spokesman Pat Goudy paid special tribute to the McGregor family and Washington State University editor-in-chief Linda Bathgate. The group then caravanned to "Kamiakin's Crossing," the northernmost point of the Palouse River between the communities of Endicott and St. John. Here Chief Kamiakin and his substantial family had resided for several years following the tumultuous period of the 1850s Columbia Plateau Wars.

As is discussed elsewhere in these pages, Kamiakin championed both traditional values and innovation, and evidence suggests the family may have established the first farm in the Palouse Hills at the crossing camp. Descendants still trea-

facing page

Endicott, Washington

sure intricately twined *wáwxpa* (corn husk) and *k'pit-limá* (beaded) bags, curved iron *kápin* (root-diggers), and dense *k'púl* (wooden mortars) for grinding roots and grain that might well have been crafted there. Traces of the old trails that cross in several directions can still be seen in the vicinity which came to be known in pioneer days as Kumtux, Chinook jargon for "Place of Understanding." Early residents of the area commonly used a route along the river pines eastward to reach fabled *Yamáštas*—"Elk Mountain," or Steptoe Butte, a longtime destination for high place spirit quests.

Yamústas—"Elk Mountain" (Steptoe Butte)   North of Colfax, Washington

Aurora Vortex

base of Steptoe Butte, Washington

As the group later viewed Nona Hengen's dramatic Steptoe Battle paintings at the St. John Heritage Museum, I mentioned that their late relative Gordon Fisher, grandson of Sam Fisher, was one of the first to tell me about the special cultural significance of *Yamástas*. He also taught listeners its proper pronunciation in sibilant Snake River-Palouse Sahaptin that frontier roadbuilder John Mullan struggled to first render in English in 1859 as "Eomoshtoss." As remains the case with ancient names for many Palouse Country landforms, however, Mullan offered little explanation of the word's meaning. Gordon, who proudly perpetuated the family name *Yosyos Tulikecíin* ("Blue Man") for a warrior ancestor, had spent summers in his youth with Sam and his grandmother Helen Fisher at Palus. He had also spent considerable time in Nespelem with Chief Kamiakin's last surviving son, Cleveland, and his wife, Alalumt'i, who had been raised at Wawawai on the Snake River. Gordon, who passed away in 2011, knew from these elders that Steptoe Butte held a central place in Snake River-Palouse cosmology. He regretted that few oral traditions had been recorded about a place synonymous far and wide with Palouse lore and geography.

Columbia Plateau *K'pit-limá Sápk'ukt* (Beaded Bag)
Private Collection

facing page

Old Palouse Barn

west of
Garfield, Washington

The Kamiakin family gathering seemed all the more timely, therefore, since Cliff Trafzer and I had recently encountered an obscure reference to century-old Snake River-Palouse oral histories in an unlikely place—the archives of the American Philosophical Society in Philadelphia.[1] Thanks to a generous Costo research grant, Cliff and I found ourselves in the elegant APS Reading Room sharing space with Lewis & Clark's original journals. Here we anxiously awaited a box of notebooks containing dictations made in 1930 by Gilbert Minthorn (c. 1870-1943) on the Umatilla Reservation to researcher Morris Swadesh; we hoped our travels had not been in vain. The young linguist conducted extensive field research with elders on several Northwest reservations as part of graduate studies at the University of Chicago. That summer Swadesh and University of Washington anthropologist Melville Jacobs visited the Thorn Hollow district on the eastern side of the reservation, where several Snake River-Palouse, Cayuse, and Nez Perce families had clustered. Here Swadesh and Jacobs met several individuals with special knowledge of Snake River-Palouse culture and language, including Minthorn and his wife, Atilapum (1867-1938).[2]

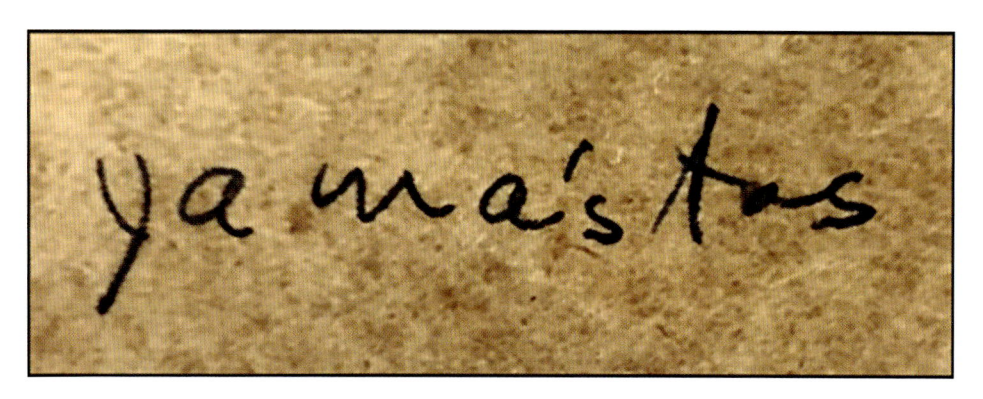

Swadesh-Minthorn "Notebook A" Title Page (1930)
Franz Boas Collection of American Indian Linguistics; American Philosophical Society

Philadephia APS curator Brian Carpenter appeared before us with a small hardboard document case, which held the three small Swadesh notebooks. Each consisted of several dozen handwritten pages with interlinear Sahaptin and English text. We opened the first volume and saw a familiar word boldly written across the inside cover—*yamástas*—and I whispered to Cliff that the trip would be worthwhile. It was as if Swadesh's hasty but legible handwriting was opening a portal to teachings handed down from the First Peoples of the Palouse since time immemorial:

minway'á hiut'sɛ´ya qáqáwa pátamaluwiya...[3]

This is how it was at that [ancient] time....

He decided and this ground was covered all over [with] water for five years.

One island named Mt. *Yamástas* [was] over there.

    No Indians named it.

        He held it right there....

Way back before my people, old story....

    Coyote he was smart,

        he knew everything,

...In the ground he started to burn fire.

...And everybody in the country learn[ed],

    were a witness....

In that time [Coyote] learned everything.

Eat just the same and then fire in that way

    he found fire and made everybody.

He knew us,

    my ancestors

        ... all of them and right here on the ground.

Everybody learned and the people grew after that.

All of them he finished that one this body [at] that time

    and that was the way he helped

        and that one used to be.

And that time came [the] big ocean all over....

[Afterward] animals and salmon and fruits and all of the roots.[4]

God named it and that one he knew him,

    all of them he name[d] it.

That time [was] before time White men came....

God's law[5] [is] that way [for] us,

    all of them that way we know that way in this world.

That [is] the way I know it used to be....

Jay Owens is a London-based researcher and writer whose work explores the clash and compatibilities of the natural and technological worlds. Her book *Dust: The Modern World in a Trillion Particles* is a sweeping exploration of science, history, and economics that invokes Bible verses and observations by Darwin to understand humanity's quest to flourish and innovate. She describes the fundamental stuff of existence everywhere but of special significance to residents of dryland regions like the Palouse, where soil, showers, and sun conspire to bring forth the miracle of seeded life. In noting the challenges of modern agriculture to sustain nation and world, Owens writes favorably about both indigenous ecological knowledge and complex technologies. She stresses the imperative for shared perspectives essential to equip future generations with tools and wisdom to confront the challenges of burgeoning growth, alternative energy, and climate change. Worlds ancient and modern met and exchanged perspectives that day in the shadow of Steptoe Butte about the meaning of *Yamástas*. Big roots run deep.

Steptoe Sunrise

from Cronk Road in Garfield, Washington

ENDNOTES

Chapter I: Place and First Peoples

1 Gilbert Minthorn, Umatilla Indian Reservation, 1930, in Morris Swadesh, "Notebook A," Franz Boas Papers, American Philosophical Society; Emily Peone oral history, 1981; and Gordon Fisher oral history, 2005. Although the Snake River-Palouse Sahaptin term *yámaš* literally means "deer," some tribal elders relate that in former times the word could refer to any large animal with antlers. Deer in myth generally is *Yamašyái*; mythic Bull Elk is *Wawu·kyayái.*

2 Alan J. Busacca, *Loess Deposits and Soils of the Palouse and Vicinity,* U. S. Geological Society of America, 1991.

3 D. F Bezdicek, T Beaver, and D. Granatstein. "Subsoil Ridge Tillage and Lime Effects on Soil Microbial Activity, Soil pH, Erosion, and Wheat and Pea Yield in the Pacific Northwest, USA." *Soil & Tillage Research* 74, no. 1 (2003): 55–63; C. R. Schroeder, "The Physical Geography of the Palouse Region, Washington and Idaho, and Its Relation to the Agricultural Economy." Unpublished Ph. D. thesis. Los Angeles: University of California, 1958.

5 Alan J. Busacca and Eric V. McDonald, *The Geomorphology and Paleopedology of the Palouse and Channeled Scabland: An Odyssey in Three Unnatural Acts: Guidebook.* Pullman, WA: Dept. of Crop and Soil Sciences, Dept. of Geology, Washington State University, 1994; John E. Allen, Marjorie Burns, and Sam C. Sargent, *Cataclysms on the Columbia: A Layman's Guide to the Features Produced by the Catastrophic Bretz Floods in the Pacific Northwest,* Portland, OR: Timber Press. 1986.

6 Willis Johns oral history, 1983.

7 Ella E. Clark, *Indian Legends of the Pacific Northwest*, Berkeley: University of California Press, 1953.

8 Peter Rice oral history, 2001.

9 Emily Peone oral history, 1981.

10 Mary Jim oral history, 1979; Eugene S. Hunn and James. Selam, *Nch'i-Wána, "the Big River": Mid-Columbia Indians and Their Land*, Seattle: University of Washington Press, 1990.

11 Charles V. Piper and R. Kent Beattie, *Flora of Southeastern Washington and Adjacent Idaho.* Lancaster, PA: New Era Printing Company, 1914; Sellars G. Archer and Clarence E. Bunch, *American Grass Book: A Manual of Pasture and Range Practices.* Norman: University of Oklahoma Press, 1953; Mary Jim, 1979.

12 Mary Jim oral history, 1979; Hunn and Selam, *Nch'i-Wána, "the Big River".*

13 Andrew George oral history, 1981.

14 Mary Jim oral history, 1979; Andrew George oral history, 1981.

Chapter II: Pathfinders and Traders

1 Gary E. Moulton, *The Journals of Lewis and Clark, Vol. V.* Lincoln: University of Nebraska Press, 1988.

2 Moulton, *Journals of Lewis and Clark, Vol. V.*

3 Moulton, *Journals of Lewis and Clark, Vol. V.*

4 J. B. Tyrrell (ed.), *David Thompson's Narrative of His Explorations in Western America, 1784-1912.* Toronto: The Champlain Society, 1914.

5 Ross Cox, *The Columbia River; or, Scenes and Adventures during a Residence of Six Years on the Western Side of the Rocky Mountains among Various Tribes of Indians Hitherto Unknown; Together with a Journey across the American Continent.* London: H. Colburn and R. Bentley, 1831.

6 W. Morwood, *Traveler in a Vanished Landscape: The Life and Times of David Douglas.* New York: Clarkson N. Potter, 1973.

7 David Douglas, *Journal Kept by David Douglas during His Travels in North America 1823-1827 Together with a Particular Description of Thirty-Three Species of American Oaks and Eighteen Species of Pinus, with Appendices Containing a List of the Plants Introduced by Douglas and an Account of His Death in 1834.*

following spread

Blue Hills

east of
St. John, Washington

London: W. Wesley & Son, 1914; Helmut K. Buechner, *Some Biotic Changes in the State of Washington, Particularly during the Century 1853–1953.* Pullman, WA: State College of Washington, 1953.

8 Cox, *The Columbia River.*

9 Oscar O. Winther, *The Old Oregon Country: A History of Frontier Trade, Transportation, and Travel,* Bloomington: Indiana University Press, 1950; Roland von Bothmer, et. al., *Diversity in Barley,* 2003.

10 Klippart, John H., *The Wheat Plant: Its Origin, Culture, Growth, Development, Composition, Varieties, Diseases, Etc., Etc. Together with a Few Remarks on Indian Corn, Its Culture, Etc.* Cincinnati: Moore, Wilstach, Keys & Co., 1860; James R. Gibson, *Farming the Frontier: The Agricultural Opening of the Oregon Country, 1786–1846,* Seattle: University of Washington Press, 1985. Columbia Department grain and vegetable lists are from Fort Vancouver Identification Books in Appendix A of Terri A. Taylor and Patricia C. Erigero, *Cultural Landscape Report: Fort Vancouver National Historic Site, Vancouver, Washington,* Seattle: National Park Service, Dept. of the Interior, Cultural Resources Division, Pacific Northwest Region, 1992. Landraces are "land strains" of mixed genetic integrity with common appearance adapted over generations to a particular geographic home area. They may change when grown elsewhere due to genetic, soil, and climatic variations and cultivation practices. A cultivar is a reproducible taxon selected for a particular attribute or set of attributes. See A. C. Zeven, "Landraces: A Review of Definitions and Classification," *Euphytica,* 104, no. 2 (1998): 127–39.

11 J. Orin Oliphant, "Old Fort Colville, Part I." *Washington Historical Quarterly* 16, no. 1, 1925. Russian-America grain reference in Appendix B of Terri A. Taylor and Patricia C. Erigero, *Cultural Landscape Report: Fort Vancouver National Historic Site, Vancouver, Washington, Volume I,* Seattle: National Park Service, Dept. of the Interior, Cultural Resources Division, Pacific Northwest Division, 1992.

12 H. Reginald Buller, *Essays on* Wheat, *Including the Discovery and Introduction of Marquis Wheat, the Early History of Wheat-Growing in Manitoba, Wheat in Western Canada, the Origin of Red Bobs and Kitchener, and the Wild Wheat of Palestine,* New York: The McMillan Company, 1919; L. H. Newman, J. G. C. Fraser, and A. G. O. Whiteside, *Handbook of Canadian Spring Wheat Varieties.* Department of Agriculture Farmers Bulletin 18. Ottawa, Canada: Cereal Division Experimental Farms Service, 1946.

13 *Spokane Times,* August 28, 1879; David Blaine letter, November 21, 1854, in Richard A. Sieber, ed. *Memoirs of Puget Sound, Early Seattle 1853–1856: The Letters of David and Catherine Blaine.* Fairfield, WA: Ye Galleon Press, 1978.

14 *Yakima Herald,* August 8, 1889.

15 James R. Gibson, *Farming the Frontier: The Agricultural Opening of the Oregon Country, 1786–1846,* Seattle: University of Washington Press, 1985; Winther, *The Old Oregon Country.*

16 Sid White and S. E. Solberg, eds. *Peoples of Washington: Perspectives on Cultural Diversity.* Pullman: Washington State University Press, 1989; Theodore Stern, *Chiefs & Chief Traders: Indian Relations at Fort Nez Percés, 1818-1855.* Corvallis: Oregon State University Press, 1993.

17 Emily Peone oral history, 1981.

18 Richard D. Scheuerman and Michael Finley, *Finding Chief Kamiakin: The Life and Legacy of a Northwest Patriot.* Pullman: Washington State University Press, 2008.

19 Emily Peone oral history, 1981; Theodore Winthrop, *The Canoe and the Saddle: Adventures among the North-Western Rivers and Forests, and Isthmiana.* Boston: Ticknor and Fields, 1863.

20 James R. Gibson, *Farming the Frontier: The Agricultural Opening of the Oregon Country, 1786–1846,* Seattle: University of Washington Press, 1985.

Chapter III: Immigrants and Exiles

1 Clifford M. Drury, *Marcus Whitman, M. D., Pioneer and Martyr,* Caldwell, ID: Caxton Press, 1937; George H. Himes (ed.). "Letters Written by Mrs. Whitman from Oregon to Her Relations in New York," *Transactions of the Oregon Pioneer Association,* 1891.

2 Paul Kane, *Wanderings of an Artist among the Indians of North America, from Canada to Vancouver's Island and Oregon, through the Hudson's Bay Company's Territory and Back Again.* London: Longman, Brown, Green, Longmans, and Roberts, 1859; Henry Warre, *Sketches in North America and the Oregon Territory,* London: Dickinson & Company, 1848.

facing page

Leonard's Bow

east of
Pullman, Washington

3 Eliza Warren Spalding, *Memoirs of the West.* Portland, OR: Marsh Printing Company, 1916.

4 Isaac I. Stevens, *Report of Explorations for a Route for the Pacific Railroad.* 33rd Congress, 2nd session, SED 78; Washington, D.C., 1860:197–99; Clifford E. Trafzer and Richard D. Scheuerman, *Renegade Tribe: The Palouse Indians and the Invasion of the Inland Pacific Northwest,* Pullman: Washington State University Press, 1986.

5 William C. Brown, ed., "The Mary Moses Statement," unpublished manuscript, 1918. W. C. Brown Collection, Manuscripts, Archives, and Special Collections, Washington State University Libraries, Pullman, WA.

6 Emily Peone oral history, 1981; Fr. Thomas Connolly, S.J. oral history, 2007.

7 Donald Meinig, *The Great Columbia Plain: A Historical Geography, 1860–1910.* Seattle: University of Washington Press, 1968.

8 John Mullan, *Report of Lieutenant Mullan, in Charge of the Construction of the Military Road from Fort Benton to Fort Walla Walla (36th Cong., 2nd sess., H.E.D. 44).* Washington, D.C., 1860.

9 Isaac Stevens, *Report of Explorations*; John Mullan, Topographical Memoir and Map of Colonel Wright's Late Campaign Against the Indians in Oregon and Washington Territories (35th Cong., 2nd sess., S.E.D. 32), Washington, D.C., 1859; Paul D. McDermott, and Ronald E. Grim. *Gustavus Sohon's Cartographic and Artistic Works: An Annotated Bibliography.* Washington, DC: Geography and Map Division, Library of Congress, 2002.

10 Edward J. Kowrach and Thomas E. Connolly, *Saga of the Coeur d'Alene Indians: An Account of Chief Joseph Seltice.* Fairfield, WA: Ye Galleon Press, 1990.

11 Leoti L. West, *The Wide Northwest: Historic Narrative of America's Wonder Land as Seen by a Pioneer Teacher, Leoti L. West.* Spokane, WA: Shaw & Borden Company, 1927.

12 Cleveland Kamiakin oral history, 1956. R. Ruby Collection, Museum of Arts & Culture, Spokane, WA; Andrew George oral history, 1981.

13 Click Relander, *Drummers and Dreamers,* Caldwell, ID: Caxton Printers, 1956; Fr. Thomas Connolly, S. J., oral history, 2007.

14 George Hunter, *Reminiscences of an Old Timer: A Recital of the Actual Events, Incidents, Trials, Hardships, Vicissitudes, Adventures, Perils, and Escapes of a Pioneer, Hunter, Miner and Scout of the Pacific Northwest: Together with His Later Experiences in Official and Business Capacities, and a Brief Description of the Resources, Beauties and Advantages of the New Northwest: The Several Indian Wars, Anecdotes, Etc.* San Francisco: H.S. Crocker and Company, 1887.

15 Emily Peone oral history, 1981; John Grant oral history, 2007.

16 Emily Peone oral history, 1981; Ben Owhi, oral history, 1919, L. V. McWhorter Collection, Manuscripts, Archives, and Special Collections, Washington State University Libraries, Pullman.

17 *Wilbur Register,* September 5, 1890; *Spokane Falls Review,* April 9, 1891.

18 *Wilbur Register,* June 30, 1893.

19 *Annual Report of the Commissioner of Indian Affairs, for the Year 1897.*

20 Andrew George oral history, 1981.

21 Floyd Honn oral history, 2006; Gordon Fisher oral history, 2005.

22 Richard D. Scheuerman and Clifford E. Trafzer, *River Song: Naxiyamtáma (Snake River-Palouse) Oral Traditions from Mary Jim, Andrew George, Gordon Fisher, and Emily Peone.* Pullman: Washington State University Press, 2015: 80–81.

23 Gordon Fisher oral history, 2005.

Chapter IV: Settlers and Ranchers

1 Richard D. Scheuerman, John Clement, and Alexander C. McGregor. *Palouse Country: A Land and Its People.* Oral history ed. Self-published, 2003

2 Kingston, Ceylon Samuel., and Jay W. Rea. *The Inland Empire in the Pacific Northwest: Historical Studies and Sketches of Ceylon S. Kingston.* Fairfield, WA: Ye Galleon Press, 1951.

3 Randall V. Mills, *Sternwheelers Up Columbia: A Century of Steamboating in the Oregon Country,* Palo Alto, CA: Pacific Books, 1947.

4 Julia Pardoe, *An Illustrated History of North Idaho.* Western Publishing Company, 1903.

5 Lyons Ferry was later acquired by W. I. Cummings and eventually by Nye and Ruth Turner who operated this last ferry service across the Snake River until its closure in 1968.

6 *An Illustrated History of Whitman County,* Spokesman-Review, June 17, 1909.

facing page

Steptoe Winter

east of
Steptoe, Washington

14 Enoch Bryan, *Orient Meets Occident: The Advent of the Railways to the Pacific Northwest.* Pullman, Washington: Student Book Corporation, 1936.

15 *Oregon Improvement Company Stockholder's Report*, 1881, Thomas Tannatt Papers, Manuscripts, Archives, and Special Collections, Washington State University Libraries, Pullman, WA.

16 *Palouse Gazette*, November 16, 1881.

17 *Palouse City Boomerang*, September 20, 1882.

18 Fred Yoder, *Pioneer Social Adaptation in the Palouse Country of Eastern Washington, 1870–1890.* Reprint from *Research Studies of the State College of Washington* 6, no. 4, 1938.

19 Jacob Adler oral history, 1973.

20 Ben and Bernice Kromm oral history, 2003; Eula Hastings oral history, 2003.

21 Frank T. Gilbert, *Historical Sketches: Walla Walla, Whitman, Columbia and Garfield Counties, Washington Territory, and Umatilla County, Oregon.* Portland, OR: Printing and Lithographing House of A.G. Walling, 1882; Robert W. Swanson, "A History of Logging and Lumbering on the Palouse River, 1870–1905." Master's thesis, State College of Washington, Pullman, 1958.

23 John Fahey, *The Inland Empire: Unfolding Years, 1879-1929.* Seattle: University of Washington Press, 1986.

24 Alexander McGregor oral history, 2010; Donald Schmick oral history, 2010.

25 Dan Morgan, *Merchants of Grain.* New York: Viking Press, 1979. The globally prominent firms Louis-Dreyfus, Bunge, and corporate Fribourg heir Continental Grain dominated Pacific Northwest grain exports through much of the twentieth century. Cargill acquired the Snake River Bunge and Continental operations in the 1990s.

26 Daniel Meissner, "Theodore B. Wilcox: Captain of Industry and Magnate of the China Flour Trade, 1884–1918." *Oregon Historical Quarterly* 104, no. 4 (Winter 2003).

27 Eddy Eng oral history, 2010; Meissner, *Theodore B. Wilcox.*

28 Meissner, *Theodore B. Wilcox*; Phyllis Kaiser, "Tacoma's Floury Past," *Tacoma: Voices of the Past.* Tacoma: Pierce County Washington State Centennial Committee, 1989.

29 Marlo Ochs oral history, 1991; Forest Garrett oral history, 1979.

30 William. O. Douglas; *Go East, Young Man: The Autobiography of William O. Douglas*, New York: Random House, 1974; Thomas B. Keith, *The Horse Interlude*, Moscow: University of Idaho Press, 1976.

31 Forest Garrett oral history, 1979; Marlo Ochs oral history, 1991.

32 *Palouse Republic*, August 20, 1893.

33 Douglas, *Go East, Young Man.*

34 I am indebted to Dennis Solbrack, Lee McGuire, Bruce LePage, Arvin Edstrom, brothers Jim and Mike Kroll, and Greg Druffel for the chronology and descriptions of Palouse Country harvesting equipment innovations. Various dates have been reported with these and other inventions since the development process takes place over years with formation of a concept, protype development, patent application and subsequent registration, and eventual manufacture. John Deere discontinued production of hillside combines in 1984 which led to a joint effort between the company and the R. A. Hanson Company of Spokane to manufacture the 7722 model in 1986 which leveled up to 45% and also featured improved horsepower to weight ratio. In the early 1990s Hillco Technologies of Nez Perce, Idaho, developed the first aftermarket mechanisms to convert new level-land combines for hillside operation. Palouse Country farmer-inventors also developed innovative tillage and seeding equipment including brothers Kyle and Cleve Wolfe's rotary rod weeder (c. 1910), the rotary subsoiler by Claude Caulkins and Lawrence Hunt (c. 1940), steel shank fertilizer applicator by Sherman McGregor, Cliff Rollins, and Chester Field (c. 1950), Arlie Hill's fold-up harrow cart (c. 1955), the deep-furrow split-packer drill by Robert Zimmerman (c. 1962), and Morton Swanson's no-till drill (c. 1974).

Chapter VI: Crossroads and Communities

1 Robert Hitchman, *Place Names of Washington.* Tacoma: Washington State Historical Society, 1985; Julie R. Monroe, *Living and Learning on the Palouse,* Charleston, SC: Arcadia Publishing, 2003.

2 Roland Bainton, *Pilgrim Parson: The Life of James Herbert Bainton.* New York: Thomas Nelson & Sons, 1958.

3 Events surrounding the tragedy were related by an employee of the local hardware store where the perpetrators sought to purchase gunpowder shortly before the killing. The worker, a relative of the victim who feared reprisals, later related the events to his son, who told it to me in 1990. A year later I was traveling by train between Washington, DC, and

facing page

Fall Pocket

looking NW from Steptoe Butte

7 June Crithfield, *Of Yesterday and the River,* Pullman: WSU General Extension Services, 1973.

8 Mildred Lautensleger oral history, 2003; Ben and Bernice Kromm oral history, 2003.

9 Jack Philleo oral history, 1979; Ruth Kirk, Carmela Alexander, Louis Kirk, and David L. Nicandri, *Exploring Washington's Past: A Road Guide to History.* Seattle: University of Washington Press, 1990.

10 *An Illustrated History of Whitman County.*

11 Faye Patterson oral history, 1996; Miriam Trunkey, *We Got Here from There: About Schools in the Vicinity of St. John, Washington, 1883–1976.* St. John, WA: Junior Women's Club of St. John, Washington, 1976.

12 Fred Yoder, "Pioneer Adaptation in the Palouse Country of Eastern Washington." *Research Studies of the State College of Washington* 4, no. 4 (December 1938); *An Illustrated History of Whitman County.*

13 Joseph DeLong, Journals, 1863–1891. Private collection, St. John, Washington; *Walla Walla Statesman,* August 7, 1868; J. B. Holt, "The Honor Roll of Whitman Pioneers," *Pullman Herald,* December 2, 1921.

14 Frank T. Gilbert, *Historical Sketches: Walla Walla, Whitman, Columbia and Garfield Counties, Washington Territory, and Umatilla County, Oregon.* Portland, OR: Printing and Lithographing House of A.G. Walling, 1882; Robert W. Swanson, "A History of Logging and Lumbering on the Palouse River, 1870–1905." Master's thesis, State College of Washington, Pullman, 1958; Oakesdale's mill is a National Historic Site and Barron's son, Joseph, operated a smaller mill in an adjacent facility until the 1990s. He was responsible for coining the popular brand name "Nutrigrain," which was acquired by Kellogg's in 1982.

15 Leoti L. West, *The Wide Northwest: Historic Narrative of America's Wonder Land as Seen by a Pioneer Teacher, Leoti L. West,* Spokane, WA: Shaw & Borden Company, 1927.

16 Robert Howard oral history, 1996; Millie E. Fronek, *Pioneering in the Lower Palouse and the LaCrosse Country,* self-published, 1973.

17 Roy Smith, *Smith Bros. Shor-iz: The History of Andrew Jackson Smith and His Family and of Pine City, Washington,* self-published, 1960.

18 Marlo Ochs oral history, 1991; Ben and Bernice Kromm oral history, 2003.

19 Frank G. Roe, *The Indian and the Horse,* Norman: University of Oklahoma Press, 1955.

20 May Terrell oral history, 2003; Canutt, Yakima, and Oliver Drake. *Stunt Man: The Autobiography of Yakima Canutt with Oliver Drake.* Norman: University of Oklahoma Press, 1997.

21 John Crawford oral history, 2005.

22 Palmer J. Wagner, *The American Appaloosa Anthology,* Colbert, WA: self-published, 1999. George Hatley, "Appaloosa Sires of the Palouse Country and the Men Who Rode Them," *The Western Horseman* (March 1954).

Chapter V: Farming and Railroading

1 Fred Yoder, "Stories of Early Pioneers in Whitman County, Washington, 1937-1937," unpublished manuscript, Manuscripts, Archives, and Special Collections, Washington State University Libraries, Pullman, WA.

2 *Palouse Gazette,* April 22, 1879.

3 *Tenth U. S. Census,* Schedule 1 (Populations), 1880.

4 Ramon Huntley oral history, 2003; W. H. Lever, *An Illustrated History of Whitman County,* self-published, 1901.

5 Mary E. Reed and Keith C. Petersen, *Virgil T. McCroskey: Giver of Mountains,* Pullman: WSU Department of History, 1983; Jim Howell, Sr. oral history, 1991.

6 *Spokan Times,* May 14, 1879.

7 *Palouse Gazette,* April 10, 1879.

8 *Walla Walla Statesman,* June 14, 1876.

9 Alexander Campbell McGregor, *Counting Sheep: From Open Range to Agribusiness on the Columbia Plateau,* Seattle: University of Washington Press, 1982.

10 Marlo Ochs oral history, 1991; Joe Smith, *Bunchgrass Pioneer.* Fairfield, WA: Ye Galleon Press, 1986.

11 *Palouse Gazette,* August 22, 1884; *Colfax Commoner,* June 8, 1894; *Colfax Gazette,* July 13, 1972.

12 Henry Villard, *The Early History of Transportation in Oregon.* Eugene: University of Oregon Press, 1944.

13 Villard, *The Early History of Transportation in Oregon.*

Cashup Dawn   from Steptoe Butte

Predawn Reds   north of Waukon, Washington

Chicago and by coincidence met the victim's grandson, who said the family had never known the circumstances of the crime.

4 Gordon Fisher oral history, 2005.

5 Glen Leitz oral history, 1994.

6 Enoch Bryan, *Orient Meets Occident: The Advent of the Railways to the Pacific Northwest.* Pullman, WA: Student Book Corporation, 1936.

7 Bryan, *Orient Meets Occident; Palouse Gazette*, May 17, 1897.

8 Joseph DeLong, Journals, 1863–1891. Private collection, St. John, Washington.

9 *Palouse Gazette*, October 7, 1887; Alisa Repp, "Palouse Empire Horseracing." *Palouse Country Magazine* 1, no. 1 (Spring 1990); John Henry oral history, 2003.

10 Richard D. Scheuerman, ed., Serious Business: A History of Whitman County Basketball, Endicott, Washington: Endicott-St. John Cooperative Schools, 1993.

11 Clinton Miller oral history, 2003.

12 Theodore Roosevelt, *Address to the National Editorial Association,* Jamestown, VA, June 10, 1907.

13 *Palouse Republic*, April 14, 1911; Commission quotations in Theodore Saloutos and John D. Hicks, *Agricultural Discontent in the Middle West, 1900-1939*, Madison: University of Wisconsin Press, 1951.

14 Gus Norwood, *Washington Grangers Celebrate a Century.* Seattle: Washington State Grange, 1988; *Palouse Basin Study*, USDA, 1978.

15 Oscar Camp and Paul C. McGrew, *History of Washington's Soil and Water Conservation Districts.* Pullman: Washington Association of Soil and Water Conservation Districts, 1969; Dennis Roe and Richard Riehle oral histories, 2003.

Chapter VII: Education and Transformation

1 Keith C. Petersen, *Company Town: Potlatch, Idaho and the Potlatch Lumber Company,* Pullman: Washington State University Press, 1987.

2 John Fahey, *The Inland Empire: Unfolding Years, 1879–1929.* Seattle: University of Washington Press, 1986.

3 Mark Carleton, *The Basis for the Improvement of American Wheats.* Washington, DC: USDA Division of Vegetable Physiology and Pathology, 1900; Donald Meinig, *The Great Columbia Plain: A Historical Geography, 1860–1910.* Seattle: University of Washington Press, 1968.

4 Stephen Jones oral history, 2003.

5 E. F. Gaines, "Wheat Varieties in Washington, 1929," *Washington AES Bulletin 398* (April 1941); Orville Vogel oral history, 1973.

6 Rafe Gibbs, *Beacon for Mountain and Plain: Story of the University of Idaho,* Caldwell, ID: Caxton Printers, 1962.

7 Johannes and Anna Marie Rothe to Phillip and Anna Green, correspondence, December 18, 1883, private collection, Endicott, Washington.

8 Henry Lueg "Journal of a Trip from St. Paul, Minnesota to Portland, Oregon." Unpublished manuscript. Manuscripts, Archives, and Special Collections, Washington State University Libraries, 1867; *Walla Walla Union,* June 10, 1878.

9 Petersen, *Company Town.*

10 Sophie Delegans oral history, 1977; James Delegans oral history, 1989.

11 Mamie Oliver, "Idaho Ebony: The African American Presence in Idaho State History," *The Journal of African American History* 91, no. 1 (Winter 2006).

12 *Fourteenth U.S. Census,* Schedule 1 (Populations), 1920.

Chapter VIII: Appreciation and Renewal

1 *Seattle Post-Intelligencer*, September 29, 1994; Governor Mike Lowry oral history, 2007.

2 Norman Wirzba, *Food and Faith: A Theology of Eating.* New York: Cambridge University Press, 2011: 17.

3 Katherine Nelson oral history, 2018.

4 Matthew Weaver, "Agriculture Draws Out the Best," *Capital Press,* April 10, 2010; Anna Blomfield oral history, 2022.

5 Among the most recent developments in farm mechanization is the application of autonomous driving capabilities to tractors and combines. Technology has also transformed bulk grain handling facilities at strategically located places like Endicott and elsewhere along railroads and river ports. With the recent merger of the local Endicott-St. John grain storage cooperative with Walla Walla and other groups to form Northwest Grain

Growers, the new entity constructed a storage and 110-car unit train loading facility in Endicott since the line there had been constructed with heavier rail weight capacity. The project called for construction of seven immense steel silos located to bring total capacity there to approximately 3,100,000 bushels. The new facility, which became operational in 2020, is designed for rapid one-day loading of trains which are capable of holding 100 tons of grain per car for a total capacity of 420,000 bushels. Grain is trucked from farms and other elevators for rail shipment and barging along the lower Snake and Columbia Rivers to Portland and Kalama for distribution worldwide.

6 Bruce Holbert oral history, 2021; Bruce Holbert, "Ordinary Days," unpublished manuscript (2021). I am indebted to the author—my longtime friend, former teacher colleague, and fellow harvest truck driver, Bruce Holbert—for permission to reprint this selection.

7 On potential benefits and risks of gene editing, see Natalie de Souza, "Editing Humanity's Future," *The New York Review of Books* 68, no. 7 (April 29, 2021).

EPILOGUE

1 The Swadesh notebooks (MS 497.3.B63c/Ps1a.1) are in the Franz Boas Collection of American Indian Linguistics at the American Philosophical Society in Philadelphia. In addition to the Minthorns, Swadesh also mentions conversations in 1930 with Pete Kalaítin (Kalyton), a member of the Snake River-Palouse Harlish Wáshīmuxsh (Chief Wolf Necklace) family.

2 The Atilapum (Atinapam) stories appear in Appendix C of Richard D. Scheuerman and Clifford E. Trafzer, eds., River Song: Naxiyamtáma (Snake River-Palouse) Oral Traditions (Washington State University Press, 2015).

3 Minthorn spoke to Swadesh in the Nez Perce language while Atilapum related her oral histories in Snake River-Palouse. The texts are substantially continuous. Versification formatting here and in other publications is more consistent with Columbia Plateau storytelling traditions and guided by the excellent work of Rodney Frey, University of Idaho professor of American Indian studies and anthropology, and Carrie Jim Schuster.

4 Minthorn lists here the elements the traditional Columbia Plateau First Foods Feast in which participants first share life-giving water followed by the "chief" sustaining sacred resources: salmon to represent fish and venison for animals, followed by plants (bitterroot, camas) and fruits (currants, berries).

5 "Law" here in Nez Perce is tamáluwit; the related term in Snake River-Palouse Sahaptin is tamánwit. Snake River-Palouse elder Carrie Jim Schuster explains, "Human beings are to be stewards or proprietors of creation. Humanity exists in ahtow' (covenant relationship, sacred trust) with the Creator through which sustenance is provided to people, animals, and plants. This is what Chief Kamiakin and Columbia Plateau leaders of the nineteenth century meant when they spoke to government officials about the 'law' (támanwit)."

SELECTED BIBLIOGRAPHY

Manuscript Collections

American Philosophical Society, Philadelphia, PA—Franz Boas Collection of American Indian Linguistics (Morris Swadesh notebooks).

Colville Indian Reservation, History and Archaeology Office, Nespelem, WA—Colville Tribal Probate Records.

DeLong, Joseph. Journals, 1863–1891. Private collection, St. John, Washington.

Eastern Washington University, Archives and Special Collections, Cheney, WA—Ceylon S. Kingston and W. P. Winans Collections.

Gonzaga University, Foley Library Archives, Spokane, WA—Verne Ray Collection.

Museum of Arts & Culture, Spokane, WA—James Davis, James Doty, Robert Ruby, and Annine Harder Collections.

Spokane Public Library, Spokane, WA—Fr. Pierre DeSmet, James Montieth, and Isaac I. Stevens Collections

Washington State Historical Society Research Center, Tacoma, WA—Levi Ankeny, John Canse, and Robert Houston Milroy Collections.

Washington State University, Manuscripts, Archives, and Special Collections, Washington State University Libraries, Pullman, WA— William Compton Brown, Herman J. Deutsch, Hutchison Studio Photographs, George Benson Kuykendall, McGregor Family Papers, Lucullus Virgil McWhorter Papers, James Orin Oliphant, George Sutherland, Cull A. White, Whitman County Historical Society, and Fred Roy Yoder Collections.

Books, Pamphlets, Articles, Manuscripts, and Congressional Records

Allen, John E., Marjorie Burns, and Sam C. Sargent. *Cataclysms on the Columbia: A Layman's Guide to the Features Produced by the Catastrophic Bretz Floods in the Pacific Northwest.* Portland, OR: Timber Press. 1986.

An Illustrated History of North Idaho Embracing Nez Perces, Latah, Kootenai and Shoshone Counties. Western Historical Publishing Company, 1903.

Annual Report of the Commissioner of Indian Affairs, for the Year 1897. Washington, DC: Government Printing Office, 1897.

Archer, Sellers G., and Clarence E. Bunch. *American Grass Book: A Manual of Pasture and Range Practices.* Norman: University of Oklahoma Press, 1953.

Bainton, Roland. *Pilgrim Parson: The Life of James Herbert Bainton.* New York: Thomas Nelson & Sons, 1958.

Ball, Carleton. "The History of Wheat Improvement." *Agricultural History* 4, no. 2 (April 1930).

Bancroft, Hubert H. *The History of Washington, Oregon, and Montana, 1845–1889.* San Francisco: The History Company, 1890.

Berry, Wendell. *The Gift of Good Land: Further Essays Cultural and Agricultural.* San Francisco, 1981.

Berry, Wendell. *The Unsettling of America: Culture & Agriculture.* San Francisco, 1978.

Bezdicek, D. F, T Beaver, and D. Granatstein. "Subsoil Ridge Tillage and Lime Effects on Soil Microbial Activity, Soil pH, Erosion, and Wheat and Pea Yield in the Pacific Northwest, USA." *Soil & Tillage Research* 74, no. 1 (2003): 55–63.

Brown, William C. *The Indian Side of the Story.* Spokane, WA: C. W. Hill Printing Company, 1961.

Bryan, Enoch. *Orient Meets Occident: The Advent of the Railways to the Pacific Northwest.* Pullman, Washington: Student Book Corporation, 1936.

Buechner, Helmut K. *Some Biotic Changes in the State of Washington, Particularly during the Century 1853-1953.* Pullman, WA State College of Washington. 1953.

Buller, H. Reginald. *Essays on Wheat, Including the Discovery and Introduction of Marquis Wheat, the Early History of Wheat-Growing in Manitoba, Wheat in Western Canada, the Origin of Red Bobs and Kitchener, and the Wild Wheat of Palestine.* New York: The Macmillan Company, 1919.

facing page

Retired Palouse Schooners

west of Colfax, Washington

Hunter, George. *Reminiscences of an Old Timer: A Recital of the Actual Events, Incidents, Trials, Hardships, Vicissitudes, Adventures, Perils, and Escapes of a Pioneer, Hunter, Miner and Scout of the Pacific Northwest: Together with His Later Experiences in Official and Business Capacities, and a Brief Description of the Resources, Beauties and Advantages of the New Northwest: The Several Indian Wars, Anecdotes, Etc.* San Francisco: H.S. Crocker and Company, 1887.

Kaiser, Phyllis. "Tacoma's Floury Past," *Tacoma: Voices of the Past.* Tacoma: Pierce County Washington State Centennial Committee, 1989.

Kaiser, Verle G. "Straight as an Arrow—The Kentuck Trail." *The Pacific Northwesterner* 23, no. 2 (Spring 1977).

Kane, Paul. *Wanderings of an Artist among the Indians of North America, from Canada to Vancouver's Island and Oregon, through the Hudson's Bay Company's Territory and Back Again.* London: Longman, Brown, Green, Longmans, and Roberts, 1859.

Keith, Thomas B. *The Horse Interlude.* Moscow, ID: University of Idaho Press, 1976.

Kincaid, Garret D. *Palouse in the Making.* Palouse, WA: The Palouse Republic, 1934.

Kingston, Ceylon Samuel., and Jay W. Rea. *The Inland Empire in the Pacific Northwest: Historical Studies and Sketches of Ceylon S. Kingston.* Fairfield, WA: Ye Galleon Press, 1951.

Kirk, Ruth, Carmela Alexander, Louis Kirk, and David L. Nicandri. *Exploring Washington's Past: A Road Guide to History.* Seattle: University of Washington Press, 1990.

Klippart, John H. (John Hancock). *The Wheat Plant: Its Origin, Culture, Growth, Development, Composition, Varieties, Diseases, Etc., Together with a Few Remarks on Indian Corn, Its Culture, Etc.* Cincinnati: Moore, Wilstach, Keys & Co., 1860.

Kowrach, Edward J., and Thomas E. Connolly. *Saga of the Coeur d'Alene Indians: An Account of Chief Joseph Seltice.* Fairfield, WA: Ye Galleon Press, 1990.

Lever, W. H. *An Illustrated History of Whitman County.* Self-published, 1901.

Lueg, Henry. "Journal of a Trip from St. Paul, Minnesota to Portland, Oregon." Unpublished manuscript. Manuscripts, Archives, and Special Collections, Washington State University Libraries, 1867.

Manring, Benjamin F. *Conquest of the Coeur d'Alenes, Spokanes, and Palouses.* Fairfield, WA: Ye Galleon Press, 1975.

McDermott, Paul D., and Ronald E. Grim. *Gustavus Sohon's Cartographic and Artistic Works: An Annotated Bibliography.* Washington, DC: Geography and Map Division, Library of Congress, 2002.

McGregor, Alexander Campbell. *Counting Sheep: From Open Range to Agribusiness on the Columbia Plateau.* Seattle: University of Washington Press, 1982.

Meinig, Donald W. "Environment and Settlement in the Palouse, 1869–1910." Master's thesis, University of Washington, Seattle, 1950.

Meinig, Donald. *The Great Columbia Plain: A Historical Geography, 1860–1910.* Seattle: University of Washington Press, 1968.

Meissner, Daniel J. "Theodore B. Wilcox: Captain of Industry and Magnate of the China Flour Trade, 1884–1918." *Oregon Historical Quarterly* 104, no. 4 (Winter 2003).

Mills, Randall V. *Sternwheelers Up Columbia: A Century of Steamboating in the Oregon Country.* Palo Alto, CA: Pacific Books, 1947.

Monroe, Julie R. *Moscow: Living and Learning on the Palouse.* Charleston, SC: Arcadia, 2003.

Morwood, William. *Traveler in a Vanished Landscape: The Life and Times of David Douglas.* New York: Clarkson N. Potter, 1973.

Morgan, Dan. *Merchants of Grain.* New York: Viking Press, 1979.

Moulton, Gary E. *The Journals of Lewis and Clark. Vol. V.* Lincoln: University of Nebraska Press, 1988.

Mullan, John. Topographical Memoir and Map of Colonel Wright's Late Campaign Against the Indians in Oregon and Washington Territories (35th Cong., 2nd sess., S.E.D. 32). Washington, DC, 1859.

Mullan, John. *Report of Lieutenant Mullan, in Charge of the Construction of the Military Road from Fort Benton to Fort Walla Walla (36th Cong., 2nd sess., H.E.D. 44).* Washington, DC, 1860.

Newman, L. H., J. G. C. Fraser, and A. G. O. Whiteside. *Handbook of Canadian Spring Wheat Varieties.* Department of Agriculture Farmers Bulletin 18. Ottawa, Canada: Cereal Division Experimental Farms Service, 1937.

Norwood, Gus. *Washington Grangers Celebrate a Century.* Seattle: Washington State Grange, 1988.

Oliphant, J. Orin. "Old Fort Colville, Part I." *Washington Historical Quarterly* 16, no. 1 (January 1925).

Oliphant, J. Orin. "Old Fort Colville, Part II." *Washington Historical Quarterly* 16, no. 2 (March 1925).

facing page

Winter Lines

south of
Reardan, Washington

Busacca, Alan J. *Loess Deposits and Soils of the Palouse and Vicinity.* U. S. Geological Society of America, 1991.

Busacca, Alan J., and Eric V. McDonald. *The Geomorphology and Paleopedology of the Palouse and Channeled Scabland: An Odyssey in Three Unnatural Acts: Guidebook.* Pullman, WA: Dept. of Crop and Soil Sciences, Dept. of Geology, Washington State University, 1994.

Camp, Oscar, and Paul C. McGrew. *History of Washington's Soil and Water Conservation Districts.* Pullman: Washington Association of Soil and Water Conservation Districts, 1969.

Canutt, Yakima, and Oliver Drake. Stunt Man: The Autobiography of Yakima Canutt with Oliver Drake. Norman: University of Oklahoma Press, 1997.

Carleton, Mark. *The Basis for the Improvement of American Wheats.* Washington, DC: USDA Division of Vegetable Physiology and Pathology, 1900.

Clark, Ella E. *Indian Legends of the Pacific Northwest.* Berkeley: University of California Press, 1953.

Cox, Ross. *The Columbia River ; or, Scenes and Adventures during a Residence of Six Years on the Western Side of the Rocky Mountains among Various Tribes of Indians Hitherto Unknown; Together with a Journey across the American Continent.* London: H. Colburn and R. Bentley, 1831.

Creighton, Jeff. *Indian Summers: Washington State College and the Nespelem Art Colony, 1937–41.* Pullman: Washington State University Press, 2000.

Crithfield, June. *Of Yesterday and the River.* Pullman: WSU General Extension Services, 1973.

Cronin, William, ed. *Uncommon Ground: Rethinking the Human Place in Nature.* New York: Norton, 1996.

de Souza, Natalie. "Editing Humanity's Future." *The New York Review of Books* 68, no. 7: p. 21.

Douglas, David. *Journal Kept by David Douglas during His Travels in North America 1823-1827 Together with a Particular Description of Thirty-Three Species of American Oaks and Eighteen Species of Pinus, with Appendices Containing a List of the Plants Introduced by Douglas and an Account of His Death in 1834.* London: W. Wesley & Son, 1914.

Douglas, William O. *Go East, Young Man: The Autobiography of William O. Douglas.* New York: Random House, 1974.

Drury, Clifford M. *Marcus Whitman, M. D., Pioneer and Martyr.* Caldwell, ID: The Caxton Press, 1937.

Durham, Nelson Wayne, and Verle George Kaiser. *History of the City of Spokane and Spokane Country, Washington: From Its Earliest Settlement to the Present Time.* Spokane, WA: S.J. Clarke Publishing Company, 1912.

Erickson, Edith E., and Eddy Ng. *From Sojourner to Citizen: Chinese of the Inland Empire.* Colfax, WA: University Printing, 1989.

Fahey, John. *The Inland Empire: Unfolding Years, 1879–1929.* Seattle: University of Washington Press, 1986.

Fronek, Millie E. *Pioneering in the Lower Palouse and the LaCrosse Country.* Self-published, 1973.

Gaines, E. F. "Wheat Varieties in Washington, 1929," *Washington AES Bulletin 398* (April 1941).

Gibbs, Rafe. *Beacon for Mountain and Plain: Story of the University of Idaho.* Caldwell, ID: Caxton Printers, 1962.

Gibson, James R. *Farming the Frontier: The Agricultural Opening of the Oregon Country, 1786–1846.* Seattle: University of Washington Press, 1985.

Gilbert, Frank T. *Historical Sketches: Walla Walla, Whitman, Columbia and Garfield Counties, Washington Territory, and Umatilla County, Oregon.* Portland, OR: Printing and Lithographing House of A.G. Walling, 1882.

Haines, Francis. *Appaloosa: The Spotted Horse in Art and History.* Austin: University of Texas Press, 1963.

Harder, Annine F. *Opportunities of the Golden West.* Spokane WA: Ross Print. Co., 1960.

Hatley, George. "Appaloosa Sires of the Palouse Country and the Men Who Rode Them." *The Western Horseman* (March 1954).

Hedges, James B. *Henry Villard and the Railways of the Northwest.* New Haven: Yale University Press, 1930.

Himes, George H. (ed.). "Letters Written by Mrs. Whitman from Oregon to Her Relations in New York." *Transactions of the Oregon Pioneer Association,* 1891.

Hitchman, Robert. *Place Names of Washington.* Tacoma, WA: Washington State Historical Society, 1985.

Holbert, Bruce. "Ordinary Days." Unpublished manuscript. 2021

Holt, J. B., "The Honor Roll of Whitman Pioneers," *Pullman Herald,* December 2, 1921.

Hunn, Eugene S., and James. Selam. *Nch'i-Wána, "the Big River": Mid-Columbia Indians and Their Land.* Seattle: University of Washington Press, 1990.

Silver Light looking south from Steptoe Butte

Winter's Isolation near Fairfield, Washington

Oliver, Mamie. "Idaho Ebony: The African American Presence in Idaho State History." *The Journal of African American History* 91, no. 1 (Winter 2006).

Olmstead, Alan. "The Red Queen and Hard Reds." *The Journal of Economic History* 62, no. 4 (December 2002).

Oregon Improvement Company Stockholder's Report, 1881, Thomas Tannatt Papers, Manuscripts, Archives, and Special Collections, Washington State University Libraries, Pullman, WA.

Owens, Jay. Dust: The Modern World in a Trillion Particles. New York: Abrams, 2023.

Owhi, Ben. Oral history. L. V. McWhorter Collection, Manuscripts, Archives, and Special Collections, Washington State University Libraries, Pullman, WA, 1919.

Palouse Cooperative River Basin Study. Washington, DC: U.S. Department of Agriculture, 1978.

Pardoe, Julia. *An Illustrated History of North Idaho*. Western Publishing Company, 1903.

Paulsen, Gary M, and James P Shroyer. "Early History of Wheat Improvement in the Great Plains." *Agronomy Journal* 100, no. 3 (2008): S70–78.

Petersen, Keith C. *Company Town: Potlatch, Idaho, and the Potlatch Lumber Company*. Pullman: Washington State University Press, 1987.

Piper, Charles V. and R. Kent Beattie. *Flora of the Palouse Region*. Pullman: Washington State Agricultural College, 1901.

Piper, Charles V., and R. Kent Beattie. *Flora of Southeastern Washington and Adjacent Idaho*. Lancaster, PA: New Era Printing Company, 1914.

Reed, Mary E., and Keith C. Petersen. *Virgil T. McCroskey: Giver of Mountains*. Pullman: WSU Department of History, 1983.

Reed, Norman. "Flour Milling in Washington." *Columbia Magazine* 22, no. 4 (Winter 2008–09).

Relander, Click. *Drummers and Dreamers*. Caldwell, ID: Caxton Printers, 1956.

Repp, Alisa. "Palouse Empire Horseracing." *Palouse Country Magazine* 1, no. 1 (Spring 1990).

Roe, Frank G. *The Indian and the Horse*. Norman: University of Oklahoma Press, 1955.

Roosevelt, Theodore. *Address to the National Editorial Association*. Jamestown, VA, June 10, 1907.

Sager, Matilda J. *A Survivor's Recollections of the Whitman Massacre*. Spokane, WA: Daughters of the American Revolution, 1920,

Saloutos, Theodore, and John D. Hicks. *Agricultural Discontent in the Middle West, 1900–1939*. Madison: University of Wisconsin Press, 1951.

Schaffer, E. C. "Wheat Varieties in Washington." *Washington Agricultural Extension Bulletin 207* (1926).

Scheuerman, Richard D., ed. Serious Business: A History of Whitman County Basketball. Endicott, Washington: Endicott-St. John Cooperative Schools, 1993

Scheuerman, Richard D., John Clement, and Alexander C. McGregor. *Palouse Country: A Land and Its People*. Oral history ed. Self-published, 2003.

Scheuerman, Richard D., and Michael O. Finley. Finding Chief Kamiakin: The Life and Legacy of a Northwest Patriot. Pullman: Washington State University Press, 2008.

Scheuerman, Richard D., and Clifford E. Trafzer, eds. *River Song: Naxiyamtáma (Snake River-Palouse) Oral Traditions from Mary Jim, Andrew George, Gordon Fisher, and Emily Peone*. Pullman: Washington State University Press, 2015.

Scheuerman, Richard D., and Clifford E. Trafzer. *The Volga Germans: Pioneers of the Pacific Northwest*. Moscow: University of Idaho Press, 1980.

Schroeder, Carleton R. "The Physical Geography of the Palouse Region, Washington and Idaho, and Its Relation to the Agricultural Economy." Unpublished PhD. thesis. Los Angeles: University of California, 1958.

Sieber, Richard A., ed. *Memoirs of Puget Sound, Early Seattle 1853–1856: The Letters of David and Catherine Blaine*. Fairfield, WA: Ye Galleon Press, 1978.

Simpson, George. *Fur Trade and Empire: George Simpson's Journal: Remarks Connected with the Fur Trade in the Course of a Voyage from York Factory to Fort George and Back to York Factory 1824-1825: Together with Accompanying Documents*. Edited by Frederick Merk. Cambridge, MA: Harvard University Press, 1931.

Smith, Joe. *Bunchgrass Pioneer*. Fairfield, WA: Ye Galleon Press, 1986.

Smith, Roy. *Smith Bros. Shor-iz: The History of Andrew Jackson Smith and His Family and of Pine City, Washington*. Self-published, 1960.

Spalding, Eliza Warren. *Memoirs of the West*. Portland, OR: Marsh Printing Company, 1916.

Splawn, Andrew J. *Ka-Mi-Akin: The Last Hero of the Yakimas*. Caldwell, ID: Caxton Printers, 1944.

Stern, Theodore. *Chiefs & Chief Traders: Indian Relations at Fort Nez Percés, 1818–1855.* Corvallis: Oregon State University Press, 1993.

Stevens, Isaac I. *Report of Explorations for a Route for the Pacific Railroad.* 33rd Congress, 2nd session, SED 78; Washington, DC, 1860.

Stratton, David H., ed. *Spokane and the Inland Empire: An Interior Pacific Northwest Anthology.* Pullman: Washington State University Press, 1991.

Swanson, Robert W. "A History of Logging and Lumbering on the Palouse River, 1870–1905." Master's thesis, State College of Washington, Pullman, 1958.

Taylor, Terri A., and Patricia C. Erigero. *Cultural Landscape Report: Fort Vancouver National Historic Site, Vancouver, Washington.* Seattle: National Park Service, Dept. of the Interior, Cultural Resources Division, Pacific Northwest Region, 1992.

Thompson, Albert W. "The Early History of the Palouse River and Its Names." *Pacific Northwest Quarterly* 62, no. 2 (April 1971).

Todd, C. C. "Origin and Meaning of the Geographic Name Palouse." *Washington Historical Quarterly* 24, no. 3 (July 1933).

Trafzer, Clifford E. and Richard D. Scheuerman. *Renegade Tribe: The Palouse Indians and the Invasion of the Inland Pacific Northwest.* Pullman: Washington State University Press, 1986.

Trunkey, Miriam. *We Got Here from There: About Schools in the Vicinity of St. John, Washington, 1883–1976.* St John, WA: Junior Women's Club of St. John, Washington, 1976.

Tyrrell, J.B., ed. *David Thompson's Narrative of His Explorations in Western America, 1784–1912.* Toronto: The Champlain Society, 1914.

Villard, Henry. *The Early History of Transportation in Oregon.* Eugene: University of Oregon Press, 1944.

von Bothmer, Roland, Theo van Hintum, Helmut Knüpffer, and Kazuhiro Sato, eds. *Diversity in Barley.* Amsterdam: Elsevier, 2003.

Wagner, Palmer J. *The American Appaloosa Anthology.* Colbert, WA: self-published, 1999.

Waldbauer, Richard C. *Grubstaking the Palouse: Gold Mining in the Hoodoo Mountains of North Idaho, 1860–1950.* Pullman: Washington State University Press, 1986.

Walton, John R. "Varietal Innovations and Competitiveness of the British Cereals Sector, 1760-1930." *The Agricultural History Review* 47, no. 1 (1999): 29–57.

Warre, Henry. *Sketches in North America and the Oregon Territory.* London: Dickinson & Company, 1848.

Weaver, Matthew. "Agriculture Draws Out the Best." *Capital Press,* April 10, 2010.

West, Leoti L. *The Wide Northwest: Historic Narrative of America's Wonder Land as Seen by a Pioneer Teacher, Leoti L. West.* Spokane, WA: Shaw & Borden Company, 1927.

White, Sid, and S. E. Solberg, eds. *Peoples of Washington: Perspectives on Cultural Diversity.* Pullman: Washington State University Press, 1989.

Winther, Oscar O. *The Old Oregon Country: A History of Frontier Trade, Transportation, and Travel.* Bloomington: Indiana University Press, 1950.

Winthrop, Theodore. *The Canoe and the Saddle: Adventures among the North-Western Rivers and Forests, and Isthmiana.* Boston: Ticknor and Fields, 1863.

Wirzba, Norman. *Food and Faith: A Theology of Eating.* New York: Cambridge University Press, 2011.

Yeager, Walter M. "The Pioneer's Problems of Land Acquisition under the Public Land Laws in Southeastern Washington: 1850–1883." Master's thesis, Washington State University, 1961.

Yoder, Fred. "Stories of Early Pioneers in Whitman County, Washington." WSU Archives, Pullman, WA. 1937.

Yoder, Fred. "Pioneer Adaptation in the Palouse Country of Eastern Washington." *Research Studies of the State College of Washington* 6, no. 4 (December 1938).

Yoder, Fred. "Social Processes of Pioneering." *Research Studies of the State College of Washington* 10 (December 1942).

Zeven, A. C. "Landraces: A Review of Definitions and Classification," Euphytica 104: no. 2 (1998).

Zeven, A. C. And T. J. L van Hintum. "Classification Of Landraces And Improved Cultivars of Hexaploid Wheats (Triticum-Aestivum, T-Compactum And T-Spelta) Grown in the USA and Described in 1922." *Euphytica* 59, no. 1 (1991): 33–47.

Oral Histories

Adams, Glen. Fairfield, Washington; May 19, 1982.

Adler, Jacob. Tekoa, Washington; January 2, 1973.

Andrews, Albert Redstar. Nespelem, Washington; June 26, 2007.

Bailey, Floyd and Barbara. Ewan, Washington; February 11, 2006.

Belsby, Louise. St. John, Washington; November 5, 1996.

Blank, Julia. Rosalia, Washington; July 30, 1980.

Blomfield, Anna. Silver City, New Mexico. March 30, 2022.

Blumenschein, Conrad. St. John, Washington; May 6, 1980.

Connolly, S.J., Fr. Thomas. Desmet, Idaho, July 19, 2007.

Crawford, John. Malibu, California. June 10, 2000.

Delegans, James. Spokane, Washington; August 5, 1989.

Delegans, Sophie. Colfax, Washington; July 10, 1977. WCHS.

DeLong, Ray. St. John, Washington; July 19, 1980.

Devlin, Leonard (Jones). Dusty, Washington; July 16, 1980.

Druffel, Greg. Colton, Washington. March 12, 2022.

Edstrom, Arvin. Fernwood, Idaho. September 3, 2016.

Emberson, Joseph. Colfax, Washington; July 28, 1980.

Eng, Eddy. Colfax, Washington; November 7, 2010.

Eng, Owen. Colfax, Washington; July 25, 1989.

Fisher, Gordon. Lapwai, Idaho, June 19 and 24, 2005.

Garrett, Forest. Spokane, Washington; March 25, 1979.

George, Andrew. Toppenish, Washington; May 5, 1981.

Grant, John. Nespelem, Washington; November 10, 2007.

Harder, Herman. Aspen Creek Ranch, Washington; May 3, 2003.

Hastings, Eula. Pomeroy, Washington; May 8, 2003.

Henry, John. Colfax, Washington; April 22, 2003.

Holbert, Bruce. Blanchard, Idaho. October 29, 2021.

Honn, Floyd. Benge, Washington; February 2, 2006.

Howard, Robert. St. John, Washington. May 12, 1996.

Howell, Jim Sr. St. John, Washington; April 9, 1991.

Huntley, Ramon. Endicott, Washington; February 8, 2003.

Jenkins, Charlie. St. John, Washington; June 12, 1970.

Jim, Mary. Parker, Washington; April 2, November 10 and 11, 1979.

Johns, Willis. Butte, Montana. July 22, 1983.

Jones, Stephen. Pullman, Washington; August 5, 2003.

Kamiakin, Arthur Tomeo. Nespelem, Washington; June 16, 1972.

Kriebel, Mahlon. Garfield, Washington; May 16, 2008.

Kroll, Jim and Mike. Colfax, Washington. February 17, 2022.

Kromm, Ben and Bernice. Colfax, Washington; May 4, 2003.

Lally, Joyce. Endicott, Washington; March 28, 2003.

Lautensleger, Mildred. Vancouver, Washington; April 20, 2007.

Leitz, Glen. Fairfield, Washington; February 24, 1994.

LePage, Bruce. Pasco, Washington. November 4, 2021.

Lowry, Mike, Washington. 2007

McGregor, Alexander. Colfax, Washington; October 29, 2010.

McGregor, Sherman. Colfax, Washington; October 15, 1972.

McGuire, Lee. Cashup, Washington. February 9, 2022.

McNeilly, Bill and Polly. Colfax, Washington; August 9, 1980.

Metzker, Ethel. Spokane, Washington; March 11, 2003.

Miller, Clinton. Ewan, Washington; April 20, 2023.

Miller, Glen and Beulah. Diamond, Washington; August 5, 1993.

Nelson, Katherine. Coeur d'Alene, Idaho. July 12, 2018.

Ochs, Marlo. Endicott, Washington; October 8, 1991.

Parrish, Dick. Benge, Washington; May 10, 1993.

Patterson, Faye. Ewan, Washington; January 16, 1996.

Peone, Emily. Nespelem, Washington; June 14, 1981.

Philleo, Jack. Cheney, Washington; November 5, 1979.

Reich, Ray and Evelyn. Colfax, Washington; May 7, 2003.

Rice, Peter. Colfax, Washington; March 3, 2001.

Riehle, Richard. St. John, Washington; May 16, 2003.

Roe, Dennis. Colfax, Washington; June 12, 2003.

Schierman, Dave. College Place, Washington; July 9, 1972.

Schmick, Conrad G. Colfax, Washington; April 14, 1979.

Schmick, Donald. Colfax, Washington; April 5, 2008; October 29, 2010.

Schnaible, Fred and Dorothy. Moscow, Idaho; July 25, 1980.

Sijohn, Cliff and Frank. Plummer, Idaho; May 16, 2008.

Slind, Oscar and Ruth. Kendrick, Idaho; August 5, 1980.

Solbrack, Dennis. Colfax, Washington. May 1, 2020.

Stueckle, J. A. Lacrosse, Washington; July 17, 1980.

Terrell, May. Cashmere, Washington, March 6, 2003.

Vincent, Audra. Plummer, Idaho. May 3, 2021.

Vogel, Orville. Pullman, Washington; October 5, 1973.

Whelan, Richard. Colfax, Washington; July 3 1, 1980.

Williams, Bertha. Tekoa, Washington; July 30, 1980.

Newspapers

Colfax Commoner	*Fairfield Standard*	*Moscow Mirror*	*Palouse Republic*	*Sprague Advocate*
Colfax Gazette	*Garfield Enterprise*	*North Idaho Star (Moscow)*	*Pullman Herald*	*St. John Advocate*
Colton News-Letter	*Kendrick Gazette*	*Oakesdale Tribune*	*Seattle Post-Intelligencer*	*Tekoa Standard-Register*
Elberton Wheatbelt	*LaCrosse Clipper*	*Palouse City Boomerang*	*Spokan Times*	*Walla Walla Statesman*
Endicott Index	*Lewiston Teller*	*Palouse Gazette (Colfax)*	*Spokesman-Review*	*Washtucna Enterprise*

Afternoon Storms

from Steptoe Butte

INDEX OF NAMES, PLACES, AND EVENTS

facing page

Summer's Morning Light

Looking south from Steptoe Butte

About the Authors

Richard D. Scheuerman, who was raised on a farm between the Palouse Country communities of Endicott and St. John, is Seattle Pacific University professor emeritus of education who resides with his wife, Lois, in Richland, Washington. His books on regional themes include *Harvest Horizons: Essays on Agrarian Themes in Western Art and Literature* and *Finding Chief Kamiakin: The Life and Legacy of a Northwest Patriot*. He has received the Governor's Writers Award, Washington State Historical Society's Robert Gray Medal, and state Excellence in Education Award.

John Clement is a landscape photographer who lives in Kennewick, Washington, with his wife, Sharon. A graduate of Central Washington University, he majored in cultural geography and geology. Clement has received numerous regional, national, and international photography awards, and his work has been inducted into the National Photographers Hall of Fame. Among his audio-visual and print productions are *Northwest Drylands: Seasons* and McGregor-Clement calendar series which feature the sublime scenery of the Columbia Plateau.

Alexander C. McGregor is a business leader, historian, and passionate advocate for the remarkable farm families of the Inland Northwest. His family has raised wheat and livestock since territorial days and serves farm families in rural communities across the region. The McGregor business has earned National Family Business of the Year honors and more than twenty state, regional, and national Environmental Respect Award distinctions. McGregor received his PhD in history from the University of Washington and taught there and at Whitman College before returning to his rural roots. His book, *Counting Sheep*, was named a Washington Centennial Book, one of the top one hundred written in the first century of statehood. He has teamed with Scheuerman and Clement on several publications and presentations. Alex and his wife, Linda, reside near Pullman, Washington.

From left to right: John Clement, Richard D. Scheuerman, and Alexander C. McGregor

Fairfield Cemetery

Fairfield, Washington

Snowed In

west of Worley, Idaho